Part

Menteth.

Forth fl.

Oriens.

Part of Sterlin-shyre.

Moore of Kippen

Loch Inche mahuno

K. of

Loch Laggan

GLOTTIANÆ PARS.

Part of Cliddis- -dail.

Blaeu map of Dunbartonshire (published 1654, drawn c1600 by Timothy Pont)

Scala Miliaria

1   2   3   4

Rorfrow

M. Govan

Clyd Flu.

200 years of
HELENSBURGH
1802-2002

Entrance to Pier Buildings, Helensburgh
Robert Wemyss, 1899 (architect's perspective drawing 53 x 83cm)
The arch was demolished in the late 1970s

200 years of
HELENSBURGH
1802-2002

HELENSBURGH HERITAGE TRUST

EDITOR
STEWART NOBLE
ASSISTANT EDITOR KENNETH CRAWFORD

Argyll
publishing

First Published by
Argyll Publishing
Glendaruel
Argyll PA22 3AE
Scotland
www.deliberatelythirsty.com

British Library Cataloguing-in-Publication Data.
A catalogue record for this book is available from the
British Library.

ISBN 1 902831 38 1

Origination Cordfall Ltd, Glasgow
Printing & Binding Cromwell Press Ltd.

CONTENTS

ACKNOWLEDGEMENTS

Grateful thanks for research and assistance throughout goes to
Mrs Alison Roberts, Helensburgh Heritage Trust
Michael Davis, Helensburgh Library
Bob Wood, Helensburgh
Alistair McIntyre, Garelochhead
Miss Patricia Drayton, Helensburgh.

Thanks for assistance in particular areas is due to
Ms Gill Aitkenhead, Helensburgh – Dr Fordyce Messer
Prof Gavin Arneil, Helensburgh – proof-reading
Roger Billcliffe, Glasgow – Art and Artists
Bobbie Brodie, Helensburgh – Railways
Dr Douglas Brown – Baird Phonovision
Rev David Clark, West Kirk of Helensburgh and other members of the local clergy
who helped with chapter 5 – Religion
Clyde River Steamer Club
Ms Lesley Couperwhite, Watt Library, Greenock – Marion, Lady Cathcart
Ms Jennifer Cruickshank, BBC Scotland – Jimmy Logan
Ms Mary Davidson, Buchanan's of Scotland Ltd – Provost Andrew Buchanan
Michael Donnelly, Glasgow – Some Architectural Gems
Donald Fullarton, Helensburgh – Out of the Past & Other Helensburghs
Helensburgh Twinning Association – Public Administration
Colin Hope, Helensburgh – Transport
Graham Hoppner and Arthur Jones, Dumbarton Library – Some Architectural
Gems & Henry Bell
Hugh McBrien, West of Scotland Archaeology Service – Glen Fruin burial site
Murdo MacDonald, Argyll & Bute Council – Public Administration
Mrs Rae Macgregor, Neil Munro Society, Inveraray – Neil Munro
Donald Matheson, James McGonigle and Mrs Veronica Stephenson, Hermitage
Academy – Schools in Helensburgh & The Crambs
Daniel H Morrow, Alexandria – War and Peace
Mrs Marjorie Osborne, Helenburgh – Street Names
James Pearson, Clan Colquhoun Centre – The Lairds & Street Names
Mrs Joan Robertson, Helensburgh – Some Architectural Gems
Ms Jean Strachan, Dunedin Public Libraries, New Zealand
Mrs Ailsa Tanner, Helensburgh – Art and Artists
Ms Bev Taunton and Ms Roz Grey, Helensburgh, New South Wales
Mike and Sue Thornley, Rhu – Art and Artists
and all the local clubs and societies who provided information for Chapter 12.

**The publication of this book has been made possible
by the financial support received from**
Argyll & Bute Council; Argyll, The Isles, Loch Lomond, Stirling and The Trossachs
Tourist Board; Helensburgh Heritage Trust; John McFall MP; National Lottery
Fund – Awards for All Programme (fees for some illustrations) and Scottish
Enterprise Dunbartonshire.

Introduction

On 28 July 1802 King George III granted Helensburgh a Burgh Charter. For several years Helensburgh Heritage Trust has felt that the bicentenary in 2002 would be too important for the town to be allowed to pass unmarked, and it was decided that one of our bicentenary projects should be the production of a book about the town. We also felt that there had been something of a gap since the last history book had appeared; in the interim many important events had taken place which have played a major part in the shaping of the town.

Compared to many other towns in Scotland, Helensburgh at the age of two hundred years is a mere child. However human children generally have their birthdays celebrated more vigorously than human adults – who indeed often wish to forget their age! So surely the young Helensburgh is entitled to its celebrations too.

And it has a lot to celebrate. We live in an extremely attractive town surrounded by very attractive countryside. Helensburgh has also been a home to many well-known people and continues to be so. Lastly, it is interesting to see how the many different strands in the town's past have come together to make it as it is today.

In many respects being editor of a book can probably be likened to lying upon a bed of nails. Nevertheless at the risk of being accused of masochism, I will admit in my quieter moments to having enjoyed the production of this book. Much of this pleasure has come purely and simply by finding out from the work of the other authors bits about this town and its people which I did not previously know. I most sincerely hope that you, the reader, will get as much enjoyment from the book as I have done.

Stewart Noble
Editor
April 2002

Lady Helen's portrait
Lady Helen Colquhoun, after whom Helensburgh was named, was a grand-daughter of the 16th Earl of Sutherland whose family lived for hundreds of years at Dunrobin Castle beside Golspie. She was born in 1717, married Sir James Colquhoun in 1740 and died in 1791. Although her husband Sir James Colquhoun named the new town after his wife about 1785, names such as Milligs continued to be used for some time

Chapter 1

Before 1802

Stewart Noble

About ten thousand years ago the last Ice Age to affect Scotland slowly came to an end. As the glaciers melted nomadic hunters moved northwards, following the animals on which they preyed. How soon they reached Helensburgh is impossible to say, but from the Loch Lomond area there is evidence of primitive farming being practised about six thousand years ago. The glaciers often carried large stones, and when they melted these boulders were left behind lying on top of the soil; such a glacial erratic is to be found just off the Upland Footpath very near its junction with the Highlandman's Road on the hillside above Rhu and Helensburgh. It obviously intrigued primitive people, because they spent a considerable amount of time gouging out cup markings on it. These date back to about 2500-1500 BC, from the end of the Stone Age to the start of the Bronze Age. The experts do not know why prehistoric man spent so long on this activity – perhaps there was some religious meaning.

Towards the north-west end of Glen Fruin near Auchengaich Farm an artificial mound can be clearly seen from the road. This used to be pointed out as the burial place of some of the Colquhouns who had died in the Battle of Glen Fruin in 1603. However in 1967 an archaeological investigation of the mound was undertaken and it was found to be a prehistoric grave dating back to the Middle Bronze Age (about 1500-1200 BC). It contained a cist with a large number of burnt bones.

What we know of early man in Scotland comes, to a large extent, from the Romans. Those they met would have been a Celtic people and evidence of their presence on either side of Helensburgh can be found in Celtic place names. 'Dun' is Celtic for a fort and Dumbarton means 'Fort of the Britons' while to the north of us it has been suggested that the name Shandon means 'Old Fort'. The Romans could never really make up their minds as to whether or not they wanted Scotland to be part of their Empire. Perhaps they found the natives a bit too wild and unfriendly, perhaps they found the climate not totally to their liking. Consequently about 139 AD they built the Antonine Wall across Central

Scotland. The western end was tantalisingly close to us, on the banks of the Clyde at Old Kilpatrick. From here they sailed round Britain and to do so they must have come down the Clyde and passed Helensburgh.

As the Roman Empire began to disintegrate the retention of peripheral colonies such as Southern Scotland and then later England became less important and over the centuries the vacuum left behind by the Romans came to be filled by other invaders. Thus during the fifth century the Scots came from Northern Ireland over the short sea route to the Mull of Kintyre and gradually spread out from there. The Vikings, meanwhile, came over the North Sea in the eighth century and spread down the East and West coasts of Scotland. They hauled their long ships over land from the salt waters of Loch Long at Arrochar to the fresh water of Loch Lomond at Tarbet. Tangible evidence of the Viking presence is to be seen in the graveyard of Luss Parish Church where there is a Viking hogback gravestone. The easy way out of Loch Lomond for them was to sail down the River Leven and then down the Clyde, once again passing Helensburgh. But like the Romans they left no evidence of their presence here.

The deaths of King Alexander III in 1286 and of his granddaughter and heir, Margaret, Maid of Norway four years later led to a third group of invaders: the English. During the Wars of Independence they captured Dumbarton Castle and on the foreshore at Havock on the western outskirts of Dumbarton one can find Wallace's Cave. Although there is no proof that he was in Helensburgh, there is a tale that Wallace swam from Rosneath to Ardencaple to escape capture. King Robert the Bruce spent his final years at his house at Cardross Mains and actually died there in 1329, but this is not the Cardross which we know today – it lay on the west bank of the River Leven about half a mile upstream from Dalreoch.

It was in the thirteenth century that the first prominent local family made its appearance, namely the MacAulays (to use one of several spellings). They built a typical tower house at Ardencaple Castle and although most of the Castle has been demolished, an old tower is still a prominent landmark today. It is located at the junction of Frazer Avenue and West King Street, but is best seen by looking straight up Castle Avenue from Rhu Road Lower. Over the centuries the MacAulays extended their ownership of the land from this base

Throughout the stormy times that characterised the reigns of the Stewart monarchs, the Earls of Lennox frequently played a prominent role; much of their power base was Dunbartonshire and they had a castle at Faslane. Furthermore Dumbarton Castle was the last piece of Scottish soil where the infant Mary Queen of Scots stayed in 1548 before she had to flee to France for her safety. However Helensburgh does not appear to have been involved in any of this.

Towards the end of the sixteenth century Timothy Pont, minister of Dunnet in Caithness, Scotland's most northerly mainland parish, drew the first ever county maps for most of Scotland. This must have been a daunting task and it was not until 1654, many years after Pont's death, that the maps were finally printed in the form of a book *Theatrum Orbis Terrarum sive Atlas Novus* by Joannis Blaeu in Amsterdam. Despite the difficulties, a large amount of detail is visible. A glance at the map of Dunbartonshire (called Levinia) reveals that some familiar names are still there to be seen, but others have disappeared. (The Blaeu map can be seen on the endpapers.)

Sir James Colquhoun envisaged Helensburgh as an industrial town for weavers

Helensburgh as such did not exist for nearly another two hundred years, but in the area many of Pont's names, although spelt differently today, are instantly recognisable; these include Luz, The Yle of Roseneth, Glen-Fruyn and Ard-moir. Like Helensburgh, Craigendoran and Rhu do not appear at all, while Cardross appears in its old location, namely on the West Bank of the River Leven where Strathleven Park in Dumbarton is today (about one mile downstream from Robert the Bruce's Cardross Mains). The modern Cardross is shown as Kilmahew.

Working from east to west through Helensburgh one finds Kammezeskan, Cougrein, Kirckmichell, Stouck, Mulligs and Mullyis (two spellings!), Arncappill and Arnkapill (again two spellings!), and Arnconnel. Interestingly the name Mulligs appears on the map in order to mark a mill, and small ruins of the old Maligmill – yet another spelling! – can in fact still be seen today in the Hermitage Park almost immediately behind the Victoria Halls. At that time these names would probably have marked individual farms, although it is possible that they were also small hamlets, particularly as farms were much more labour-intensive in those days and accommodation may well have been provided for the farm workers in the shape of bothies. The spelling of placenames only became standardised with the introduction of Ordnance Survey maps in the mid-nineteenth century.

Map-making could perhaps be regarded as a sign that people were starting to live in more civilised times. However the Battle of Glen Fruin between the Colquhouns and the MacGregors in 1603 proves that this was far from the truth.

In the seventeenth century the MacAulays had been disposing of more and more of their lands locally and in 1705 what was to become Helensburgh was sold to Sir John Schaw of Greenock.

Forty years later when Bonnie Prince Charlie launched his Jacobite rebellion, there were still no roads north of Dumbarton and Helensburgh did not exist. However the Prince's defeat the following year heralded a greater feeling of security throughout Britain. Perhaps it was this feeling that encouraged Sir James Colquhoun in 1752 to buy the lands of Milligs for £6,500 from Marion, Lady Cathcart who had inherited them from her father, Sir John Schaw only shortly before.

Sir James did nothing with the land for several years and then on

11th January 1776, six months before the Americans made their Declaration of Independence, he placed an advertisement in the *Glasgow Journal*.

> Notice: – To be feued immediately, for building upon, at a very reasonable rate, a considerable piece of ground, on the shores of Malig, opposite Greenock. The land lies on both sides of the road leading from Dumbarton to the Kirk of Row. The ground will be regularly laid out for houses and gardens, to be built upon according to a plan, etc. There is a freestone quarry on the ground. For the accommodation of the feuars, the proprietor is to enclose a large field for grazing their milk cows, etc.
> NB – bonnet makers, stocking, linen and woollen weavers will meet with encouragement. There is a large boat building at the place, for ferrying men and horses with chaises.

Despite Sir James's plans, development on the ground was very slow to materialise and for a while it was merely known as The New Town. However he later decided to name it after his wife, Lady Helen Sutherland and thus the town of Helensburgh finally acquired the name by which we know it today.

Lady Helen was a granddaughter of the 16th Earl of Sutherland whose family have lived for hundreds of years at Dunrobin Castle beside Golspie. She was born in 1717, married Sir James in 1740, had three sons and six daughters, and died in 1791; her portrait may be seen in the Council Chamber in Helensburgh's Municipal Buildings. Around that time it was quite fashionable for landowners to name towns after members of their family, and local examples are Alexandria and Renton, both of which are named after members of the Smollett family of Cameron House on Loch Lomondside. It is not certain when the change of name to Helensburgh actually occurred, but some light can be shed on the matter from the old parish registers of births, marriages and deaths. Thus the name Helensburgh first appears in 1785 and is in common use after 1792. However names such as Milligs continued to be used after the latter date for some time. (The spelling of Row was changed to Rhu in 1927.)

These then were the beginnings of the small settlement which was to receive its Burgh Charter from King George III in 1802. •

CHAPTER 2

The Year of Our Lord 1802

DAVID ARTHUR

There were no cataclysmic events which might have ushered in the year 1802 and so welcomed the emergence of Helensburgh, no events of world shattering importance that might highlight the appearance of a new burgh. Nonetheless those years of the first decade of the nineteenth century were in many ways a watershed, a watershed between a relatively stable world of conservative practice and a new century that was to see major changes that would alter not just the balance of power but bring in new and more radical thought and ideas. It was, in short, a period that ushered in great changes, and while the arrival of a new burgh in the West of Scotland may have happened unnoticed in the larger world, the birth of Helensburgh coincided with the movement of great tides in the history of the world. With the birth pangs of the new infant burgh in that year it is useful to place this happening in the wider context of **The World of 1802**.

The successful rebellion of the Thirteen Colonies in **America**, starting in 1776, had closed off the colonial ambitions of Europe in that part of the world. Because the American continent was closed to British developments she had been forced to transfer her attention to the East, and not just to India but further beyond to the Pacific in particular.

At this time an ideal geographic position as a centre of trade routes built on the impact of the Industrial Revolution, allied to the pugnacious acquisitiveness of her people, was to give Britain the opportunity to build an empire that was to cover almost a third of the globe by the twentieth century. The loss of the American colonies was a loss indeed but there was still Canada, and more importantly the West Indies. From the West Indies came sugar and the huge profits of the slave trade, profits that in today's money dwarf those of most of the huge conglomerates. It was cities like Bristol, whose 'bricks were cemented in the blood of slaves', where the money lay. But Scots too made money, mostly from the ownership of plantations in the islands of the Caribbean and from shipping. Britain itself was not to abolish the slave trade until 1807, though the Mansfield judgement in 1772 and Knight's case

Neil Macleod

A slave is said to have escaped from an American trading ship anchored off Helensburgh, cheered on by the local populace.

Donald Fullarton

Robert Story (1818-1848) was a freed slave from West Africa who lived for many years in Rosneath and is buried there

six years later had made illegal the actual status of slavery in England and Scotland respectively.

A story is told that around 1820 a slave jumped ship from an American trading ship anchored off shore from Helensburgh. He was being rowed ashore in a small skiff, but was pursued by another boat. His cries attracted a small crowd to the beach, their threats deterred the Americans and so he was free. There is also a freed slave's grave in Rosneath chuchyard.

But Britain was already looking further to **the East**. India had always been the source of large profits and many Scots made their fortunes with the East India Company; the redoubtable Clive of India was one example who was able to retire to Musselburgh with his huge fortune. The defeat of the French in the last years of the eighteenth century had opened the door to giving 'John Company' a virtual monopoly throughout the whole of India.

In **Australia** the first convict settlement had been founded in 1788 at Botany Bay, the modern Sydney. While at first the colony was devoted to being a penal base – and a viciously brutal one it was with flogging and hanging common practices – soon other settlers arrived. The most important one was Robert Macarthur, the son of a highland chieftain, who had fought at Culloden. Macarthur was instrumental in introducing sheep to New South Wales, and immensely profitable it was to prove. So profitable indeed that it brought him into conflict with the local government, in the form of the Governor, one Captain Bligh. Bligh incidentally has the unique distinction of being at the centre of three rebellions, once at the naval mutiny of the Nore, the second on the *Bounty* and the third in New South Wales!

In 1802 **New Zealand** was dangerous territory because of the fearsome Maoris! The islands did, however, serve as bases for both whalers and sealers, once again many of whom were Scots seamen.

In **Europe** the Revolution in **France** in 1789 had brought to an end the rule of the Divine Right of Kings but had also sown the seeds of many of the modern concepts of individual rights and of individual freedoms. The French Revolution had let loose some frightening new ideas which would shake the world.

This was a year of relative peace, at least of peace for a short time, as the Peace of Amiens in 1802 was the brief dividing point in the period of wars between the European powers and France. Napoleon, not content with the role of First Consul, was on the verge of grasping the title of Emperor, the weakening Austro-Hungarian Empire bestrode a large part of Central and Eastern Europe, and Turkey was lapsing into the 'Sick Man of Europe' with the consequent appearance of the nationalistic vultures of the new Balkan states ready to pounce. What has sometimes been referred to as the Second Hundred Years War between France and Britain still had thirteen years to run, the most vicious period of that conflict covering the Peninsular campaign, Trafalgar and Waterloo still lay in the future.

The upstart Napoleon had abilities as an astute social thinker. This, along with his military awareness, had made astonishing changes to French life with the remarkable reorganisation of its whole society through the Code Napoleon. By 1802 he was ready to start on his grand idea to be the master of the whole of Europe.

The concept of a nation such as **Germany** simply did not exist apart from the growing power of the northern Kingdom of Brandenburg-Prussia. The great empire that was **Spain** no longer caused the rest of the world to tremble, and the result of the Napoleonic War with the defeat of France would open the way for the new and mighty empire of Britain. The forces of nationalism which were to shape Europe, and in particular Germany and Italy, were only just beginning to take shape.

In Britain the forces of the Industrial Revolution were driving her to become the engine room of the world while the changes of the Agricultural Revolution were slowly changing the face of the British countryside. The Younger Pitt had been briefly ousted as Prime Minister and the long troubled reign of George III while not yet drawing to a close was in a twilight time of his periodic spells of madness.

Scotland and England had been united since the Treaty of Union in 1707 for almost one hundred years, and the benefits, whatever may be argued today, were undeniable in the opening of wider markets to Scottish merchants. At the turn of the century the French Revolution, far from opening a new era of freedom, saw instead a tightening of the grip by a central government terrified by what had happened across the Channel. The laws on both sedition and treason had been dramatically tightened and the Combination Acts of 1799 put a clamp on any group movements that might cause trouble.

The 1745 Jacobite rebellion had had many unfortunate effects in **Scotland**, much more indeed than the catastrophic destruction of the clans and the banning of tartan and the pipes. It also caused a fatal misunderstanding of the complicated relationship over land between a clan chief and his clansmen which had led to the handover of all clan lands into the personal ownership of the chief. The effect was that large areas of Scotland could then be used or misused at the whim of the new owners. One result over the succeeding century was the arrival of the Cheviot sheep and the clearance of acres of land and the consequent arrival of refugees from the Highlands into the new cities and towns and, of course, widespread emigration particularly to Canada and the Carolinas. The most ruthless of these events in Sutherland and the West Highlands lay in the future but the removal, for example, of the Men of Ross had already taken place in 1797. It should be made clear that none of this affected the Helensburgh area, the clearances being far to the north.

The eighteenth century saw two major social revolutions – the Agricultural and the Industrial. Taking the former first, in Scotland there were two systems of farming, that of the croft, which still continues today in the North and the West, and the group farm. Those who could find no place on the land found that the towns offered the only place to go. In turn this provided the power for the Industrial Revolution. The steam engine, the product of the happy partnership of Matthew Boulton and James Watt in 1774, became the driving force for the new world of power. Allied to the damp and wet climate of the west coast of Scotland the conditions were right for the growth of the textile industry and David Dale, a successful banker, invested his money in cotton mills at New Lanark, Blantyre and later in Oban. He and his son-in-law, Robert Owen, set new standards for the treatment of their workers with the new model village at New Lanark. Even so, that one good example cannot hide the grim fact that the lot of the average worker, male, female or child, was brutally hard and the expectation of life was desperately short. Shipbuilding played an important part in the industry of the West but it was still confined to wooden ships, the change over to iron and to steam, as with the first commercial steamship the *Comet*, still lay in the future.

With the increasing wealth of the merchant and mill-owner class in Glasgow came a new development, the move to the country, a move to affect much of the surrounding countryside round Glasgow – Killearn, Kilmacolm and, of course, Helensburgh.

In political terms, the government of the United Kingdom was entirely in the hands of the aristocracy and the landed ones in particular, for both the right to vote and the right to stand as an MP rested totally on the possession of land. Sadly it has to be recorded that Scotland perhaps suffered worst in the United Kingdom from this system and in the words of authors on the subject Scotland at that time was regarded as simply 'one large rotten burgh'. The patronage for that situation lay in the hands of one Henry Dundas, the 1st Viscount Melville, or as he was better known – the uncrowned King of Scotland, and in turn the patronage master for the Younger Pitt.

The years 2002 and 1802 share much of the same appearance in one respect – the emptiness of the River Clyde. While the Mersey and the Severn share the attraction of facing to the West, more importantly both rivers benefit from deep water access, where the Clyde until the end of the 1700s was beset with shoals and shallow water – the fact that Dumbarton, thanks to the Rock, served as capital of the ancient Kingdom of Strathclyde is explained by that problem. While the fortress-like crags of Edinburgh and Stirling were obvious defensive sites, unfortunate Glasgow had nothing but a ford to commend it. Despite that handicap Glasgow did flourish and by 1670 it was the second city of Scotland, both in size and in importance. Thanks to the ports lower down the Clyde like Greenock and the specially built Port Glasgow, the city prospered.

It is easy to forget that life for most people, apart from the wealthy, in the early nineteenth century, whether in the towns or the country, was harsh and always on the edge of subsistence. 1789 saw an attempted riot by the Calton Weavers which failed and there were the Bread Riots in 1800.

From the 1670s Glasgow became the centre of the tobacco trade and the prosperous, red-coated tobacco barons could be seen walking in the city, and by 1790 the Merchant City was being built. With the revolt of the Americans and the loss of much of that trade, fortunately Glasgow was not totally dependent on tobacco alone as the business in sugar and linens was growing. There are still reminders of those days, firstly in the magnificent Mitchell Library in Glasgow, the gift of the Mitchell family whose cigarettes were the Four Leaf Clover, and secondly in the high building, seen across the Clyde in Greenock, of the old Tate & Lyle sugar factory.

Although **Helensburgh** in 1802 had sufficient population to justify the granting of the Burgh Charter, it was nevertheless a very much smaller place than it is now. A map produced in 1776 by Charles Ross of Greenlaw for Sir James Colquhoun shows the proposed Town of Maligs bounded by the Glenan Burn to the west and the Millig Burn to the east. According to the 1799 Statistical Account of Scotland the Parish of Row – of which Helensburgh constituted only a very small part – had a population of only 1000 (486 males and 514 females). It goes on to say that there is 'one village in the parish, lately built, which contains about one hundred souls' – presumably this was Helensburgh.

There was therefore just a straggle of houses along the seafront, with the occasional farm inland where, because of the introduction of sheep over the previous twenty to thirty years, there was less heather and more grass to be seen. The people generally spoke English, but many understood and frequently used Gaelic.

Partly because it was so small, transport links to Helensburgh were poor. Some twenty-five years previously a road classified as a highway had been built from Dumbarton through Rhu to Portincaple, but by modern standards it was a very rough track. Travel by sea was a very good alternative, although the steam power of Henry Bell's *Comet* was still ten years in the future. The Statistical Account noted that the people of the parish were fond of the seafaring life, but not the military life.

Sir James Colquhoun's attempt twenty-six years earlier to develop the town as a centre of textile production had failed; farming and fishing were the principal sources of employment, although there were a few craftsmen around the area. Labourers were earning between 10d (4p) and 1 shilling (5p) per day. Because the town was largely self-sufficient, much of the food produced locally had to be processed and preserved locally; thus two of the earliest recorded occupations were the miller (to grind the corn and grain) and the cooper (to produce barrels in which food could be stored). And the presence of whisky stills would, of course, have given the cooper a bit of business too!

To 'feed the inner man' there were religion and education. The first church in Helensburgh had been built three years previously, but the first school was still five years in the future, although there had been one at Rhu for at least fifty years. The Statistical Account recorded that 'the people in general are not expensive, a few individuals are much addicted to dram drinking; and the young people, especially the females, fond of dress, and more expensive in that way than their circumstances can well afford'. Some things never change!

So, the world of 1802 which saw the emergence of the burgh of Helensburgh was a different one to that which we view 200 years later. The growth of popular democracy and of radicalism lay far ahead. The world of 1802, while the forces of a new industrialisation were beginning to take effect, was still a conservative society in which the land, in the hands of the aristocracy, and in particular the Scottish church held a position which enabled it to control the country in ways that would seem foreign to the citizen of the twenty first century. At the same time there was the opportunity for the growth and development of new structures and of new ways of life.

CHAPTER 3

The Lairds
PAT MITCHELL

The MacAulays of Ardencaple Castle

Although the history of Ardincaple Castle (to use an older spelling of the name) is indelibly linked with the MacAulays, they were not the original inhabitants – MacArthurs from the shores of Loch Awe had been there earlier. Perhaps the Viking raiders who had destroyed Dumbarton Castle in AD 870 and were a threat in the Clyde until late in the thirteenth century had put paid to the MacArthurs.

The Ardincaple lairds and many other landholders came into being with the introduction of the feudal system. This displaced the clan system which was based on the principle that land, the basis of life, belonged to the people in common, not to individuals, and each clansman, irrespective of rank, was duty bound to assist another if the need arose.

The Anglo-Norman King David I of Scotland (1124-53) imposed the European feudal system on a stunned Scotland – or at least that part up to the Highland line where the Scots (Anglo-Saxon) tongue gave way to the Gaelic. Under this sytem the King owned all the land, which was then divided up and granted to Earls who in turn could grant land to Lairds. The Lairds would then assess their tenants' incomes from farm produce etc and demand a tithe, or tenth part, paid in kind.

King Malcolm IV, the son of King David, created the Earldom of Lennox, making Alwyn the 1st Earl in 1155. About 1225, Aulay, the son of Alwyn, 2nd Earl of Lennox was granted many lands in an undated charter from Maldouen, 3rd Earl of Lennox. Ardincaple was mentioned in another undated charter and Morice de Ardincaple appears in the records of the Bishop of Glasgow in 1294.

The view of historians is that Ardincaple Castle had been built in the twelfth century. It is worth noting that there are two clans called MacAulay – the MacAulays of Ardincaple whose ancestors had been cadets of Clan Gregor; and the totally unrelated MacAulays of Lewis, Sutherland and Wester Ross who were of Norse descent.

In 1296, following Edward I of England's savage retaliation to King

Neil Macleod

Clan MacAulay coat of arms. The motto translates as 'Sweet Danger', while the boot may be linked to Sir Aulay MacAulay MP's appointment as Commissioner on the regulation of footwear prices in 1608

Ardencaple Castle ancestral home of the MacAulays was originally built in the twelfth century. The retaining wall in this picture still stands at the head of Castle Avenue

John Balliol, two thousand nobles swore fealty to Edward, appending their seals and ribbons to parchments, collectively given the name of the Ragman Roll. Morice de Ardincaple's signature and seal were there. But when William Wallace rebelled against Edward, the Battle of Stirling Brig ended in a rout of the English army which had a large Scottish backup including Malcolm, Earl of Lennox and Morice de Ardincaple. At great personal risk, they and a small number of other Scots nobles changed sides in what had become the Wars of Independence.

Blind Harry, the Scots bard, later told of Wallace and his followers being guests at Malcolm, the Earl of Lennox's castle at Faslane following Wallace's sacking of Dumbarton and Rosneath castles, both garrisoned by the English. It is likely that near neighbour and comrade Morice de Ardincaple would have been there also.

Another story, probably apocryphal, tells of Wallace narrowly escaping from his pursuers by leaping on horseback from a rock onto the shore at Rosneath and then swimming the half mile across the mouth of the Gareloch to Cairndhu Point (where Kidston Park now is).

Morice de Ardincaple and the other Lennox lairds joined a few others in 1314 at the Battle of Bannockburn where King Robert the Bruce's army routed the English. The Earl of Lennox and Morice and fellow lairds must have returned home to a rapturous welcome. With such staunch friends, Bruce made the Vale of Leven his home.

Aulay of Ardincaple, 9th Laird, was a beneficiary of a generous ruling from James IV to the heirs of those who had died at Flodden in 1513, whereby they were excused from the duty payable on the purchase of land; this enabled Aulay to acquire further lands. These included Faslane, Milligs, Kirkmichael and Ardoch.

Alexander, 10th Laird, was the first to employ the surname MacAulay consistently, as a result of which the family became known as the Clan MacAulay. This would have been around 1530. While the Clan MacAulay were in the ascendancy in the sixteenth century, by contrast the Earls of Lennox were in decline.

Throughout the sixteenth century the power of the MacAulays continued to grow, and when King James VI of Scotland became James I of England in 1603, the Duke of Lennox wished Aulay to accompany him to the English court, and the King gladly agreed. Some years later Aulay MacAulay received a knighthood, followed in 1608 by his becoming the first MP for Dunbartonshire. In the same year both he and Semple of Fulwood became Commissioners in the regulation of the prices of footwear. Significantly a boot with spur became the MacAulay coat of arms. Under his stewardship Clan MacAulay had steadily increased in influence, wealth and prestige.

The fifteenth Laird was another Aulay, and he inherited the title about 1645-48. Initially he demonstrated a keen interest in the area, paying by himself for the building of the Church, manse and glebe of Row, yet still able to purchase land elsewhere despite Scotland's economy plummeting at that time. This benevolence was soon to change and rumours abounded that he was a waster. He died in 1675. We begin now to see the sad decline of the MacAulays. His son, Archibald, sold Milligs, Kirkmichael, Buchanan and Drumfad to Sir John Schaw of Greenock.

By the mid-eighteenth century Ardincaple Castle's roof had collapsed and it had become uninhabitable forcing Aulay, the 19th Laird, to move to his remaining property at Faslane. When he had to sell that too, he took refuge in a humble cottage at High Laggarie where he died, a childless pauper in 1767. Before his death he sold Ardincaple Castle and its remaining policies to John, the fourth Duke of Argyll, who appointed Robert Adam as architect to convert the Castle into a castle mansion. Work proceeded apace between 1762 amd 1774 and there arose two towers and a centre portion between them, the stone being quarried from the moor above Ardincaple Farm.

The crumbling rocky bluff facing seawards was heavily reinforced by stonework in 1806 but the north-west portion of the Castle was destroyed by fire in 1830. When commissioning repairs the Duke made other additions, these including the Argyll Tower, bearing his coat of arms, the only remaining portion of the former Castle complex.

In 1862 Sir James Colquhoun (the fourth Baronet) bought Ardincaple, but in 1923 the MacAulay name reappeared when Mrs H MacAulay-Stromberg purchased it. She made great improvements both to the interior and gardens but died in 1931. In 1927 she made a donation to Helensburgh's Victoria Infirmary, recorded in gilt lettering in the entrance hall.

Mr JD Hendry later owned the Castle and feued the fields in front for the building of houses. The mansion house with its fine timber screening attached to the internal walls, and coal-fired central heating, must have been a pleasant place to live, as his daughter attests.

By the autumn of 1940 all that had changed. Ardencaple Castle had been requisitioned and converted into offices by government agencies. Wrens (female naval staff) appeared. Dart boards were attached to the timbered walls. The war effort resulted in deterioration of the fabric, internal and external. Unoccupied after 1945 steadily the decay accelerated, leading to the Castle's demolition in 1957-59, and so to the loss to Helensburgh of a major part of its heritage.

Only the Argyll Tower survives. The rest of the Castle made way for naval housing. The Tower was retained because of its usefulness as a mount for transit lights to assist naval vessels in navigating Rhu Narrows, but it is now redundant for that purpose.

There have been moves to re-establish Clan MacAulay, these having been initiated by Iain MacAulay of Drumbeg in Sutherland who has sought possible claimants to the Chieftainship in a number of countries, and has organised clan gatherings in Scotland in order to spread the message and engender clan spirit.

The Colquhouns of Colquhoun and Luss

Colquhoun coat of arms as sited on Rossdhu gates, near Luss

After the demise of the MacAulays the next lairds of significance to Helensburgh were the Colquhouns. As the name suggests, the Colquhouns of Colquhoun and Luss were the result of the coming together of two families: the House of Colquhoun and the House of Luss. The history of both goes back to at least the twelfth century but, typically of that time, what we know today of their early history is only vague. Furthermore following their history over the centuries can be confusing, as succeeding generations have often used the same first names and they have added to the number of their titles. Thus for example they became Colquhouns of Colquhoun and Luss only from 1368. Many were knighted and in 1625 they became baronets of Nova Scotia (a hereditary title); following a complicated and disputed succession this title went to another branch of the family, but then in 1786 they became baronets of Great Britain.

The House of Colquhoun had its origins in the parish of Old Kilpatrick, east of Dumbarton. Umfridus de Kilpatrick (1190-1260) was granted the lands of Colquhoun in 1246 by Maldouen, 3rd Earl of Lennox in token for his military service. Umfridus, proud of his exalted station, now called himself de Colquhoun, a laird in his own right.

But where is this place called Colquhoun with its quite unique name? It is thought that de Colquhoun built a castle near Middleton Farm about two thirds of a mile (1km) north of Milton on the A82, although no castle is seen there today. Just over the Milton Burn, south east of the farm are the remains of the Old Chapel of Colquhoun, while the burn has been referred to as the Colquhoun Burn and the village as Milton of Colquhoun. The extent of the estate originally was about 2000 hectares.

During the Wars of Independence Ingelramus (3rd of Colquhoun, 1280-1308) did not side with the English and consequently Robert the Bruce richly rewarded him and his son, Humphrey, with lands. Ingelramus was granted lands in Stirlingshire, and Humphrey was knighted and given a charter to the barony of Luss. It is interesting to note that the names Umfridus (Humphrey) and Ingelramus appear alien, indicating a non-Celtic ancestry. Humphrey however became a favourite name for the Colquhouns over the following centuries. In 1368 Sir Robert of Colquhoun (son of Sir Humphrey) married a lady known only as the Fair Maid of Luss; he thus became the 5th of Colquhoun and the 7th of Luss. At some point around this time the Colquhouns abandoned their castle near Milton and by around 1380 had built another one at Dunglass on the shores of the Clyde near Bowling – the ruins of this castle are still clearly visible from the river.

The first recorded Laird of the House of Luss was Maldouen (1150-1220). He was probably near kin to the mighty Earls of Lennox, whose lands covered an area similar to Dunbartonshire. His was a sacred family, Celtic married priests and hereditary guardians of St Kessog's pastoral staff. Godfridus (Godfrey) 6th of Luss (1345-1385) was the father of the Fair Maid, whose marriage to Sir Robert of Colquhoun united the families.

Unlike the MacAulays, the Colquhouns were not to feature directly in the story of Helensburgh for many years. However, some links do date back to the medieval period. One story in particular concerns Sir John Colquhoun, 10th of Luss (1408-1439), who was made Commander of Dumbarton Castle by King James I. The King asked Sir John if he could take the Castle from Duncan, Earl of Lennox. 'Could you do it?' the King asked. *'Si je puis,'* Sir John is said to have replied. He thought up a ruse by which he could achieve this without bloodshed. A hart was to be captured, then released before the gates of Dumbarton Castle to be pursued by a hunting party with hounds, while an assault group waited in nearby woods. The mock hunters invited the castle guards to join in the chase, which they gleefully did, so allowing the castle to be taken. The King devised for Sir John the crest of a hart's head with two dogs with the motto in French *'Si Je Puis'*, If I Can. *'Si Je Puis'* is now part of the crest of Helensburgh Community Council and was also part of the Burgh Council coat of arms, along with the hart's head and one dog.

Likewise the words 'Cnoc Elachan' (Gaelic for Armoury Hill) came to appear in the coat of arms of the Burgh of Helensburgh. This was a call to arms of the Colquhouns and reflects the stormy times through

Neil Macleod

which people lived for many hundreds of years. The coat of arms also had a small medallion at the foot which signified the granting of a baronetcy of Nova Scotia to Sir John Colquhoun in 1625.

Those troubled times are best exemplified by the story of the Battle of Glen Fruin, but in recounting it one must be aware that it is difficult to disentangle myth from fact. In November 1602 two young MacGregors became benighted in Colquhoun lands and requested food and shelter. Being refused traditional Highland hospitality and finding an empty hut, they killed a sheep for their supper and, being discovered, were tried and executed by the Laird, Alexander (17th of Luss) – as he was entitled to do as a free baron. The result was a retaliatory raid by the MacGregors, who made off with cattle, sheep, goats and horses. Furthermore two Colquhouns died and Alexander accompanied a large group of 'widows' mounted on palfreys (side-saddled ponies) to Stirling Castle, bearing shirts dipped in sheep's blood on spear points. King James VI, being squeamish, granted to Colquhoun Letters of Fire and Sword. This led to a violent reaction by the MacGregors and to the Battle of Glen Fruin on 7 February 1603.

There were about three hundred MacGregors and Camerons.

Neil Macleod

Figures vary as to how many Colquhouns there were, some claiming as many as eight hundred, but possibly about half that number. Like the MacGregors they had help from other lairds, but not the MacAulays. The battle started on the ridge at the head of Glen Fruin overlooking the Gareloch. The Colquhouns soon retired down towards the Glen itself, having suffered early losses. Their plight became desperate when their downhill flight towards Croit and Strone farms brought them into a second conflict with a force which had been hiding in the small tree-girt ravine of the infant Fruin Water. What is certain is that the Colquhoun forces lost many more than the MacGregors – indeed the Records of the Privy Council give the number of Colquhoun dead as eighty. As a result of the battle James VI ordered the proscription of the MacGregors, and they were persecuted for another two hundred years.

Legend has it that about 40 captured scholars from Dumbarton were murdered by their guard at the Battle of Glen Fruin, and that the event was commemorated annually at the College of Dumbarton for many years in the manner depicted. But of course, history is often determined by the ultimate victors!

A story which arose from the battle was that the MacGregors had taken prisoner about forty scholars from the College of Dumbarton who had come to watch the anticipated success of their fathers in the battle, and who were then killed by their guard. However there was no mention of the massacre in the various indictments against the Clan

MacGregor at the time, but Allan Oig McIntnach (McIntosh) of Glencoe is referred to in the records of the Privy Council as having been charged in 1609 with having assisted Clan Gregor and of 'having murdered without pity forty poor persons, who were naked and without armour'. It was said that the College of Dumbarton, for a long time after the battle, had a memorial service on each anniversary, yet the Smollett family of Dumbarton and later of Cameron House on the shores of Loch Lomond, who were associated with the College and who suffered a loss in the conflict, never made any reference to this memorial service, said to have been held right up to 1757. The approximate site of the battle is commemorated by a cairn, which has recently been restored by Helensburgh Heritage Trust.

Scandal enveloped the Colquhoun family when Sir John, the 18th of Luss and the 1st Baronet of Nova Scotia, got into financial difficulties compounded by his interest in the Black Arts and necromancy. He then crazily eloped with his wife's sister. Tried in his absence for witchcraft, abduction and incest he was 'put to the horn' and his land reverted to the Crown in 1634. He had been excommunicated, and was to be remembered as The Sinister Laird of Luss. He died in exile in Italy. However, Sir Humphrey Colquhoun of Balvie made large repayments of the debts and arrangements for clearing off the balance. King Charles I then made a grant of the estates to Sir Humphrey and transferred to him later all titles and honours held by his disgraced brother. Sir Humphrey deserves great credit for saving the Colquhouns and consequently has recently become recognised by many as the 19th laird of Luss, although for various reasons others deny him this title. However the current Laird, Sir Ivar, recognises Sir Humphrey as the 19th Laird, and so this practice is followed for the rest of this text and throughout this book.

Sir James Colquhoun, 26th of Luss and 1st Baronet of Great Britain, succeeded to the title in 1732. Eight years later he married Lady Helen Sutherland; she was the granddaughter of the 16th Earl of Sutherland, and was born in 1717 and died in 1791. He was a Captain in the Highland Regiment, the 'Black Watch', and his bravery in war in Flanders led to his promotion to the rank of Major. He was severely wounded and sent home in 1745 to recuperate, but by 1746 he had recovered sufficiently to lead the hunt for escapees from the army of the Young Pretender, Charles, following their defeat at Culloden.

Sir James retired from the army in 1748 and took every opportunity to expand his estates; thus the Colquhoun connection with Helensburgh began. It was in 1752 that Sir James purchased the lands of Malig from Marion, Lady Cathcart, the daughter of Sir John Schaw of Greenock, but for many years did little with them. The most fundamental change on his estates was due to his son, also James, while Sir James was still laird. Young James introduced 'black-faced' Linton sheep to Glen

The memorial cairn for the Battle of Glen Fruin stands by the road at the head of the Glen

Mallochan above Luss in 1769; they expanded from a small flock to 7,800 in another twenty-four years. Consequently many crofters became redundant. The news of the revolution in farming methods – and the profits to be made from its adoption – spread like wildfire, Lady Helen's family in Sutherland becoming notorious disciples. It is said that Sir James founded Helensburgh in order to provide cottage industries to give work to the unemployed crofters. However his main aim by advertising in the *Glasgow Journal* of 11 January 1776 was to attract wealthy feuars to the new township which he later called 'My Lady Helen's Burgh' after his wife. The crofters from the Colquhoun estates would have sought work in Glasgow, Paisley or Greenock. Those further north and west were shipped, 'for their own good', overseas, their homes burnt down, in the Highland Clearances. Deserted clachans, now rubble, litter the Highlands. The disappearance of Scotland's native woodlands has been attributed to sheep being allowed to feed amongst trees.

It was in 1773 that a new mansion house was built at Rossdhu on the shores of Loch Lomond; it replaced the nearby 15th century Rossdhu Castle (the ruins of which can still be seen today). Lady Helen had mixed feelings about moving – 'it was a lucky hole!' she said tearfully on her departure.

Over the succeeding years the Colquhoun family became the biggest landowners in Dunbartonshire, and they also came to exercise increasing influence on the development of Helensburgh. Thus for example in 1834 Sir James, the 28th of Luss and 3rd Baronet, made a grant to Helensburgh Council of the vacant ground eastward of the granary for the improvement of the pier. Kidston Park, the East King Street playing fields and the East Bay esplanade were all in whole or in part gifts from various Colquhouns. Furthermore, they frequently served as Honorary Presidents of many Helensburgh clubs and societies. In 1902 when Helensburgh celebrated the centenary of the granting of its Burgh Charter, Sir James, the 30th of Luss and 5th Baronet, donated the splendid Celtic cross which stands in Colquhoun Square.

Sir Iain Colquhoun, the 32nd of Luss and 7th Baronet, was a remarkable man. Choosing the army as his career, he won the British Army Lightweight Boxing Championship. While serving on the front during World War I he permitted his soldiers to fraternise with the Germans on Christmas Day 1915, as a result of which he was court-martialled and sentenced to death. King George V pardoned him and back he went to the front. Because of his bravery during the war he was awarded the DSO, and then a bar to it. During much of his time in the trenches he even kept a fairly tame pet lion there! Later he became the founder Chairman of the National Trust for Scotland.

Since then the Colquhouns have granted a 100 year lease of Rossdhu House and it is now the clubhouse for the splendid Loch Lomond Golf Course. Sir Ivar, the 31st of Colquhoun, the 33rd of Luss, and the 8th

Baronet of Great Britain now lives at Camstradden, immediately to the south of the village of Luss. Luss Estates still continue to have an important influence on Helensburgh as they are the feudal superiors for much of the town, and at the time of writing they are the centre of much controversy because they have proposed the construction of a large supermarket at the pierhead.   ●

CHAPTER 4

Public Administration

KENNETH CRAWFORD AND NORMAN GLEN

On 11th January 1776 an advertisement appeared in the *Glasgow Journal* to the effect that Sir James Colquhoun of Luss was offering land, divided into areas known as Feus, for occupation by people who would wish to build houses and set up businesses. This was the time of the Scottish Enlightenment when many estate owners were setting up new villages and towns on their land – often specifying a simple grid system of straight lines for the planning of the roads and buildings. Here, the streets followed the shore line of the River Clyde and others were at right angles. The area had no name other than the old place of Muleig (which was described in 1865 as an old spelling) later to become Millig or Milligs.

1776

The Statistical Account of Scotland in 1791 records that:

> In Row the air is sharp and healthy but the climate, like that
> of every other Parish near the mouth of the Clyde, is wet. In
> consequence of the heavy and almost incessant rain which
> falls in the harvest and winter months the lands are for a
> long time drenched in water and less valuable.

However by January 1794 there were seventeen houses recorded in the 'town' with a gross annual feu duty of £8.18s.6d (£8.93). Indeed it is said that the whole shore, from the pier to the eastern boundary (probably where Craigendoran Avenue now is) had been offered for £1 but refused as being 'too serious a speculation!'

1794

By the turn of the century the settlement must have developed a personality of its own and therefore a need for some control of civic affairs, for on 28th July 1802, King George III granted a Royal Charter of Resignation and Novodamus in favour of Sir James Colquhoun, Baronet. This created a Burgh of Barony called Helensburgh and authorised a weekly market and four annual fairs. The Council was enabled to have a Provost, two Bailies, and four Councillors. It is not known what, if anything, happened immediately because the first four pages of minute book no. 1 are blank, and the first meeting of which a record survives was not until 12th September 1807!

The 'Feuars' agreeable to the charter named Hendrey (sic) Bell as Provost and the Council was attended by the Town Clerk, John Gay and Depute Clerk, Robert Colquhoun. The meeting may have been of some ceremony for, in his excitement, the scribe minuted that there was a need for a road and side path in the 'City' of Helensburgh and instructions were given for estimates to be obtained. It must be said that the term City has never been used since!

All the subsequent minute books are still in existence and another interesting feature of these early Council times is that uniforms were provided for two officers, who were instructed to attend Church with the magistrates. The Town Officer, John Campbell, was fined for failure to attend Church on a Sunday in 1808 and in February the following year Provost Henry Bell was warned that he would be fined if he failed to attend Church. Henry Bell was also elected Provost in September 1808 and September 1809, but the last record of his attending a meeting occurs the following month. Thereafter the Bailies appear to have run the town until Jacob Dixon was elected Provost in 1811. Furthermore Henry Bell ceased to be listed as a voter after 1809, presumably because he was no longer the owner of property.

In November 1807 land was purchased from James Smith for the building of a town house. Although an offer to build it for £260 (or £245, if 20 feet [6m] was kept off the steeple) was received from John Bremander, the proposal was discontinued, and £80 compensation paid to Sir James Colquhoun for not taking up the Feu. The Turnpike Trusts were exacting tolls at Millig and Drumfork. A contract to build a market was let in the following year. By 1810 the population was 500 persons and the Theatre, where the Municipal Buildings now are, was well supported, but the income from the letting of the Annual Fair Customs was only five shillings (25p). The old town hall housed a library in 1816 and a reading room was opened in Clyde Street in 1830.

However, the spread of education had not extended the democratic process to many people – to vote a man had to own land of a value exceeding £33.6s 8d sterling (£33.33p). It was believed that a wealthy man could influence the result of an election by dividing some of his land between friends who in return would vote as instructed. The Reform Act of 1832 extended the franchise so that the wishes of the majority of male residents were more likely to be heard.

On 27th July 1833 a survey of the boundaries of the burgh was carried out and large stones of wrought freestone having 'BB' cut in them were placed in position wherever the line changed direction 'in order that the boundaries may be known in time coming.' A lengthy written route appears in the minutes as does the list of people attending, including the Bailies, Councillors, Feuars and tradesmen 'besides a great many other young and middle aged persons to witness the proceedings.'

George Maclachlan of Young's Place, 3, East Princes Street was the first of three generations to be town clerk – an era of service to the town that lasted for 110 years.

1807

1833

30

The day ended with a regatta attended by the Northern Yacht Club which was won by Provost Smith's cutter the *Amethyst*.

The pier, or rather, a stone dyke, had been built in 1816, lengthened by thirty yards (27m) in 1822 and taken over by the Burgh Council in 1830. Due to the enterprise of Provost Smith, a piece of land to the south-east of the pier was purchased, and the Committee of Management considered erecting a bazaar or market place. However, an offer by Sir James Colquhoun in 1834 to make a grant to the Council of all the vacant ground eastward to the Granary was on condition that the feu should not be sold or built upon, but it should be kept clear for the future improvement of the pier and for the accommodation of passengers.

The first National Census of Scotland took place in 1841 and revealed that the Burgh's 2,229 persons contained an imbalance of 916 males to 1,313 females. Was this because of a preponderance of servant girls or were the men away at sea? However, 1844 began a period of steady progress with the Helensburgh Joint Stock and Gas Light Company seeking permission to lay its pipes in the Maitland Street area although it would be two years before the Council authorised twenty four gas lights to be placed in the streets. A scheme to license porters to carry goods on the pier and elsewhere was introduced and required them to wear a brass badge. It continued in force until 1938 by which time, perhaps, the licensing of taxi-cabs took over.

1841

The following year saw a private Act confer the status of Police Burgh and the appointment of a force of Superintendent, at a salary of £160 per annum, and nine men to be administered by the Provost and Bailies with nine Commissioners. The Police Rate was 6d (2.5p) in the £ plus 3d for street lighting but, as some lamps were not yet in place, a rebate of 1d was allowed. Residents also paid a parish poor rate.

A crisis of some sort occurred on 22nd July 1847 when all the Councillors resigned simultaneously. At the election on 7th November all were re-elected although Richard Kidston replaced Peter Walker as Provost. Storm conditions prevented the Clerk from attending a later meeting.

The civic authorities must have felt that the Rhu Churchyard was insufficient for the needs of the growing Burgh as in November 1849 it identified a part of Kirkmichael Farm as suitable for acquisition for the purpose of constructing a cemetery.

By the 1851 Census the population of the Burgh was 2,895. Bad weather and frost was said to be the reason for poor time-keeping by the town clock on the Old Parish Church tower and this was discussed with the Ecclesiastical Trustees in April 1853 – this may be the clock that greets travellers on the sea front today. Now the tower is the Tourist Information Centre, and a major overhaul of the clock took place in 2001.

Possibly the shortest term of office came in 1853 when James Smith was elected Provost for the second time, on 9th September and resigned on the 24th as he was moving house!

In 1854 there were problems with the water supply from the wells and a committee was set up to enquire into the propriety of applying to the Superior for a grant of land for a reservoir. This may have been too embarrassing as it would be twelve years before the first public water supply came from Mains Hill reservoir. However, the Council did make Rules and Regulations regarding streets, roads, drains and sewers, but it noted that the solum of all streets and roads in the Burgh was the exclusive property of Sir James Colquhoun.

On 6th April 1857 Sir James wrote to the Clerk of the Council describing the purchase by his grandfather of the Barony of Millig from the daughter of Sir John Schaw of Greenock, (he had purchased it from the Clan McAulay in 1705, but had failed to implement any development plans) and his decision to lay out a new town. It was a friend of his who had suggested that the town should be called after his wife, Lady Helen, granddaughter of the 16th Earl of Sutherland. And so Helen's Burgh it had become!

At about the same time, Provost William Drysdale persuaded Sir James to grant ground at Glenfinlas & Adelaide Streets for a recreation ground which is now the East King Street Public Open Space. The Council then ordered the construction of the new cemetery at the Eastern extremity of its area, but became conscious that the drawback was that King Street had still not been fully opened up! Initially access had to be by the Dumbarton Road to Drumfork toll and then Old Luss Road. The Justice of the Peace Court was held on the last Saturday of each month. Attending on the Court would be George Maclachlan of Young's Place, 3, East Princes Street. The first of three generations to be town clerk – an era of service to the town that lasted for 110 years.

In May 1860 the Reverend John Bell of the Episcopal Church reported to the Council that a public meeting had called for trees to be planted in the streets. Later that year, the Council gave support to a petition presented to the Electric Telegraph Company asking it to lay another line for commercial use along the railway. On the cultural side, though not a Council matter, William Battrum advertised that he had established a link with Mudies London Library with about 1,000 volumes at his premises in East Princes Street opposite the railway station. He also had a subscription reading room with newspapers and reviews from London, Edinburgh and Glasgow.

A longstanding joke was to describe something or someone being 'as ugly as the town hall!'

The 1861 census of population again recorded an increase – 4,613, but with an imbalance of almost three females for every two males. Although there was a continued demand for new houses, building was slow for want of a regular water supply. Three years later the cholera outbreak in Glasgow reoccurred but it was stated that in Helensburgh 'after nearly twenty years of effort on the part of the corporation nearly all of the streets are in good condition, though not so well lighted as they ought to be, are better than in most country towns.'

On 26th March 1868 the Mains Hill reservoir was opened by Mrs Breingan, the wife of the Provost, and the town used its first public piped water supply. It had taken twelve years from a positive decision on the need and even longer from a proposal by Henry Bell!

The census of 1871 revealed that the 2536 males were again outnumbered by 3,428 females – a population increase in ten years of more than a thousand. The piped water scheme must have been appreciated for an additional pipe from Glen Fruin was laid in 1872. The obelisk to commemorate the life and work of Henry Bell was put up on the sea front esplanade at a cost of £900 – forty two years after his death!

When the Duke of Argyll appeared to be about to sell a sea front site for residential use in 1877, William Kidston obtained financial support from Sir James Colquhoun and others to enable its purchase for a public park and in order to preserve the integrity of the West Bay. The agreement at the time was that it should not be named after any of the subscribers, and it was known as Cairndhu Point. However, in 1889 Mr Kidston left money to support the maintenance of this feature and requested it became known, as it still is, as Kidston Park.

Sites for a new town hall were debated, in Colquhoun Square and in King Street, but in 1878 the present Municipal Building, in Scots Baronial style, was built at the corner of Sinclair and East Princes Streets at a cost of £6,000, on the site of the long disused theatre. Three years later the Town Council proposed the building of esplanades on both the east and west bays and Sir James Colquhoun offered to contribute one quarter of the cost.

A major complaint in January 1895 was made by Mr JR Fleming who was concerned at the danger caused by people tobogganing in the streets.

Also, in 1881, the census showed further population growth to 7,693 persons, and this time there had been much debate as to the appropriate questions to be asked of the public. It seems that the replies given may not always have been accurate, however. Helensburgh claimed 1,581 inhabited houses, 211 vacant houses and 39 in course of building with 4,411 female and 3,282 male residents, of whom 235 were Gaelic speakers.

Controversy arose after the General Election in 1880, for the defeated Liberal, Mr John William Burns, alleged 'bribery, cheating and personation' on the part of the successful candidate Mr Archibald Orr-Ewing (Conservative). The Court of Session appointed Lords Ormidale and Craighill to try the case, but agreed that it should be heard in the Municipal Buildings, convenient to the Queen's Hotel, there being no premises of sufficient luxury for their lordships near to Dumbarton County Court. In the event, an out-of-court settlement was reached with agreement that the electoral malpractice had taken place, but not to such extent as to affect the result!

Judges, lawyers and interested parties entering the Municipal Buildings for the 1880 Electoral fraud case

Neil Macleod

The nineteenth century ended with the alteration and renovation of the Victoria Halls to mark the 62nd year of the Queen's reign and the 80th year of Her Majesty's life. West King Street was the site chosen by Rhu Parish Council to erect Chambers in 1899 which today provide an elegant setting for civil weddings.

In 1901 the Council had Committees for Finance, Waterworks, Streets, Cleansing, Lighting, Police and Parliamentary Bills, Victoria Halls, Parks and Buildings, Fire Brigade, Sanitary and Public Health, and Harbour. The Gas Corporation had a Clerk, Treasurer, Manager and four County Councillors.

1902

An offer by Sir James Colquhoun to donate a Celtic Cross as an ornament and to mark the centenary of Burgh status was accepted. It was placed in Colquhoun Square where it now is, though at one time it was in the centre of the roadway, becoming a traffic hazard. Local architect and watercolourist AN Paterson was commissioned to design an extension to the Municipal Buildings taking the building further up Sinclair Street. This contained a Police Office, with Cells, Fire Station and an entrance to the Court Hall which was at first floor level. The external finishes of the building are worth examination with stone handcuffs, a cat, and the date inscription.

Adrian Kidston offered to convey land in James Street, already used for recreation in 1907, on condition that it be preserved in all time as a place of recreation for the people. As it still is. Provost DS MacLachlan received a Gold Chain of Office in 1907 and in 1911 the Council

The Council objected in 1899 to the idea of a poster board outside the railway station so as to save the town from 'hideous disfigurement.'

acquired from the Estate of the late Miss Susannah Cramb at a cost of £3,750 the house and grounds at Hermitage which were subsequently laid out as a public park and recreation ground. Messrs R&W McMurrich donated the flywheel from the steamship *Comet* and Henry Bell's blacksmith's anvil to be placed in the park, where they remained until 2002.

The Housing and Town Planning etc Act 1919 authorised local councils to provide housing and was enthusiastically adopted by the Burgh Council and the need for two and three apartment houses was discussed in February of that year. The Local Government Board had advised that additional power to requisition land was being investigated. An architect, George Paterson, was engaged in March and throughout the summer negotiations took place with Luss Estates. Land at Ardencaple was thought suitable at a price of £1,750, and by December the Scottish Board of Health had approved a scheme cost of £63,200. The foundation stone of the first council house was laid by Mrs Duncan, wife of the Provost on 5th July 1920.

Further development in the Ardencaple area was under consideration in 1921 when the Burgh Surveyor was instructed to prepare a Town Planning Scheme. Other developments were considered at Claverton Nursery (at Adelaide and East Princes Streets), West King Street, Columba and Colquhoun Streets and West Argyle Street (later called Whitelands). This latter was selected and a compulsory purchase order made for enough land for twenty four houses. The building of council houses then continued for many years. However in 1925 the Scottish Board of Health ruled that the cost of building a two-room council house must not exceed £358 or a three-room £412. The architect had to omit fireplaces in back bedrooms and reduce their height.

The impressive War Memorial in Hermitage Park was completed in 1923 designed by AN Paterson after a campaign led by J Whitelaw Hamilton, his father-in-law. Ceremonies to mark the ending of hostilities and subsequently to remember those who lost their lives in various conflicts have been held annually in the park at 11 am on the Sunday closest to the 11th day of the 11th month.

On the sea front near to the Pier a Putting Green was opened in 1925 and has been operated by the

Kenneth Crawford

The Celtic Cross in Colquhoun Square was donated by Sir James Colquhoun to mark the centenary of the burgh in 1902

An outbreak of smallpox in 1901 caused the erection of a Smallpox Hospital in King Street at its east end at a cost of £1,000 and resulted in the cancellation of Showground lettings.

Council ever since, with the exception of the war years, when air raid shelters were sunk under the land. Due to the liability to easy inundation however they were hardly, if ever, used. A year later, Mr and Mrs Andrew Buchanan made a generous benefaction to the Burgh – Bailies' Robes and Chains of Office. This was followed, in 1928, by the building of the Open Air Swimming Pool at the side of the Pier Head, for which they paid the cost.

1928

Only in 1928 did all persons including women over the age of 21 and resident, become entitled to a vote in local government elections. Since 1918 women had had to be over 30, and property owners or married to property owners.

In 1929 major administrative changes took place, with the Dunbartonshire County Council taking over the responsibilities of various Parish Councils, School Boards and committees. Its 73 members each served for three years and were divided into 28 for the landward (or more rural) areas and 45 for the burghs, sub-divided between large burghs and small burghs – such as Helensburgh. Of course, the Burgh Council continued to be the local authority, but with some reduction in its powers. The County Council declared a precept for its funds from the Burgh annually, which then added its own needs and collected the general rates from the property owners of the Burgh. For the financial year 1933/34 the County demanded a total of £38,180.11s.

In 1933 the Council received a report on future housing needs; to replace houses unfit for human habitation 76 were required and to deal with overcrowding a further 12. The following year the building of 80 at Kirkmichael Farm was agreed. Two years later the London & North Eastern Railway offered to sell land at Alma Place (at East King Street between Grant and Charlotte Streets) and upon this tenements were built.

To celebrate the Silver Jubilee of the reign of King George V in 1935, the interior of the Victoria Halls was renovated by the Burgh Council, but the cost was the gift of Provost Andrew Buchanan JP, another example of the generous practice of local people contributing to major expenditure which would otherwise fall on the ratepayer.

To mark the death of the eminent scientist John Logie Baird on 14th June 1946 the Council passed a resolution and arranged for the embedding of a plaque, which is still on the wall of the Municipal Buildings in East Princes Street. Another major benefaction occurred in this year when, in memory of William Anderson (1854-1928) and his wife Annie Templeton (1858-1928), the Anderson Family gave Drumgarve, John Street, to the Town for use as a Public Library. The house had been home to three generations of their family from 1870 and the public library, known as the Templeton Library, served the town well until replaced by a purpose-built building in 1998. The same family developed the front lawns by the erection of four houses to be

Only in 1928 did all persons including women over the age of 21 and resident, become entitled to a vote in local government elections.

On 3rd June 1940 the Council contributed to the effort for World War II by removing iron railings from Kidston Park, James Street playground and Colquhoun Square.

36

Argyll & Bute Council

To commemorate his 60 years of service as Town Clerk the Council commissioned Sir James Guthrie to paint George Maclachlan's portrait in 1906 – although the sitter was liable to fall asleep while posing! (Oil on canvas, 90 x 69cm)

Miss Janet R Young was elected the first (and only) Lady Provost of Helensburgh in 1958 and she served for three years.

known as Drumgarve Court for occupation by 'indigent gentlewomen'. This scheme was extended by the Town Council which erected eight additional houses in the 1960s.

1962

In 1962 the Council celebrated the one hundred and fiftieth anniversary of the construction of the first commercially successful passenger-carrying steam-powered ship in Europe – the *Comet*. Provost J Macleod Williamson donned period dress and carrying an umbrella believed to have belonged to Henry Bell, escorted the Secretary of State for Scotland on the crossing from Port Glasgow to Helensburgh Pier. They were on board a replica of the *Comet* built for the purpose by Sir William Lithgow at his shipyard in Port Glasgow.

The only Royal Visit by the Monarch to the town occurred in 1965 when HM the Queen inspected the redecorated Municipal Buildings.

The public water supply was in need of an upgrade and the Council accepted a tender for the construction of a new water system Filter House in 1966; however, it also agreed that it would then transfer its undertaking to a new Water Board. Thirteen Water Authorities were set up by government to amalgamate 199 local Scottish water works.

Off street parking was provided in the period 1967 – 1975 when the land previously used as a railway goods yard, and cleared sites in the centre of the block between Sinclair, Princes, Colquhoun and King Streets, also land in Maitland Street and land reclaimed from the sea adjacent to the Pier were so designated.

The Burgh Council elected Alastair H Paterson to be its first and ultimately, only, Honorary Burgess for his services to the community, but sadly he died only seven weeks later. He had been a sportsman, was a long serving and conscientious councillor and the son of AN Paterson, the local architect.

On 16th June 1970 Norman Macleod Glen was elected Provost. As he was re-elected in both 1971 and 1974 he became the last Provost of Helensburgh. On taking office he declared his two aims, firstly to ensure a public sewerage scheme for the town and secondly, to build a covered swimming pool. During some of his retirement, Mr Glen lived at Queen's Court, formed from the Queen's Hotel, built as the Baths Hotel, the home of Henry Bell. Fittingly, there are still two Provosts' Street Lamps in front of this celebrated building which record the fact that the First and Last Provosts lived in the building.

Public sewerage and drainage of the area had been commenced in 1929 but only became completely effective in 1974. In 1970 all the sewers discharged untreated into the sea only a few yards below the low water mark. As will be imagined the penalty for all to see and smell was a filthy beach on many occasions. Much research took place before it

It was reported to the Council in 1968 that 80% of its 958 houses had been damaged by the most severe storm in the history of the Burgh.

became apparent that discharge into the sea between Ardmore and Greenock was least likely to result in the flow returning. A main pipe with pumping stations was laid along the sea front from Kidston Park to Ardmore which picked up all the outflows.

Extensive house building was required by the growing town in the early 1970s, the Ministry of Defence constructed houses at Churchill and Ardencaple and the Council built more than 200 at Johnson Court, Maitland Court, Old Luss Road, Mossend Place and Cove Place. Consideration also had to be given to a looming problem of an increasing number of elderly residents. Twelve cottages, known as Birch Cottages, were eventually built by Bield Housing Association in co-operation with Dumbarton District Council on an allotment site at the north-west corner of Hermitage Park. The same Association were later to build Waverley Court on the site of St Joseph's Primary School in West King Street.

At the same time Government was arranging for much larger authorities to be created – it had concluded that 400 Scottish Burgh and County Councils should be reduced to 65, although the two tier system was thought to be essential.

The Final Kirking of the Burgh Council took place on 11th May 1975 at the Old and St Andrew's Parish Church in Colquhoun Square when eleven Councillors and seven Officers were lead by Provost Glen and the Colquhoun Pipe Band to repeat a ceremony which had preceded each Civic Year. Thus was marked the end of 173 years of the Helensburgh Burgh Council. A scroll is displayed in the porch of the West Kirk signed by those who attended.

1975

The replacement administrations were to be the Strathclyde Regional Council based in Glasgow and Dumbarton District Council. The Local Government Act clearly defined the responsibilities of each, but they had much wider interests than the small towns within their areas. Strathclyde ensured that the pier remained viable by dredging the sea bed to facilitate the regular sailing of pleasure steamers. A further large area adjacent to the pier and on its Eastern side was infilled and ultimately became a car and coach park accessed from the foot of Sinclair Street. By this time the precept for Council services had risen to £1,650,012. Some more locally based representation was restored in 1976 when Helensburgh Community Council was set up to ascertain local opinion and to convey views to the appropriate service provider authorities.

A period of stagnation commenced in which local government resources were concentrated upon the improvement of infrastructure in areas to the east of Helensburgh and not within the town. Public buildings and roads were not regularly maintained and development proposals tended to be ignored or refused. Financial restructuring also

By 1975 the Government had concluded that 400 Scottish Burgh and County Councils should be reduced to 65.

Kenneth Crawford

The Baths Hotel which became the Queen's Hotel is now Queen's Court – the middle name can be clearly seen at the top of the building. The inscription on the pair of Provost's lamps in front of the building states:

These Lamps Mark
the Home of
Henry Bell and Norman Glen
The First
and Last Provosts
of Helensburgh

was introduced by the Government which probably gave it more control over services which really are of local importance. All councils were required to put out to public tender the provision of services and their own direct labour departments had to change their systems to allow them to prepare and submit a competitive tender on commercial lines.

After a long campaign and much co-operation between various interests the new covered swimming pool on the sea front came into use on 8th November 1976, although the opening ceremony, by James McKinley JP, BA, MCIT, was not until 25th March 1977. As 30% of potential users were thought to be likely to come into town from the rural areas the County Council had contributed to the cost but public subscription had raised £10,000 by various means. The total cost of the pool was £300,000 plus £20,000 for the car park both in front and on the newly infilled land at the rear. The intention had certainly been that the open air pool would continue in use during the summer months but, after one season, Dumbarton District decided that it should close and, to the regret of many residents, it was boarded up and left to become an eyesore and remain derelict for many years.

In 1983 Helensburgh acquired its only twin town. Dumbarton District Council signed an agreement with Thouars, a French market town of similar size situated on the River Thouet about ten miles (16km) from its junction with the River Loire. When Argyll and Bute Council took over in 1997 the twinning agreement was re-signed by them.

As part of the process of finding its feet and role, in 1985, the Community Council prayed to the Lord Lyon King of Arms and received a grant of its own Ensigns Armorial based upon the Arms which had been granted to the former Burgh Council in 1929 continuing from the Seal of the Burgh recorded as having been authorised in 1857. The motto surmounting the crest '*Si Je Puis*' means 'If I Can' and is reputed to have been the reply of a Colquhoun Chief when asked by the King of Scots to recapture Dumbarton Castle from enemies. At the time when King James I of Scotland had appointed the Clan Chief to be Governor of the Castle, it is said that his troops pretended to be hunting a stag and thus contrived to close in on the castle and take it.

In the arms the stag is a symbol of battle honours and the helm indicates the rank of a Baronet. Below this the black St Andrews cross and the Greyhound on the left were from the Colquhoun Crest. At the base a further motto '*Cnoc Elachan*' was the battle cry and gathering place of the Colquhouns, Armoury Hill. On the right hand side, the three gold stars on a red shield originated from the Sutherland family arms, acknowledging that Sir James had named his new town after his wife, Lady Helen Sutherland. A coronet signifies a Statutory Council. The black cross and gold stars are continued in the Arms of Argyll and Bute Council.

A planning proposal to reclaim more land from the sea adjacent to

Burgh coat of arms prior to 1929

1985

Helensburgh Community Council coat of arms

Helensburgh's Provosts 1807 – 1975

1807-09	Henry Bell
1811-28	Jacob Dixon
1828-34	James Smith of Jordanhill
1834	James Bain
1835	John McFarlane
1836	Richard Kidston
1837-39	James Breingan
1839	James Bain
1840-49	Richard Kidston
1850-53	Peter Walker
1853	James Smith of Jordanhill
1854-57	William Brown
1857-63	William Drysdale
1863-69	Alexander Breingan
1869-77	Thomas Steven
1877-84	John Stuart
1884-90	William Bryson
1890-93	John Mitchell
1893-96	Alexander Whyte
1896-1902	Colonel William Anderson VD
1902-08	Samuel Bryden
1908-11	David S Maclachlan
1911-12	Adrian MMG Kidston
1912-18	James D Bonnar
1918-27	Major John F Duncan VD
1927-30	Ronald R Herbertson
1930-36	Andrew Buchanan
1936-41	J Russell Martin
1941-44	John Somerville
1944-45	William A Ferguson
1945	John Somerville
1945-52	William B Lever
1952-55	Alexander Gordon CIE
1955-58	John M Jack
1958-61	Janet R Young
1961-70	J McLeod Williamson
1970-75	Norman M Glen TD

the car park and behind Tower Place for the purpose of building a large food supermarket was pursued for over three years by the Scottish Co-op but was finally rejected, on appeal, by the Secretary of State in 1995. By the 1990s the appearance of neglect of the town had reached a stage which could no longer be ignored, and Dunbartonshire Enterprise stepped in, and in the interests of job creation designed a comprehensive upgrade plan for the West Bay Esplanade. This was not implemented in its entirety but in 1994 a refurbishment did take place. The sea wall became safe to walk on with increased seating, flower beds were introduced and the bust of John Logie Baird, which had been hidden in Hermitage Park, achieved a prominent position. Then the long derelict outdoor swimming pool was finally cleared away and 'temporary' redevelopment as a children's play area greatly enhanced the entrance to the pier.

Once again Government had become unhappy with the statutory local government arrangements made in Scotland by its predecessor. Another reorganisation was proposed, to abolish all of the 1973 divisions and create single tier, all purpose councils. In Helensburgh, a movement grew to separate the town from whatever authority would also contain the town and politicians of Dumbarton. The sensible alternative was to join Argyll, a vast area covering the West of Scotland, but at the same time so very much smaller in population and financial background than Strathclyde had been. The Community Council maintained a non-political stance on the idea but supported a referendum held by Dumbarton District Council with the help of the *Helensburgh Advertiser* local newspaper. A substantial return showed that the residents were of the view that an alliance with Argyll should be made.

By 1996 it seemed likely that the changes in local government would deprive Dumbarton District of its more affluent, income producing, areas, and it commenced a programme seeking to change the opinion of the electorate. In case it did not succeed, however, some asset stripping ideas were also put forward! A new, purpose built library for Helensburgh was proposed, a joint user scheme with A Trail & Son Ltd was devised to utilise the site of the former St Bride's Church with a development of Housing Association flats and a Public Library. To great acclamation building commenced but it did not occur to anyone that the library building construction was just that – a full residential scheme for occupation plus the shell of a building which could, perhaps, be finished internally as a Library (at a later date) by someone else!

The East Bay Pavilion, long derelict, unsightly, and a danger to intruders and others was advertised nationally for sale for a restaurant or a variety of possible uses. Three tenders were received and a firm of architects was favoured, but local opposition developed and a long drawn out battle of public meetings, claim and counterclaim about the

1996

By 1996 likely changes in local government led to Dumbarton District seeking to commence a programme of asset stripping !

history of the site and the conditions upon which it was owned by the District Council lasted four years.

In the last few days before ceasing to exist, on 31st March 1997, Strathclyde Regional Council found the means and opportunity to engage a suitable vessel to 'level the sea bed' around the pier. This enabled continuity in the sailings of the *Kenilworth* ferry service to Gourock and Kilcreggan and summer sailings by PS *Waverley*, whose operators had been reporting the silting up of the bed.

Reorganisation took place on 31st March 1997 and Helensburgh became a part of a new unitary authority, the Argyll and Bute Council, administered from Lochgilphead. Many cartoons and comments were published about the cost and effort likely to be needed to visit the Headquarters some seventy miles away. However a scheme of decentralisation was envisaged by the statute and a local office was set up, together with a new internal area boundary extending from Cardross to Garelochhead and Arrochar and including the peninsula of Rosneath and a substantial part of Loch Lomond side. The six local councillors started monthly meetings in public at various public halls. The former medical practice centre was refurbished as Scotcourt House to house local staff thus providing public access. A former mansion at Rhu, Blairvadach, was converted into offices for Planning and Environmental departments with the result that more administration is accomplished locally than had been the case for many years.

1998

In 1998 a small upgrading of the pier began with the installation of navigation lights, and pedestrian lighting columns. The ferry across the Clyde became year round and offered four crossings daily. The Victoria Halls were redecorated by the Council and new flooring greatly enhanced the facility for dancing. In 1999 new decking, seats and a small shelter again added to the practical use of the pier. Another improvement scheme was the installation of sixteen custom built and designed street lighting columns in Colquhoun Square to replace the post-war concrete pillars with their yellow sodium lighting. Each carries plaques relating to town history and the lantern is surmounted by a golden replica of Henry Bell's *Comet*.

The year 2000 saw the occupation and reopening of the ground floor of the Municipal Buildings by Lomond Enterprise Partners and the undertaking of an upgrade to the Court Hall to bring it back into use for its original purpose as a District Court. This latter had been forced upon the Council by a ruling of the Court of Session that it was not legitimate for Argyll & Bute to rent court space outwith its area, in Dumbarton, and that it had to provide a Court facility within its own administrative area to dispense justice for its inhabitants.

During the same year the saga of the derelict East Bay Pavilion continued even though the prospective tenant architects had long since gone away, and the Council had decided that the best option was to demolish the building. Early in 2001 the East Bay Pavilion was razed to the ground by the Council, perhaps ending years of controversy, but planning consent was granted for a supermarket on the sea front, in the knowledge that the Scottish Executive would be almost bound to 'call-in' the application for decision at national level. As expected the Executive announced a public inquiry later that year.

A committee to consider upgrading the landscaping of Colquhoun Square was set up by the Council. Local residents also formed a committee to create a vision of the future of the town with a view to shaping the Structure Plan, required to be drawn up by Argyll and Bute Council. Another group of residents were protesting at the severe reduction in Public Toilet facilities available for visitor and public use. The Council maintained that it had no statutory duty to provide toilets and insufficient funds to maintain them voluntarily.

A 'livery colour' of maroon and gold was adopted by Argyll and Bute Council for use on street furniture – litter bins, lamp posts and safety rails – the designer lighting column scheme was extended and a set of direction indicator finger posts installed with the aim of giving a unified appearance to Helensburgh town centre.

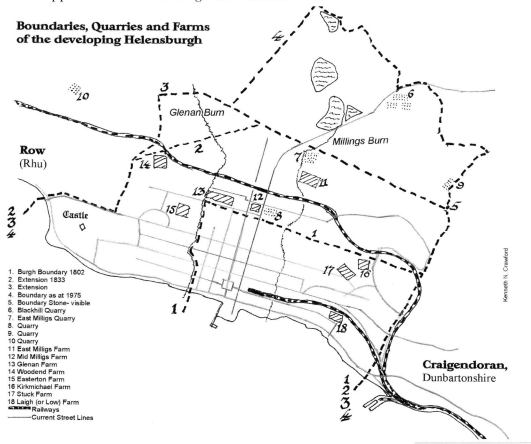

Boundaries, Quarries and Farms of the developing Helensburgh

Row (Rhu)

Glenan Burn

Millings Burn

Castle

Craigendoran, Dunbartonshire

Kenneth N. Crawford

1. Burgh Boundary 1802
2. Extension 1833
3. Extension
4. Boundary as at 1975
5. Boundary Stone- visible
6. Blackhill Quarry
7. East Milligs Quarry
8. Quarry
9. Quarry
10 Quarry
11 East Milligs Farm
12 Mid Milligs Farm
13 Glenan Farm
14 Woodend Farm
15 Easterton Farm
16 Kirkmichael Farm
17 Stuck Farm
18 Laigh (or Low) Farm
▬▬▬ Railways
——— Current Street Lines

The Row Heresy – farewell sermon preached in a field by Rev John McLeod Campbell in 1828

The chain of events leading to the Row Heresy was indicative of the history of faction and division in the Church of Scotland played out in Helensburgh and throughout the country.

The church in the background of this illustration is a representation of the old Row Church as it might have been in 1828, well before William Spence designed the pinnacled octagonal tower which was erected in 1851

CHAPTER 5

Religion

ANNE GRAY

Garelochside was a rough place in the eighteenth and the early nineteenth centuries. Public Houses had increased in number, illicit stills flourished, smuggling was commonplace and church attendances were dwindling. In those days, in addition to responsibility for spiritual guidance, the Church was responsible for the education and moral welfare of the people of the parish.

The parish system existed long before the Christian era. In Roman times it was a geographical unit of civil administration and the early Christian Church first introduced it into Scotland in the thirteenth century. The Parish of Row was created in 1648 from lands belonging to the ancient parishes of Cardross (the Mother Church of which was Glasgow Cathedral) and Rosneath (the Mother Church of which was Paisley Abbey). It extended from Camis Eskan in the South East to Loch Longside and upwards into Glen Fruin. A new church had to be built in Row for the new parish and the money for this was provided by the fifteenth Macaulay, Laird of Ardencaple, who also gave land for the manse and garden. The church was completed in 1649. No longer would the people have to cross the narrows to worship in Rosneath.

In early days there had been Chapels of Ease in Glen Fruin, Faslane and Kirkmichael. Those were chapels which did not have the full status of a church but were places of worship for the people to attend when it was not convenient for them to attend the Parish Church. In common with such chapels all over the country in post-Reformation days, they were neglected and fell into a state of disrepair. The new church with its minister and Kirk Session would have to shoulder the responsibilities of the large parish alone for the next 150 years.

The minister and Kirk Session did what they could to look after the spiritual needs and the moral welfare of this unruly population. Less serious offences were punished by fines or public rebukes with the offender sitting on the repentance stool. For more serious offences they could excommunicate the offender. In the past this had meant that the civil authorities would almost certainly refuse to allow the offender to work, thus plunging him and his family into a condition of poverty and social ostracism. This extreme penalty was withdrawn by the civil authorities at the beginning of the eighteenth century.

At the beginning of the nineteenth century there was an upsurge of free-thinking which affected religious as well as secular matters. Helensburgh, after a slow start, was beginning to grow and this growth would be more rapid as travel became faster. Although there were many public houses in Helensburgh at the beginning of the nineteenth century, there was no church and, on Sundays, the 'guid folk' had to set out on foot in all weathers to attend worship in Row. But groups were beginning to meet in houses and this would develop in different ways.

The first development started in 1799 when two young men from the Society for the Propagation of the Gospel at Home were walking through Helensburgh after an unsuccessful missionary journey in the Highlands (because they could not speak Gaelic). They were invited to hold a service in the town on the following day and from then on students from Rev Greville Ewing's theological training establishment in Glasgow visited the town on a regular basis.

By 1802 the group was strong enough to build the first church of Helensburgh – **The Tabernacle**. This was a small plain building built on ground at the corner of West Princes Street and James Street that was so marshy that stepping stones had to be laid up to the door. There was no comfort, the floor was the bare earth and the seats hard and high. Immediately there was dissension between groups favouring different independent movements and this led to a vote which was in favour of the **Congregational** movement. Part of the congregation departed and it is said that they demanded the return of the money they had subscribed towards the building fund – a sum of £90. The story goes that this money was eventually found and the matter resolved.

The first minister left after five years to join the Baptist Church and the second minister also left after five years to take a charge in Falkirk from which he also joined the Baptists. For eleven years they had no minister but a small nucleus of the congregation stayed faithful and they were well served by students from Glasgow Theological Academy who took the Sunday services. They were rewarded in 1824 when Rev John Arthur accepted the call to be minister. He was the only minister in Helensburgh until 1827 and thereafter was one of only two ministers in the Burgh for a further fifteen years. He gladly gave his help wherever needed to members and non-members alike and he founded both day and Sabbath schools.

The original Tabernacle building served for nearly fifty years, with the addition of a large gallery and a wooden floor. In 1851 it was decided to demolish it as there had been extensive outbreaks of dry rot. A new church was built on the site but it also fell victim to dry rot. It was replaced in 1884 with a new church built adjacent to the old on the

Neil Macleod

Park Church

Built in 1862 as the East Free Church to alleviate overcrowding in the Kirk in the Square, it changed its name to Park United Free Church in 1900, and then to Park Church in 1929, each time as a result of denominational mergers within Scottish church life

The confusing threads of secession and subdivision – the 'card trick' episode at Park Church surrounded a dispute about standing for worship and sitting for prayer

Neil Macleod

south east corner of West Princes Street and James Street. The second church now serves as a capacious church hall.

The next church to be built was **The Kirk in the Square** but to understand the composition of the congregation of this new church in Colquhoun Square it is necessary to go back to the early days and disentangle the confusing threads of secession, subdivision and union.

The first to secede from the Church of Scotland were the Cameronians who seceded in 1681. They had been Covenanters and were rigidly Calvinistic. They were later joined by the Hebronites and together they formed the Reformed Presbyterian Church. There is no record of a branch of this church in the Helensburgh area.

The first major secession was in 1733 when Ebenezer Erskine of Stirling led a group out of the Church of Scotland to form the **Associate Synod**. They were protesting against the reinstating of Patronage which had taken place in 1712 with the passing of the Patronage Act. This meant that once more lay patrons, such as the local laird, had the right to appoint ministers to charges – in other words, the congregation no longer had the right to call their own minister. The denomination grew rapidly but in 1747 argument broke out about their attitude to the Burgess Oath. The point of contention was that in the oath administered to Burgesses there was a reference to '. . . the true religion presently professed within this realm'. This was interpreted by some as a reference to the Established Church and, as they could not agree, the denomination split into **Burghers** and **Antiburghers.**

Unfortunately this was not the end of disagreement. A further point

1825 saw the building of the first church in Colquhoun Square, aptly called 'The Kirk in the Square'.
The present building was constructed in 1853 but suffered a major fire in 1924. Today, after changes of denominaton and mergers with other churches, it is known simply as 'The West Kirk'

Neil Macleod

at issue was whether or not the seventeenth century Covenants were binding forever. The arguments gave birth to the **Auld Licht** and **New Licht Burghers** in 1799 and the **Auld Licht** and **New Licht Antiburghers** in 1820. The New Lichts were more liberal than the Auld Lichts in their thinking and in 1820 they came together to form the **United Secession Church**.

In the meantime another parallel group had been led out of the Church of Scotland in 1752 by Thomas Gillespie and two others who felt that religion should be kinder and gentler than the fierce Calvinism of the other seceders. The resulting denomination was called the **Church of the Second Secession** or the **Relief Church**. It was formed 'For the relief of Christians oppressed in their Christian privileges'. This was a very united body which welcomed all believers to the Lord's Table irrespective of denomination. In 1847 they joined with the Church of the United Secession (previously New Licht Burghers and New Licht Antiburghers) to form the **United Presbyterian Church**. This denomination was to be represented in Helensburgh by the **Church of St Columba.**

The Auld Lichts remained and it was the successors of the early group who came together and, in 1822, started to worship in a tent on rising ground above King Street. This was the first Presbyterian meeting place in Helensburgh. In the winter they moved to a room in the Granary and the congregation prospered. In 1825 they erected their first church which was a basic barn-like building. It was erected in what is now Colquhoun Square but in those days was largely an unfenced quarry with pits which used to fill up with water in rainy periods. The authorities eventually erected a fence when an unfortunate old lady fell into one of the pools and was drowned.

Two years later their first minister, Rev John Anderson, was called to the charge. Mr Anderson was a man of strong personality whose leadership was readily accepted by the congregation. In 1839 most of the congregation followed his advice and were received into the **Church of Scotland**. Some, however, could not accept this and they joined with other seceders, thus becoming part of the group that was to become the United Presbyterian Church.

For years there had been rumblings of discontent in the Church of Scotland throughout the land and the Evangelical party had been getting stronger. Matters came to a head when, at the opening of the General Assembly in Edinburgh in 1843, the retiring Moderator, Dr David Welsh, quit the Moderator's chair saying that he could not regard it as a free Assembly. He walked into the street followed by many ministers and elders and they walked in procession down Hanover Street to Canonmills to the cheers of the people. **The Disruption** had begun and the Church of Scotland was about to become splintered. It would never regain the authority it once enjoyed in the community.

There were only two Church of Scotland congregations in the Helensburgh district and they went in different directions. The minister and most of the congregation of Row Parish Church stayed with the establishment and those who seceded worshipped in a large granary in Rhu until **Shandon Free Church** was built in 1844.

The other congregation was the **Kirk in the Square** who had just been received into the Church of Scotland four years previously. Under the strong leadership of their minister, Rev John Anderson, nearly the whole congregation left the established church and, after paying £400 for the building, the church became the **Free Church**. In 1853 the foundation stone was laid for a new building in Colquhoun Square which was dedicated later in the year. It was built partly of stone from the adjacent quarry.

So once again, after only four years, there was no Church of Scotland congregation in Helensburgh, and Row was the only place of worship for those faithful to the Auld Kirk. But the Church of Row had been having its own troubles.

In 1825 they had called Rev John McLeod Campbell to be their minister. He was a well qualified twenty-five year old son of the manse who was a fluent Gaelic speaker. This was necessary for Row was largely a highland parish. He had a major task before him and set about it with true Christian zeal. He did not subscribe to the Calvinist teaching that Christ did not die upon the cross for all mankind but only for the elect because some had been decreed from all eternity to be consigned to an eternal destruction. John Campbell preached: 'Salvation is the free gift of God to all who are willing to receive it.'

Soon the crowds came to hear him preach and many turned again to the faith they had rejected. But the Establishment did not appreciate his teaching and even some of his own people formed a cabal and began an intrigue against him which soon blossomed into a national scandal and the appearance of the word 'heresy'. **The Row Heresy** had begun and was to shake the very foundations of the Church of Scotland. A formal complaint was made against him in the winter of 1828 and this was found proven by the Presbytery and Synod and referred to the General Assembly.

At the General Assembly John McLeod Campbell defended himself vigorously but to no avail. After debating all night the Assembly reached a decision at 6.15am and pronounced against him by 119 votes to 6 with many abstentions. He was accordingly deposed as a minister of the Church of Scotland and automatically stripped of his priestly and pastoral functions and forbidden to enter any of the Church's buildings 'to preach therein'. After the sentence was pronounced his father, minister of Kilninver, said those memorable words:

> Moderator, I bow to any decision to which you think it right
> to come. I am not afraid for my son. Though his brethren
> think it right to cast him out, the Master whom he serves
> may not forsake him and whilst I live, I will not be ashamed
> to be the father of so worthy and blameless a son.

John McLeod Campbell preached his farewell sermon in a field to large numbers of those who so recently had been his parishioners. He was presented with a chalice inscribed: 'To the Rev J McLeod Campbell to show the continued devotion and faith in his teaching of some Row parishioners'. He travelled the country on horseback preaching to huge congregations and later formed a congregation in Glasgow. He published two books – *The Nature of the Atonement* and *Thoughts on Revelation* – and was awarded an Honorary Doctorate of Divinity by Glasgow University. At his graduation it was said: 'The University has done what in them lies to reverse the sentence of the General Assembly.' When his health failed he went to Rosneath where, from his house, he could see his former parish with the tower of the new church built in 1851. He died in 1872 at the age of 72. In the nave of the present day Rhu Church there is a fine memorial window.

The only other church to be built before the great watershed of the Disruption was the **Episcopal Church**. As early as 1814 an Episcopal congregation existed but there are no clear records until 1841 when Mr William Nimmo ordered a small apartment in William Street to be fitted up as a temporary Episcopal chapel. In 1842 a plain stone chapel, the Holy Trinity Chapel, was built on a site at the corner of William

The Row Heresy was to shake the very foundations of the Church of Scotland

The tympanum of St Michael and All Angels Church

Kenneth Crawford

Street and West Princes Street. In 1851 a day school was added to the chapel and in 1857 the Parsonage (now Rectory) was built. By 1866 the congregation had outgrown Holy Trinity Chapel and it was decided to pull it down and erect a larger church in its place. In 1868 building of the present church was completed and it was dedicated to **St Michael and All Angels** after the pre-Reformation chapel in Faslane. The school made a very important contribution to education in the area and even after the Education Act of 1872 was passed, obliging the School Board to provide education, the Episcopal school remained open for a further forty years. As time went on there were various additions to the church buildings – the church hall and a new vestry in 1912 and the church tower in 1930 when the new bells rang out for the first time at the service of dedication. The side chapel was built in 1950 and dedicated to the Holy Trinity. The Church is busy and prosperous and has had an influx of new blood with the coming of the Navy to Faslane bringing members of the Church of England to the area.

Now a period of church building began with four new churches erected in Helensburgh within fifteen years of the Disruption. The first was the **United Secession Church** (later to become **United Presbyterian** and today known as the **Church of St Columba**) which was dedicated in June 1846. This denomination had been formed by the union of the New Lichts and the Relief Church (see above) but, having no meeting place of their own, they had been worshipping in the Kirk in the Square. In 1839, however, this church was received into the Church of Scotland and they could not accept this and so they had to find a meeting place in Helensburgh or walk to Dumbarton to worship. Mrs Margaret Bell, the widow of Henry Bell, was a moving spirit in this group and she invited them to meet in her Baths Hotel (now Queen's Court at 114 East Clyde Street) for worship. When the congregation became too big they moved to the theatre at the corner of East Princes Street and Sinclair Street where the Municipal Buildings now stand. They petitioned the United Presbytery of Glasgow praying to be formed into a congregation. This petition was quickly granted and the church dates its beginning from 1844. It was then a United Secession Church but from 1847 onwards it was United Presbyterian.

The first church at 2 West King Street was known as the **Wee Kirk** and is now a commodious hall much used, not only by the Church but also by other organisations in the town. It was replaced by the present church at the corner of Sinclair Street and West King Street in 1861. Two churches and a manse were built between 1844 and 1864 at a total cost of £7,000.

The next church to be built came to be known later as the **Old Parish Church**. With the defection of the Kirk in the Square to the Free Church there was, once again, no parish church in Helensburgh. The minister of Rhu helped out by taking weeknight services but the need for a Parish Church in the fast growing town was urgent. A site was found on the seafront at the foot of Sinclair Street and on the 23rd May 1847 the church was opened. In 1862 it was erected (*sic*) into a Quoad Sacra Parish Church to be known as the **Church and Parish of Helensburgh**. The church opened a successful day school which, however, was closed after twenty five years as a result of the passing of the Education Act in 1872.

The congregation in the Kirk in the Square (the **Free Church**) prospered and grew to such an extent that they had to look for further premises. They started by having services in Grant Street led by a lay missionary then, in 1862, built the **East Free Church** (now **Park Church**) at the corner of East King Street and Charlotte Street, and the Free Church now became the **West Free Church**. Twelve years later there was a major internal conflict in the East Free Church which has been referred to as 'the Card Trick'. The old custom was to stand for prayer and sit for praise but one Sunday anonymous printed cards were handed out to the congregation advising them to abandon the old custom and sit for prayer and stand for praise. Most followed this advice but not all. The next communication to the congregation was signed by six elders who held that the handing out of an anonymous card by unauthorised individuals was not consistent with Presbyterian order and advised that '. . . all who are in health should continue as heretofore. . .'

This was a period of full church attendance and as the population grew the need for another Church of Scotland congregation became apparent. In 1867 the elders and trustees of the Parish Church met to consider the setting up of a preaching station and as a result they rented a large room in William Street which they fitted up with a pulpit and forms at a total cost of £18. Shortly after they appointed John Baird as Probationer at a stipend (salary) of £80 per annum. His son, John Logie Baird was to become world famous as the inventor of television.

A year later they petitioned the Presbytery to let them have an ordained ministry for Mr Baird had now been a probationer for a year. The Presbytery pointed out that they must have a constitution so a Presbytery committee met with the managers in January 1869. A constitution was agreed but Presbytery would not accept it unless they changed one phrase. This phrase was: 'The right of voting in the election of a minister shall be vested in the communicants, Male and Female.' The Presbytery demanded that the words 'male and female' should be replaced by the words 'male only'. The congregation insisted that the original wording should stand and a deputation of managers went to the March Presbytery meeting eventually persuading it to agree. A pioneering blow for women's suffrage had been struck in Helensburgh.

In 1868 the church had ordered an iron building at a cost of £510.5s (£510.25) and it was erected on a piece of ground fronting William Street. When the church opened it was officially named the **West Parish Church** and on 19th August 1869 Mr Baird was ordained, eventually serving this church for a total of forty-two years. In 1873 the congregation started to raise money for a replacement for the iron church and by the end of 1876 they had £3,900 of the estimated £6,200 required. The site of the Iron Church was not available for a permanent building but they eventually found a site at the corner of West King Street and John Street and decided to lay the foundation stone. The new church was opened on 10th March 1878

Helensburgh by the 1880s had five Presbyterian churches where not even one had existed forty-four years earlier. In addition there was a **Roman Catholic** church, a **Congregational** church, a **Baptist** church and an **Episcopal** church.

There was no **Roman Catholic Church** in Helensburgh until 1880. After the Reformation came to Scotland in 1560 the Roman Catholic Church had to go underground and to all intents and purposes disappeared from the scene but groups were meeting secretly. The earliest recorded local meetings were in 1865 when a group met in a hall in East King Street where the supermarket is now. The original name was **St Brigit's** but two years later this was changed to **St Paul of the Cross**. In 1880 a chapel with school was built in Grant Street where the present halls are (between East Argyle Street and East King Street). Now the final name change took place and the church was renamed **St Joseph's**. The present stone church at the corner of Lomond Street and East King Street was opened in 1912 and for forty three years had

no sister church but in 1955 St Mahew's Chapel
in Cardross was restored and reopened for
worship. Twelve years later St Gilda's Church
was opened in Rosneath.

The **Baptist Church** came to Helensburgh
earlier. In 1833 Robert Dickie, a Glasgow
businessman, came to live in Helensburgh and
formed a group of 'Scotch Baptists' – a group
that rejected trained ministers and shared
ministry among the elders. They worshipped
in a house in William Street then built a chapel
in Mr Dickie's garden and for baptism used a
pool in the East Burn which ran through the
garden. This was a harmonious group until

St Joseph's Church

towards the end of Mr Dickie's life when signs
of dissension became apparent. He died in
1862 and the numbers declined until there was
nothing left. In 1876 a Baptist Church started
in Dumbarton and some walked there from
Helensburgh. In 1889, however, eleven Baptists
engaged the Masonic Hall and eventually,
largely due to the faith and perseverance of Mrs
George Chapman, the decision was taken to
form a new church. Another important figure
at this time was Mrs Elizabeth Sale, a retired
missionary from India, who was noted for her
zeal and generosity.

Baptist Church

In 1886 the present church building at 7
East King Street was completed. Apart from a
short period in the 1950s the church has been
self-supporting and has contributed to the
Baptist Missionary Society, World Relief
Organisations, the Baptist Union and the wider
work in Scotland.

As the years went on it became plain that
the existence of different denominations had
provided a focus for dissension rather than
peace, so the Church decided to enter into a
new phase. The Free Church and the United
Presbyterian Church united in 1900 to form the
United Free Church and the three Free Church
congregations in Helensburgh were now known
as the **West United Free**, **St Columba United
Free** and **Park United Free**.

The **West United Free Church** had come

St Columba Church

a long way from the barn-like structure beside a quarry. The 1853 building was imposing and the erstwhile quarry was now an elegant square. But on 24th February 1924 the church was almost entirely destroyed by fire. The congregation held together, much help was given by other churches and the church was restored and re-dedicated in 1926.

In 1929 the United Free Church and the Church of Scotland united under the name of the latter. Dissenters to this Union were known as the **United Free Church Continuing**. The West United Free Church was now known as **St Andrew's Church**, the West Parish Church became **St Bride's**, the church on the seafront became **Helensburgh Old Parish Church** and the other churches became simply **St Columba Church** and **Park Church**. The breach created by the Disruption was finally closed in Helensburgh.

By the middle of the twentieth century, attendance at Church was dwindling and it became clear that the town could no longer support five churches of the same denomination. When Helensburgh Old Parish Church became vacant in 1956 a union took place with St Andrew's Church to form the charge of **Old and St Andrew's**. For a further three years both churches were used for worship then the Old Parish Church building was closed. Subsequently it was acquired by the Huts and Canteens Committee of the Church of Scotland and converted into a hostel for Royal Navy personnel. It was opened by HRH Princess Margaret on 29th March 1959 and continued to serve as a hostel until 1968. The building then lay empty and became derelict until, in 1982, it was sold to A Trail & Son Ltd., a local builder who requested planning permission to demolish the building and build a block of flats on the site. This was eventually granted on condition that the clock tower was left standing and reconditioned. The tower became the Tourist Information Centre and later in the 1980s the Tower Place flats were built on the site.

In 1981 St Bride's Church was united with Old and St Andrew's Church to become the **West Kirk**. Later, St Bride's Church was demolished and a library and flats were erected on the site in West King Street. In Rhu there was a linkage between Rhu and Shandon churches in 1954 and this led to full union in 1971. Shandon Church continued in use until 1981 and is now converted into dwelling houses. Following the pattern of union, the **Congregational Church** became part of the **United Reformed Church** in April 2000.

The **Bethesda Evangelical Church** sprang from the same origin as the Baptist Church. It was in 1850 that John Bowes, who really regarded himself as one of the Brethren, began to visit and preach in the Baptist Church. In 1859 he reported that the Eastburn chapel was overflowing and moved meetings to the Ragged School where he was said to have audiences of more than 500 'and many responding emotionally'. In 1860 division finally took place, possibly over the issue of the requirement of believers' baptism for membership. In 1931 Bethesda Hall at 30 Colquhoun Street was bought and the church is still active and has a full programme of services and of evangelical, social and missionary activities. The persuasion of this church is the **Open Christian Brethren** which is fundamentalist and believes in the two alternatives – eternal life or everlasting damnation. They believe that the Bible is the Word of God and inspired by the Holy Spirit and they believe in Baptism of Believers by immersion and have Communion every Sunday. The church is controlled by its elders and deacons.

The **First Church of Christ, Scientist** was the latest church to come to Helensburgh. It had its local beginnings in 1910 when three Christian Scientists started meeting every Sunday morning and held a Sunday School on Sunday afternoons for the families. When war broke out in 1914 two of the families moved away and services stopped. Ten years later, in 1924, two students of Christian Science started to give bible readings and soon the public asked to join. As numbers increased they had to rent a hall and in 1927 they held their first service in the Masonic Temple. In 1946 they bought a plot of ground at 138-144 West Princes Street and raised the money for the church which was built in 1956 by A Trail and Son. Premises for a Christian Science Reading Room were bought at 106 West Princes Street. Every church maintains a reading room where members of the public are welcome to enquire about Christian Science. They may read, borrow or purchase the Bible, *Science and Health* with *Key to the Scriptures* by Mary Baker Eddy, and the *Christian Science Monitor*.

There is a small but significant group of families in the area belonging to the **Moslem** faith. For some time unsuccessful attempts were made to set up a place of worship in Dumbarton where, in addition to worship, the children and young people could be educated in the teachings of the Prophet Mohammed. In the meantime, the men attended the Mosque in Glasgow and the women taught the children. After many disappointments the community eventually found premises within their means in Dumbarton and, since Autumn 2000, an imam (priest) has come from the Glasgow Mosque to spend two hours every week teaching the children.

Finally, there is a worshipping community in the Churchill Estate which had its beginnings in the early 1970s along with the building of the estate for personnel of HM Naval Base Clyde at Faslane, and their families. For some years both Anglican and Roman Catholic congregations met in Church House in Churchill Square, one of the rooms being named the **Chapel of the Holy Spirit**. In 1996, part of the NAAFI complex was transformed into **St Margaret's Church** to provide a more adequate place for worship. The Church is served by the Chaplaincy Team from the Naval Base, its main Sunday use being by the Roman Catholic community for Mass. On occasions it is used by the Church of Scotland and Anglican Chaplains for worship and meetings.

This account would not be complete without reference to music in the churches. After the Reformation, music in the church was held to be sinful and there was even a period when organs were destroyed. The early churches in this account had no instrumental music and even the introduction of a harmonium merited much discussion and heart-searching. Praise was led by a Precentor with the congregation seated. The Precentor was a very important man who, when a psalm was announced (hymns were not acceptable in those days), used his tuning fork to find the key and proceeded to sing the first line and then was joined by the congregation. The success of this depended greatly upon the musical talent of the Precentor which varied widely.

The first pipe organ in the Burgh was installed in the Congregational Church in 1865 at a cost of £170. The West Parish Church introduced a harmonium in 1871 after considerable argument and this was replaced by an organ in 1898. In 1878 St Columba was the next church to introduce instrumental music. Rhu Church installed its first organ in 1880. It was rebuilt in 1903 and again in 1957. In the West Free Kirk praise was led by a succession of precentors until 1883 when instrumental music was 'made permissive' by the Free Church and a few years later the first organ was installed. The present organ was installed in 1925, during restoration after the fire. In 1891 there was great argument in Park Free Church but after a vote a harmonium was installed. In 1900 this was replaced by a pipe organ which was rebuilt in 1963. The Old Parish Church installed an organ in 1900.

Helensburgh has a fine musical tradition. The West Kirk is ideally suited for choral and orchestral performances and runs a musical series 'Sunday at Seven' which is much appreciated. The United Reformed Church is also noted for musical performances.

The religious scene in Helensburgh during its two hundred years began with no churches at all and rose to a peak of eleven. Two then closed, but one opened, giving a total today of ten, three of which are of the same denomination. Who knows what the future will bring? As ministers of the Church of Scotland retire or resign the future structure of the church is always considered. There are no signs as yet of any union between denominations but the ministers show a good example to their people. They meet weekly for breakfast when they discuss matters of common concern and interest. All the denominations participate and the circle is widened in the Ministry Forum which includes retired ministers and meets monthly. Could this be the beginning of greater union?

Chapter 6
Schools in Helensburgh and District
David Arthur

Scotland has always prided itself on a particular national identity which the Scots have believed to stem from at least three prime and unique areas – the Law, the Church and its Education. For a nation relatively poor in natural resources, such a deficit has been more than made up in large measure thanks to its school system, its intellectual output and through the entrepreneurial enthusiasm and inventiveness of its people. It is only necessary to justify that with the inventions of television by John Logie Baird, the telephone by Alexander Graham Bell, and penicillin through Alexander Fleming. In the nineteenth century half the doctors in the UK had been trained in Scotland, and it was even joked, not without a large measure of truth, that the whole administration of the British Empire was the responsibility of the Scots.

A bewigged Scots dominie

In the Labour Government of 1997 the three great Offices of State, those of Prime Minister, Chancellor and Foreign Secretary were held by two Scots and a man educated in Scotland. Even today a casual listen to radio and TV soon identifies the Scots burr, whether it be on government, business, medicine, the unions or in education. The 'lad o' pairts', the name given to the upwardly mobile young man, while often exaggerated, was held to be an icon for the Scots. It was remarkably true that Clydebank Public Library was the one most used throughout the UK, from which followed the emergence of Red Clydeside and its well-read leaders.

Three hundred and fifty years ago, despite John Knox's aim that there should be one school in every parish, in this area only Rhu, which included of course present day Helensburgh, had one small building set aside as a school. To the twenty-first century child with his or her brightly lit classroom, cheerful wall-coverings, neat desks or tables and the ever present computer screens, that tiny school must seem not just a world away but almost a nightmare scenario in a third world country. The building had only small windows which let in little light, an earthen floor, virtually no heating apart from the one large open fireplace behind the teacher, a row of desks and a large barrel-like contraption in which the bewigged dominie (the term used for the teacher) would sit in small measure protected from the draughts. Close by, hanging on two nails by his desk were a switch (cane) and the dreaded two-pronged tawse (leather strap).

The discipline which these imposed was brutal and immediate, and child rights were a thing for the long distant future. Learning was by rote, with the emphasis on the ability to read, to use number and to have a knowledge of the Bible, usually based on the famous Shorter Catechism. The latter was a small booklet of question and answer about the Bible to be learnt by heart. Gaelic interestingly was the language of learning.

By 1696 the teacher was earning a salary of between 10 guineas (£10.50) to £11 per annum though it was not till 1803 that a house with garden was provided. The teachers of the time were often trained for the ministry and being unable to find a parish then took to teaching and could also use their talents to serve during church service as precentor (leader of the singing of the psalms in the absence of musical instruments), and as parish clerk. One teacher, John Arrol of Row, added to his income by money-lending and it was this part-time occupation that resulted in his murder by a Dumbarton man in 1760.

Education and the system of education in Scotland at that time were still primitive, but it was noted in 1796 that 'even day labourers get their children a good education. . . an advantage which the Scots as a nation enjoy over the natives of other countries.' There was, however, a footnote to all this and it was that 'the want of proper schoolmasters accounted for much bigotry and ignorance'.

It was not until the 1800s that education in Helensburgh took off with the building of a school in 1807, though it was to be financed by fees from the pupils. That method of financing would have failed to make ends meet in its first year but for the good fortune of the sale of a silver watch. The burgh soon had a population of 1400 with eight schools, while in contrast the number of inns in the town had also burgeoned from eleven to thirty! Despite that odd statistic it was noted in the Statistical Account of 1851 that there were 'many respectable and educated people' in the burgh, that all children of the town were within reach of a school, and – a remarkable feature – that no-one born in the parish and who had reached the age of ten was found to be unable to read.

In the 1800s schools sprouted. John Hunter opened one at the

Neil Macleod

The beating of the bounds

corner of William Street and Princes Street, and there was another in the old Town Hall. There was also a 'Ragged School'. One interesting feature of the curriculum was an annual event – 'the Beating of the Bounds'. This exciting event probably involved each boy being provided with a birch stick and being taken to beat the boundaries of the Burgh, which in turn, involved beating the stones that marked the bounds. However, Donald MacLeod in his book, *A Nonogenarian's* (sic) *Reminiscences of Garelochside and Helensburgh* (1883) states that during 'the Redding of the Marches' the boys themselves were actually beaten by the dominie! He recounts:

> Some of the boys operated on howled, others sulked and
> bore it quietly, or with a ghastly grin; none seemed to
> appreciate it, and all went as captives from one point to
> another, a tear-stricken and despondent mob, until the last
> point had been reached, and the last item of instruction had
> been duly implanted in the seat of knowledge.

In explanation of this the purpose was to provide an interesting lesson in local geography! The boys were rewarded with a respectable 6d (2.5p), while the adults, men only, had a more acceptable whisky.

In 1833 the Colquhouns funded an infant school for fifty children and in 1845 Springfield Academy in James Street offered both boarding and day facilities for girls, though this changed in 1864 to offer education to boys – and in its curriculum there was to be included

SCHOOLS

dancing, calisthenics (a form of gymnastics), together with fencing and military drill. For boys there was already, in the 1830s, a school in the manse at 6 Glenan Gardens, West Argyle Street and this had the added attraction that the boys could guddle for trout in the Glenan burn. Meanwhile in 1856 the Rev John Arthur started a boarding school for boys in Campbell Street. By this time, to add to the educational facilities, there was a Helensburgh Public Library and there were even more schools, these being run by the various religious denominations – Baptist, Episcopal and Roman Catholic. The mainstream schools, however, were very much under the control of the established Church of Scotland.

The School Board Act of 1872 changed all this with the handing over of the control of the schools in the state system to School Boards, though the local parish ministers still held great power. The churches have retained this power even to the present day, with alternative education being provided for Roman Catholics and with most Education Committees co-opting a minister from a local parish. At this point in time Hermitage Public School in East Argyle Street was started with a proposed population of 500 youngsters; latterly it was just known as Hermitage School. It stood between Sinclair Street and Grant Street, where Hermitage Primary School now stands. A new building was put up in 1880 which was a magnificent example of the late Gothic style, and other buildings were added over the succeeding years. It had its own secondary and primary departments, and in addition there were three primary schools at Grant Street, Clyde Street and James Street to act as feeders for the upper school. The schools were funded with fees of between 10d (4p) and one shilling (5p) per term, though this seemed to be no major obstacle even to poorer families – parents were expected to provide jotters and books, but desks and ink were provided by the school! The Hermitage School rules of 1916 stated that 'firearms, ammunition, and catapults are . . . forbidden'!

Lack of accommodation proved to be a growing problem even before World War II and in times of need the Victoria Halls and Hermitage House (in Hermitage Park) were used for lessons. Consequently in 1946 the decision was taken to build a new larger school, but it was actually another twenty years before this was to happen, by which time the overcrowding was even worse. The new school was given the name of Hermitage Academy and was built on a large site at Colgrain, the old Hermitage School was then demolished the following year, and Hermitage Primary School was built on its site. However even before the Academy opened, the building was already too small for the ever increasing roll. As a result an adjoining building of nearly the same size was built in 1973.

With the 1872 Act all the denominational schools disappeared, with the exception of St Joseph's for Roman Catholic children, which acts

George Outram & Co Ltd

Hermitage School

Built in 1880 in late Gothic style this building served generations of
Helensburgh scholars as the local secondary school until its replacement by a
new building in 1976 and its demolition in 1977. Hermitage Primary School
now stands on the site in East Argyle Street, although the janitor's house in the
foreground of the picture still remains

today as a feeder for Our Lady and St Patrick's School in Dumbarton. Today the feeder schools for Hermitage Academy are Hermitage Primary, Colgrain, John Logie Baird, Rhu, Luss, Arrochar and all the schools on the Rosneath Peninsula.

Perhaps because Helensburgh had a relatively wealthy population and because Britain still had, in the last part of the nineteenth century and the first half of the twentieth, a large Empire covering almost a third of the globe, this situation meant that a large number of Scots were employed overseas. For both reasons the burgh offered a number of private schools, often with boarding facilities for the children of parents who worked abroad. While this account describes a large number of schools in the area that were privately funded it should never be forgotten that the large majority of the young people of the area were, and still are, educated within the mainstream state system.

> The burgh offered a number of private schools, often with boarding facilities for the children of parents who worked abroad in the days of Empire

The town itself grew over this period from a population of 672 males and 717 females within the parish of Rhu in the 1830s, increasing to 2895 in 1851, but with little change in the first part of the twentieth century – 9703 in 1921, 8,893 in 1931 and 8760 in 1951. It was to be the arrival of the Clyde Submarine Base and the attendant increase in trades and professions which drove the population up to the present 15,000. This increasing change within a relatively small community created many complications for the educational system. One factor of difficulty in educational terms has been a constantly changing population group, either because of businessmen who were transferred to the West of Scotland for a 2-3 year term, or because of naval and military staff who were also posted into the area for a similar relatively short spell.

By the middle of the 1900s education within the state system was completely free of any charge. The schools were controlled by the then County Council of Dunbartonshire, a county which stretched from Arrochar in the west to Cumbernauld in the east. The structure of control worked through an elected Education Committee serviced by its appointed officers – the most senior being the Director of Education. Education was and is strictly regulated through a centralised system monitored by the Scottish Executive and its team of Her Majesty's Inspectors, the curriculum is clearly laid down and all teaching staff must be registered with the General Teaching Council.

While there was a brief period of change in the structure of local government from the 1970s with Helensburgh and Dunbartonshire becoming part of the larger Strathclyde Region, this reverted to a smaller grouping with the move of Helensburgh into Argyll and Bute in 1997. In practice these moves have made little difference to the actual running of the schools and their curriculum. In other ways though, a multitude of changes have been made, particularly in the examination system, and such changes are not yet over. The national move in 1970 to a comprehensive system, whereby the division of schools into selective academic and non-selective vocational came to an end, had little impact on Helensburgh. Hermitage, while it had its more selective academic streams, had also included all pupils in the area.

As the twenty-first century dawns the provision of schools within the burgh has become much simplified. There are non-denominational primary schools within the town itself at John Logie Baird, Hermitage, and Colgrain, while St Joseph's caters for the Roman Catholics, and Rhu and Cardross cover the wider part of the area. Hermitage Academy is the secondary school with over 1700 pupils and 100 teachers, while older Roman Catholic pupils have the option of travelling to Dumbarton to Our Lady and St Patrick's. Pupils in the area with learning difficulties and special needs are ensured excellent state support in the well-equipped Parklands School at the corner of Charlotte Street and East Montrose Street.

Hermitage has two famous authors among its former students in Helen Macinnes (1907-84), a writer of exciting thrillers and known as 'the queen of spy writers', and AJ Cronin whose 'Dr Finlay' transferred so successfully to TV.

A look at the period of the late nineteenth century reveals a formidable list of private schools in large houses – Ardenlee for young gentlemen, Ashmount for young ladies, Barwood, Glenfruin House, Springfield Academy, Kintyre Villa and Colquhoun House for young ladies, with Larchfield for boys. There was, of course, still the small school for boys in the Manse in West Argyle Street – with trout! There were, too, a number of small Dame schools – these were small schools for young children run by ladies; perhaps among the best known of these, certainly to those still alive today, was Miss Ottman's.

Many of the famous names of families which lived in Helensburgh received their early education at one of the independent schools. In the school lists can be found the Crambs (although interestingly there are still Cramb

Lomond School

Larchfield School, 1926

Robert Houston (etching)

Kinnear House at 31 Charlotte Street (c1910) was principally a boarding house for the senior girls of St Bride's School; today it is private housing

Elliott & Fry

medals at both Lomond and Hermitage), the Andersons, the Blackies of publishing fame, the Sloans who lived in Dalmore House and made their money with a coastal shipping company, and of course the Kidstons.

Of all the
independent
schools the most
enduring were
Larchfield and
St Bride's

Of all the independent schools the most enduring were Larchfield and St Bride's, but even these have disappeared being amalgamated in 1978 into Lomond School. On the other hand in the first year of the twenty-first century financial pressures brought the collapse of Keil School in Dumbarton, together with its junior department at Park Lodge at 17 Charlotte Street, Helensburgh. Larchfield probably had its beginnings in Campbell Street with the Rev John Arthur but more successfully in 1846 through the Rev John Wardlaw. Initially the school took boys right throughout their whole school time but latterly evolved into a boys preparatory school feeding boys into the public school system. Among its best known students were Sir James George Frazer, author of *The Golden Bough*, Jack Buchanan, star of stage and screen, and of course the great inventor, John Logie Baird. Among its staff, for brief periods, were the famous poets (and future Poets Laureate), C Day Lewis and WH Auden, who followed the tradition of unqualified teachers filling in before or after college.

St Bride's was founded in 1895 but became the leading girls' school that it was in 1901 and was part of the Girls School Company which included St Columba's School at Kilmacolm and Park School in Glasgow. The Company was established by a group of prominent Glasgow businessmen who wished to ensure a good education for their daughters. Unlike Larchfield which was in one building, St Bride's spread throughout the town with the main school housed at 10 Stafford Street and the junior school at Clarendon (89 James Street), and with boarding houses in Ashmount (8 Millig Street – now the Headmaster's house), Burnbrae (58 Campbell Street) and Lansdowne (1 Victoria Road). A small number of boys were accepted in Primary 1.

There now remains only one local independent school, Lomond with 450 boys and girls from both primary and secondary, following the closure in 2000 of Keil School. Lomond, while a relatively recent amalgamation, has proved to be a success despite hard times for other independent schools. What could have proved to be a disaster was a fire in the main St Bride's building in 1997; it was turned to good use with the construction of a fine new red stone building at the top of John Street which gave the chance to bring together in one building senior and top primary pupils. The old Larchfield building and grounds at 37 Colquhoun Street were sold and turned into flats.

While this record of the schools in Helensburgh has dealt with both the state and the independent sector, there is another area of great interest. It was common in the eighteenth and nineteenth centuries for charitable bodies to establish schools for children who faced major family problems – examples of which were the ragged schools in England, George Heriot's in Edinburgh, Robert Gordon's in Aberdeen and of course Hutcheson's in Glasgow. Along similar lines of charitable activity it is not always recognised that over 6,000 boys owed their start in life to the two ships moored in the Gareloch – the *Cumberland* and then the *Empress*.

The first, the *Cumberland*, was endowed by twelve prosperous Glasgow merchants and anchored off Kidston Park in 1869 (complete with a special pier) and targeted at boys aged between 12 and 14 who faced the risk of being drawn into crime. For twenty years the *Cumberland* provided full-time training and learning until tragically in 1889 it was burnt to the waterline. For a full day the flames burnt fiercely. Fortunately as a memorial in Rhu churchyard states 'no young lives were lost' but four boys were later charged with 'incendiarism'! Once again the Royal Navy were able to provide a ship, the *Empress*, to replace the burnt-out hulk. The *Empress* remained until the 1920s giving a tough and sometimes brutal training to the 300 boys on board at any time. Discipline was harsh and the teaching offered consisted of the standard 3Rs (ie reading, writing and arithmetic), drill, seamanship and, interestingly, music. There were two excellent bands, a brass one and one for pipers. 'Marching through Georgia' became the signature tune for these bands which were much in popular demand for special occasions.

Of those who passed through the ships, some went into trades, many into the Merchant Navy and even some into the Royal Navy. This is a story that is an unusual relic to be included in education, but not one that should be belittled. The great ships in their black and white, and the boys in their uniforms were very much a part of the local scene. For these boys this was possibly their only chance to break out from a city which at that time could offer them little. It must not be forgotten too that their contribution to the local economy cannot have been small, their supplies collected weekly, in particular the bread and cakes from Maclachlans, the Wednesday treat at the film matinee in the La Scala cinema, and even the offerings of sweets and cigarettes which were scrounged from the locals who rowed out to the moorings of a Sunday.

There can be no doubt that Helensburgh has been fortunate in its educational heritage. From the tiny primitive cottage in the Parish of Row and the Ragged Schools of the burgh to the present provision of good state schools with the alternative for those who wish to attend Lomond, the opportunity for the 'lad – or lass – o' pairts' to reach the top has never been greater. Schooling has moved away from the past with its rigorous concentration on the Bible, on grammar and number to the computer, the overhead projector, science labs, and school visits to Germany and France.

Over 6,000 boys owed their start in life to the two ships moored in the Gareloch – the Cumberland and then the Empress

The bewigged dominie or teacher of the 1700s and even his successors in later centuries would not recognise their modern counterpart with computers, except perhaps in a similar devotion to encouraging his or her pupils to achieve the best of which they are capable. Scotland still prides itself on the quality of its educational system and while this may not be quite as true today as it was, it still offers to its young people a high standard that stands them in good stead in the world. •

Skyviews of Leeds

St Bride's School before the fire in 1997

Kenneth Crawford

Hermitage Academy at Colgrain. At the time of writing the buildings shown here are scheduled for replacement once funds become available

CHAPTER 7

Commerce

JOHN ASHWORTH

The lands, which became Helensburgh, had been purchased by Sir James Colquhoun in 1752 from Marion, Lady Cathcart (the daughter of Sir John Schaw of Greenock) for the sum of 6500 English pounds.

In 1802 the proprietor of the new town, James the 25th Laird of Colquhoun, sought to obtain a Charter elevating the village to a Burgh of Barony and in a petition to King George lll recalled the following:

> I have established a village called Helensburgh that there
> was a convenient market place in the said village and several
> necessary accommodations for the purpose of giving
> encouragement to trade, industry and manufacture, which
> were carried out there on a considerable extent.

It is apparent from the information that we have that these claims were a little on the creative side of accuracy, but the purpose was achieved and the town was awarded a Free and Independent Burgh of Barony status.

The council levied tolls and duties for the weekly market on Thursdays and four annual fairs. These did not bring the hoped for prosperity to the town as can be gleaned from the fact that the revenues from them were knocked down to one R McNeill for the princely sum of five shillings (25p). The fairs continued until the 1850s doing business in the way of selling cattle and hiring servants. They were occasions of festivity for the early natives with their travelling showmen, jugglers, acrobats, minstrels, tightrope dancers, gingerbread dealers and candymen. The customer weaver, the itinerant tailor and travelling shoemaker used to journey around the country for work.

The area at that time was known as Millig, which refers to the Mill that stood on the burn in what is now Hermitage Park behind the Victoria Halls. The Milligs Burn today starts as an overflow of the reservoirs at the top of Sinclair Street and works its way down, emerging on the foreshore to the east of Maitland Street. The Mill, from at least

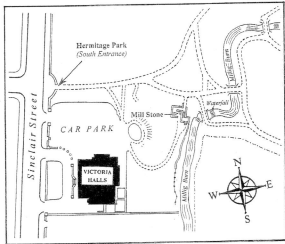

Malig Mill Stone and three stone wreaths set into the remaining mill wall in Hermitage Park

the early 1700s, was operated by a Robert Lennox who milled corn (ie oats), barley and malt and this was significant in that it serviced at least seven farms which covered the hillside that is now modern day Helensburgh. Some trade was done by bringing grains in and out by sea, passing them through the Granary, which until recent times stood at the foot of Sinclair Street.

The lower area of Hermitage Park, which is now a bowling green and tennis courts, was a mill lade or pond where the Milligs Burn came in at the upper end and discharged at the lower end over the water wheel of the Mill.

The farms were basically subsistence farms, in the early days tenanted by a number of people, but progressively over the years they came down to one tenant in most of them. The Colquhouns, who owned these lands, made extremely minimal income from letting farms. Scotland was recovering from a financial and cash crisis and many estate owners were forced to sell their estates at distressed values. It seems safe to assume that Sir James Colquhoun was not immune to these pressures and that his way of alleviating financial hardship was to offer land to be feued, which would potentially bring in many times the rents available from the letting of farms. He was probably influenced in this by seeing how effectively the towns of Greenock and Gourock were evolving across the water by encouraging manufacturing and trading.

From those early days until 1980, there was on the foreshore at the bottom of Sinclair Street, a large ugly building known as the Granary, which was in the 1700s a malt barn facilitating grains being brought in and taken out by boat. The Granary has performed many roles in its time, apart from its prime function as a malt barn. In the days before the churches were constructed it was used for worship. About 1900 grain merchant RS McFarlane diversified by first of all converting part of the building into a garage, but more importantly by establishing McFarlane's Gareloch Motor Service Company Ltd, which was probably the earliest motor bus company in Dunbartonshire, and predated the introduction of tramcars. By 1906 the company had a fleet of at least six buses, which operated services to Dumbarton, Garelochhead and Clynder along with tours to Aberfoyle and the Trossachs.

In 1934 the premises were converted into a restaurant, which was very popular with tourists and with local ladies as a meeting place for coffee and afternoon tea, and many local couples arranged their wedding receptions to be held there. It was greatly missed when it closed. It lay empty for several years before being demolished in 1980. Since then a public house has been built on part of the site.

Apart from the granary and the mill, before the nineteenth century the only other buildings were the ferryman's cottage at Drumfork and Drumfork House on Old Luss Road, which was a drovers' inn. Along the foreshore were nine single-storey thatched fishermen's cottages and at the westerly end of what is now Helensburgh, where Kidston Park is now designated, there was the Cairndhu Inn and two fishermen's cottages. The Cairndhu Inn was kept by the Duke of Argyll's ferryman. The six-oared ferryboat was housed there and was used to row the Dukes of Argyll and their visitors between the Dukes' two castles at Ardencaple and Rosneath.

In the early 1800s the Ardencaple Inn was built by the Duke of Argyll. The old Cairndhu Inn was demolished and much of its stonework was used in the construction of the new Inn. The Ardencaple Inn was one of the stages where horses were changed on the coaching run from Glasgow to Inveraray. It was also used by visitors to the Argyll family at either of their residences. Horses and carriages were put up there and in these old coaching days it was a bustling, thriving place. Its use as an inn was discontinued about 1870 and it became Mrs Drew's private mansion until it reverted to being a hotel, the Ardencaple, about 1900.

At the time of the first Statistical Account in 1791 the population

Illicit stills were an important part of the local economy, as the name Whistler's Glen in Rhu can testify

Herring fishing was a productive trade in the early nineteenth century, and the cured fish was stored in barrels made in a cooperage at the foot of Maitland Street – this carved stone can still be seen in the wall there

of the Parish of Row was recorded as being 853, of which 100 were in the newly formed village of Millig. The minister also recorded that there were about eleven ale or whiskey hoofs (*sic*), only one of which could properly be called an inn. Distilling must have been taking place and there were two legitimately recorded establishments, one at the foot of Whistler's Burn, where the house called Aldonaig stands, and one next to it at Broomknowe. There were nine workmen's cottages up the glen and further up again a dam which held back the water to supply the distillery. There was a small harbour at the foot of the burn, where small boats were beached after bringing in the malted barley from Helensburgh.

The name Whistler's Glen came from the practice of signalling the approach of the Gauger or Exciseman. Smuggler's Way is the route by which the whisky was smuggled out of sight. The distilleries seem to have fallen into disuse about 1830.

There was a distillery at the foot of Maitland Street, run by Stein and Company, who also owned the biggest distillery in Scotland, the Saucel Distillery in Paisley. The Helensburgh distillery could produce 400 gallons per week of the finest malt whisky. The lease of the Helensburgh distillery was thus advertised in 1838 – 'the water is the best quality for making fine malt whiskey being collected over nearly three acres (1.5 hectares) of moss in a long dam'. We can assume that the moss was the millpond in what is now Hermitage Park.

As all over Scotland, there were many small stills in the glens, up the Glenan Burn, in Glen Fruin and at Bannachra. There are many tales of adventures with the Gauger's men and cunningly executed plans to take the whisky to neighbouring towns where the receivers lived. It is recorded that, in 1832 when the population of Row parish had reached 2,000, there existed thirty public houses and a traveller from one end of the parish to the other often progressed very slowly.

The most economic trade was probably the herring fishing, for several months of the year a very productive industry. There was a small market for fresh fish, but most of it had to be cured before being despatched to Glasgow. John Gray had a cooperage at the foot of Maitland Street, which was kept busy producing barrels for the cured herring. The cooperage was washed away in a storm and all that remains today is a carved stone set into a wall.

The town's reputation for sea bathing brought many visitors and it was noted in the *Helensburgh Directory* for 1834 that there were 217 householders in the area of which 126 offered lodgings ranging in accommodation from 1-14 rooms and that everything was subservient to house letting. In springtime the row of whitewashed houses fronting the beach broke out in an eruption of tickets bearing the legend 'To Let Furnished'. The houses had previously been lime washed inside as well as externally, the furniture polished up and the landlady eagerly awaited the arrival of the strangers. *Fowler's Guide* states:

> So beautiful is the town that it is no surprise that the crowds
> flock in to enjoy the fine beaches and the celebrated fresh
> water springs, the town can provide almost every luxury
> required by civilised life and some of these are shipped in
> from the sophisticated metropolis of Greenock by ferry.

The *Directory* recorded that the population increased by 50% in summer months and ran an advertisement for carrier services to and from Glasgow, Dumbarton and Garelochhead twice weekly.

The Tontine Hotel was one of the first hotels, being a hotel, an inn and a coaching centre now known as the Imperial Hotel. The name Tontine is worthy of comment, as it is fairly common – there is a Tontine Hotel in Greenock. The name derives from the eighteenth century when an Italian called Lorenzo de Tonti used it to describe the type of financial arrangement whereby a project was financed by subscribers making a loan, from which each was to receive an annuity for life. The annuity increased as the other subscribers died off, until the last survivor received the whole sum. It would appear that this was the basis of funding for the construction of what is now the Imperial Hotel.

Henry Bell obviously saw the potential of Helensburgh and built the Baths Hotel in 1806. Having built and commissioned the *Comet* in 1812 he was advertising a programme for his steamboat passage from Glasgow and Greenock to his private jetty. The Baths Hotel later became the Queen's Hotel, a social centre of the well-to-do in Helensburgh until the 1980s when it was converted into flats, now known as Queen's Court.

The first public building in Helensburgh was the theatre, on the site of the present Municipal Building. While actors strutted and fretted their art upon the stage, magistrates held court and by 1840 there was a public library and a grocery store in there as well. One can assume that the grocery store was merely a centre for exchanging produce, barter being the main means of trading. James Breingan, who was Provost at the time, was trading from his premises in East Clyde Street as a grocer and wine and spirit merchant. He was also the Postmaster and Procurator Fiscal.

A sure sign that prosperity had arrived was the introduction of banks. The first bank was a savings bank promoted by James Smith of Jordanhill in 1827 which was managed by Peter MacCallum, the draper. In 1841 a branch of the Western Bank of Scotland was set up, but in 1857 its premises and business were taken over by the Clydesdale Bank under the management of Mr Orr. Shortly afterwards they built and moved to the present premises in James Street. The Union Bank of Scotland arrived in 1856 and in 1861 moved to the building in Colquhoun Square. The Bank of Scotland had its premises at 10 West Clyde Street by 1865 and later built 36 West Clyde Street.

In the early 1800s most of the development of the town took place to the east of what is now Sinclair Street and beachside mansions were built there by prosperous Glasgow merchants (a merchant is distinguished from other businessmen in that his main concern is seaborne traffic). By the mid 1850s with the advent of the railway through the east side, the development started taking place for the wealthy residents to the west of the town, and the eastern end became more industrialised with the gas works being developed there together with the slaughterhouse, aerated water factory and other trades. A single storey building, beside a decrepit slipway, at the west end of the East Bay was the boat shed for the Helensburgh Rowing Club. Now 86 East Clyde Street, it has been variously used as a dance room, a tea shop and is currently a small shop.

The area behind the buildings along Clyde Street was, in the earliest days of the town, a drovers' road bringing cattle along the foreshore to the slaughterhouse on the east side of the town and possibly onwards to Drumfork Ferry. The line of this can just be made out within the amalgam of buildings between Clyde Street and what is now Princes Street. This was a congested area of habitation with small cottages, and the alleyways which remain can just be traced behind Clyde Street. Gradually these became unsanitary and were disused as people moved into the newer terraced houses and tenement buildings.

About 1810 green fields extended all the way down the slopes to Clyde Street except in that portion of Princes Street around Colquhoun Square. The east and west burns, apart from two stone bridges in Clyde Street, were spanned by small wooden bridges or crossed by stepping stones. Even in later periods, the streets running up from Clyde Street, with houses and villas on both sides, were merely indicated by incipient

Waldie's Pend,
32-34 Sinclair Street
c.1908

sidewalks and rows of trees as formalised roads had not yet been constructed.

In 1845 a survey was made of Helensburgh streets and this recorded many shortcomings in the matter of footpaths. Clyde Street as far as Adelaide Street had no footpath on the north side as all the properties encroached upon the street. The lower end of Maitland Street was for the most part under rubbish and nettles, and John Street and Glenfinlas Street were not yet properly formed. Water ran across Princes Street, and King Street was impassable from the west. The path at the lower end of James Street at The Tabernacle required dressing and levelling and Colquhoun Square was in very bad order, with no footpath around it and more of a nuisance than an asset. Dunghills created a nuisance in several places and about half of Adelaide Street had been fenced in by residents and planted with trees.

In the 1850s there were twenty-nine dwellings on the site in James Street of the present children's playground. Known as the 'Barracks', these properties were owned by the North British Railway Company to house their navigators or 'navvies' employed on constructing the railway system. The dwellings were demolished in 1895 and laid out as a playground in 1907 then fenced and further improved in 1999.

As the town expanded, larger more fashionable houses started to appear at the westerly outskirts, namely in the 1860s and 1870s the magnificent stately homes of Cairndhu House and Ferniegair House, still slightly out in the country. More houses were beginning to appear up the hill to the north. Horses were the power of the day and behind Princes Street were stables and coach houses. Coaches and horses entered the premises of Waldie's Transport Company from the east side of lower Sinclair Street, stables were at first floor level, reached by a ramp, while the coaches, carriages and workshops were housed below. Waldies operated from here until the mid 1960s.

The company of William Battrum set up opposite the railway station in 1860. They were printers and publishers and published the *Directory of Helensburgh* for the first time in 1863. This contained a wealth of information on the town. William Battrum also had a music shop in Sinclair Street. The business opposite the station was bought by Samuel Bryden and James Macneur around 1875 and continued to publish the Directories and Guides until 1970. Macneur & Bryden also published the *Helensburgh & Gareloch Times* until the 1980s. They were booksellers, newsagents and estate agents as well as selling sports equipment and artist's materials. Samuel Bryden was Provost from 1902 to 1908.

From the Trades section of the Directories one can see that manufacture was not predominant in the town. From 1900 there was a shoe factory in Rossdhu Place on West Princes Street, which up to World War II employed twenty one people. The remnants of the building and its drive shaft can still be seen. They were not the only boot and shoe manufacturers, but it is not possible from the records to deduce when manufacturing gave way to shoe repairing or they just became shoe shops. There were at least two or three aerated water factories. One, The Lily Springs, was at 67 James Street on the site now occupied by RM Prow (Motors) Ltd, coachbuilders and repairers. In James Street the ruins of the prewar toffee factory can still be seen. This was Eman's, who advertised their Celebrated Helensburgh Toffee and High Class Tearoom at 75 West Clyde Street.

In 1913 there were fifteen refreshment rooms in the town and twenty confectioners. There were thirteen grocers, ten wine and spirit merchants and thirteen tobacconists. In addition there were thirty dressmakers, thirty gardeners, fourteen milliners and fourteen joiners and glaziers. Urie's China and Glassware shop, set up in the 1890s, continues to trade in its good old fashioned way in West Clyde Street.

The firm of JG Burgess, painters and decorators, was founded in 1878 by Alexander Bisland and still continues in business today. The builders A Trail and Son make their first appearance in the Directory in 1913 and James Williamson, builders, in 1939.

It was a feature of most businesses in those days, and indeed through to the 1960s, that goods were delivered to your home. Most shops employed a message boy who rode a bicycle and delivered the goods within the hour anywhere in the town and surrounding area. It was recounted in very recent times by one of these original message boys that it was their practice, when out of sight of their proprietor, to gather in one of the streets behind the town and exchange their loads, so that one boy would go to one area rather than each boy trying to cover the whole community. That way much effort was saved. It is not known whether the proprietors knew of this practice or encouraged it.

After many decades of stability changes started to come in the 1960s, when the first minor supermarket was opened by William Low and Company on the lower part of Sinclair Street. This was the start of convenience shopping and put pressure on the butcher, baker and greengrocer. Worse was to come when in the early 1980s the goods yard at the rear of the station was given over to the building of a supermarket, which, after various changes of ownership is now the Co-op. This offers the full range of consumables and other goods, including pharmaceuticals and is much used by the local population at the expense of local traders. Those with motorcars can go to the even larger supermarkets of Dumbarton and further afield.

From the 1970s onwards the rate of change increased rapidly and many of the small individual traders ceased business. Also, their premises were taken over by new businesses, which, for whatever reason, did not seem to last for very long and the use of shops chopped and changed each year. Traditional features like the public houses were converted into multiple off-licence groups and building societies. The ultimate sign of the decline of the independent trader is the advent, during the 1990s, of charity shops, of which there are seven at the present time.

At the time this book is being prepared there is a debate raging as to whether a supermarket to be built on the pier car park is a desirable and necessary feature. The community seems to be divided as to the merits of this proposal, which would include an up-to-date leisure centre. It would certainly change the image of the traditional sea front of Helensbugh.

Given the ups and downs of trading in recent times, Helensburgh is extremely fortunate in that a number of small independent traders are still with us. Very few small towns can boast three butchers, a fishmonger and a greengrocer. We have two hardware shops, a television and audio shop and, uniquely, two independent booksellers. We have

Mac's Model Railroading and Dolls Houses, lovely gift shops and, of course, Dino's Radio Café which still makes its own Italian ice cream.

One point which should never be forgotten is that the town of Helensburgh on its own has not created the wealth of Helensburgh. From the time of Henry Bell's *Comet* Helensburgh increasingly became a place which acquired its prosperity from elsewhere. Initially this was through Glasgow businessmen building villas for use at weekends and during holidays, and then after the arrival of the railways more and more Glasgow businessmen started to commute to the town on a daily basis. This continues today.

There is also the role of the public sector to be considered. The naval bases at Faslane and Coulport particularly are major employers of both service and civilian personnel, while of course public authorities such as Argyll and Bute Council and the National Health Service provide many jobs and hence much prosperity for the town. A third source of wealth is the large number of people who have decided to retire to Helensburgh, having spent their working lives elsewhere. Without all these groups bringing in wealth from outside, Helensburgh would be a very different town today.   ●

CHAPTER 8

The Geology of the Lands of Malig

ALISON ROBERTS

Helensburgh lies just to the south east of the northern branch of the Highland Boundary Fault, which separates the Highlands from the Lowlands of Scotland. The boundary between Helensburgh and Rhu follows the line of the fault for a short distance.

Earthquake activity throughout the world occurs at tectonic plate boundaries where the faults are geologically active. The Highland Boundary Fault is not such a fault. It ceased to be active hundreds of millions of years ago when the Midland Valley dropped down between two large normal faults. Nevertheless minor tremors do occur in the Helensburgh area from time to time, caused by settlement of the land and the differential hardness of the rocks on either side of the fault.

Helensburgh is in the Lowlands. The rock, which underlies much of the town is Upper Devonian Sandstone. It was laid down by fast flowing rivers bringing debris from high mountains around three hundred and sixty million years ago. That is a couple of hundred million years before the dinosaurs walked the land. Because of abrasion very few fossils have ever been found in our rock and these were found by experts. The rock is mainly red and pink in colour as desert conditions prevailed at the time it was laid down. It is a mixture of sandstone of various grades and conglomerate, a pebbly puddingstone. The sandstone cleaves into nice layers, which is good for building, but some is hard to break up. The lumpy conglomerate is full of pebbles, which fall out, making it an unsatisfactory building stone. Nevertheless the local rock has been much used for building and can be seen in the town's older houses, such as the West Kirk Office in Colquhoun Street. The rock is well exposed at Kidston Point, on the Rosneath shore and at Ardmore.

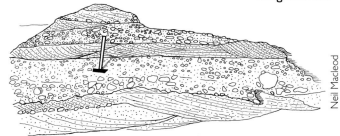

Sandstone and conglomerate

Neil Macleod

Looking South West
along the Highland
boundary fault

The Highland rocks to the north west of the fault are, in contrast, grey in colour, some are quite silvery due to the presence of the mineral mica. They are the hard rocks, which underlie much of the Highlands, giving rise to the rugged mountain scenery. They are about another two hundred million years older than the rocks of the Lowlands. Earth movements millions of years ago have uplifted them so that here they are tilted to face south east as can be seen on the shores of the Gareloch and Loch Long. Metamorphism of the rock has caused slate to be formed in places and the scar of a massive and long abandoned slate quarry remains behind Clynder. There were some much smaller slate quarries near to the old Rhu reservoirs. These slates are excellent for roofs and can be seen all over the town in their various colours, purple, grey or green.

A mere two million years ago the Ice Ages began, which ground down the mountains and carved out the valleys. In Scotland we only have evidence of the final stages, about ten thousand years before present. The Spit at Rhu is an internationally known site which provides some of that evidence. Loch Lomond, Glen Fruin and the Gareloch and Loch Long were all carved out by glaciers moving south. As the glaciers began to melt they dropped their load of clay, sand and gravel so that Loch Lomond was cut off from the sea completely and the Spit at Rhu all but cut off the Gareloch. Some deposits at Rhu are blue clays which contain the shells of marine creatures only found today in the Arctic.

The large boulders, which lie haphazardly on the beach around Helensburgh and Rhu, and which are such a hazard to yachtsmen, were brought down by the glaciers and deposited as they melted, as was the cup marked boulder on the Upland Way. These boulders are known as glacial erratics.

The principal deposit is boulder clay, which as its name implies, is a sticky clay containing pebbles and boulders. It is difficult to dig and gives rise to a great deal of mud. There are areas of gravel and sand deposits, which are much easier for gardeners and farmers to work.

As the ice melted and ran into the seas, the sea level rose. The land, relieved of its burden of ice, was uplifted. This happened intermittently causing a series of changes in the relative levels of land and sea. The result is a terrace of beach deposits, inland of the present shoreline, and raised beach cliffs. Lower Helensburgh from King Street seawards and the Ardencaple estate are on the former beach terrace.

Clydeview Eventide Home and the ruins of Ardencaple Castle stand on a raised beach cliff above the ancient shoreline.

The red sandstone of the cliff can be seen exposed inland of the road from Cardross to Dumbarton and also at Portkil, eastwards from Kilcreggan.

Walking up Sinclair Street or Colquhoun Street you will come to a steep bit between King Street and Argyle Street, which represents the cliff, at Queen Street is another steep bit and just above the Highland Railway is another.

The famous notice which appeared in the *Glasgow Journal* in January 1776 reads 'to be feued immediately for building purposes at a very reasonable rate a considerable piece of ground upon the shores of Malig.' The word Malig means a mill, and the remains of the mill are still there behind the Victoria Halls.

The notice continues, 'There is a freestone quarry on the ground.' The map of the time indicates that there was a quarry where there are bowling greens at present, on the east side of Sinclair Street at Abercromby Street. The stone from the quarry made a passable building stone, but because of its varying hardness it cuts into blocks of uneven size so that for building there has to be infilling of rubble between the blocks. This stone was used for all the old fishermen's cottages of the original Helensburgh and it is easily recognisable. It is from this same local stone that, in 1846, the Old Parish Church was built. The church tower, which survived demolition in 1968, is the home of the Tourist Information Centre.

Records show that in 1858 a minister of the Episcopal Church entered into a feu contract for part of the lands of Easterton of Ardencaple to build houses. The feuar was permitted to get stone for the building from a quarry in the Barony of Millig. This could have been the quarry at the bowling green or it could have been at East Milligs, where a quarry was opened at about this time

The West Kirk in Colquhoun Square was built in 1858, mostly from the same local sandstone. The fine quoins, sills and mullions would have been brought in from elsewhere and the porch was not added until forty years later. At the time the Church was built it would have stood isolated but for a few stone cottages.

Much has been written about a quarry in Colquhoun Square. In fact there were numerous small quarries in lower Helensburgh. This area, as we have seen, was built on the old abandoned shoreline and

Variously coloured stones in the wall of Kirk Cottage, Colquhoun Street, are infilled with rubble

Kenneth Crawford

penetrating the soil were outcrops of crumbly conglomerate rock the same as that seen at Kidston Point today. More fortunate feuars had such an outcrop on their land which they were able to exploit for rubble which could be used to fill the spaces between the uneven building blocks. Much more importantly the rubble could be used as bottoming to give horses, carts and people some chance of negotiating the ever present mud. This is the type of small quarry, of which there were many, which existed in Colquhoun Square at that time.

The major excavations for building stone were much further up the hill, at East Milligs, and the remains of this quarry are still visible in the woods beside the Milligs burn. An even larger quarry was created later at the Blackhill, now infilled and better known to us all as the Coup or Public Service Amenity Site. Golfers are aware of the large hole in the ground where once there was a quarry on the lands of Kirkmichael Farm, now the golf course. These quarries all yielded the same sandstone of varying colour and hardness, cutting to various sizes, which was used in the churches and early buildings and in stone walls.

The coming of the railway brought economic expansion across the land and thereafter the growth of Helensburgh was rapid. In common with other towns and villages buildings began to lose their local character. Now that there was rail transport building stone could be economically brought in from other places, the transport of minerals being far more profitable than the transport of passengers.

Stone from the huge Dalreoch quarry, near Dumbarton, was much used and is almost indistinguishable from our own Helensburgh stone. Also brought in was stone from Overton, above Dumbarton, which is paler in colour. Bonhill Quarry yields a dark red stone which can be seen in some of the tenement buildings in the lower part of the town. We know that 102 West Princes Street, and possibly some other buildings, were built of a red sandstone of a younger age, brought in by sea from Arran.

The ideal building stone is a freestone, one which is virtually uniform and can easily be cut into large rectangular blocks. It is easy to carve into steps and lintels and decorative motives. Such a stone, belonging to the Carboniferous System, younger than the Devonian and containing the coal seams, underlies much of Glasgow. It is pale honey coloured and very attractive and has been used in many of the prestigious buildings there. It is likely that this is the sandstone which was used for the Municipal Buildings, the Victoria Halls, the Post Office and many of the fine houses which were being built further and further up the hill.

Bricks would be transported by rail as there is no suitable clay for brick making in Helensburgh. Slate from Luss and Aberfoyle has the same variety of colour as our own local slate, so that it is not possible to know whether such a roof is local or not. Ballachulish slate, on the other hand, is darker and more uniform in colour.

The Monument to Henry Bell on the esplanade was raised in 1872. At that time it was claimed to be the largest single block of red Aberdeen granite to have been erected in Scotland. The Celtic Cross in Colquhoun Square, gifted by Sir James Colquhoun, is also a pink granite, but finer grained than that of the Bell Monument and unpolished.

It is interesting to walk around the town and try to identify the various building stones used. Often a house has a fine sandstone front but the gable ends and the backs are built of local stone or even brick for cheapness. The great stone walls are mostly of local stone.

Helensburgh expanded above the West Highland Railway to take advantage of the fine views from above the raised beach cliff. The variety of style and building materials of the grand houses is quite amazing. Probably some of the red sandstone came from Dumfries to be set off with English roof tiles. Among the English and Italianate mansions came suddenly the Scottishness of The Hill House, finished in traditional harling. Nevertheless the house is actually built of local stone beneath the harling, presumably for economy. The roof is Ballachulish slate.

These large houses all had their own gardens, some had as much as an acre, which was used to grow flowers and produce for the 'big house'. Gardeners had to be employed and many were provided with a home in the grounds as were coachmen and later chauffeurs. The *Helensburgh & Gareloch Times* of September 1888 refers to the 'garden robbing season' when youths made free among the apple trees.

In the twentieth century the cost of labour increased so much that many quarries became uneconomic and closed down. Natural stone became an expensive luxury, used only for cladding, and concrete has taken its place. More recently, however, good looking synthetic stone is being used to good effect as in the pink stone of the new Library and the new Lomond School, rebuilt after the fire of 1997 destroyed the original red sandstone building.

The air in Helensburgh is fresh and unpolluted, not only because of its proximity to the sea and the hills, but also because the town has plenty of green spaces. Most of its streets have wide grass verges planted with trees and there are fine stretches of grass on the sea front and at Kidston Point. There is the Walker's Rest, at the top of Sinclair Street, woods and playing fields at Churchill and more playing fields at the East End Park. We have bowling greens and the large area of playing fields, just outwith the boundary, at Rhu Road Higher. Beside these are the Duchess Woods, which now have a network of footpaths, and, of course, the Hermitage Park.

Due to lack of maintenance and adequate policing, Hermitage Park is no longer as attractive as it was. On the plus side, we now have good interesting footpath walks around the town and more are planned for the future. Cycle paths are also planned.

In addition to Duchess Woods there is the the Helensburgh Upland

Way which starts at the car park behind The Hill House and leads along the burgh boundary by the Blackhill Plantation. It then turns uphill, past the cup marked rock, to join the Highlandman's Road, which goes from Glen Fruin to Rhu. Once up there one can take to the hills in many directions.

Recently the Skating Pond at the top of Sinclair Street has been upgraded, there is a car park and a comfortable path goes around the pond. It is also possible to walk to higher levels around the two main reservoirs from where there are extensive views,

I recommend taking a geological map with you to the hills because one can see so much of the geology of Scotland in microcosm. On a clear day one can see all the way to Arran and pick out Holy Island and the granite peaks of Goat Fell and recognise the 'Sleeping Warrior'. In a different direction one can see Loch Lomond and look along the line of the southern branch of the Highland Boundary Fault as it follows the islands across the Loch all the way to the Conic Hill.

One can take a glimpse of the fertile U-shaped valley of Glen Fruin, with its scattered farms, populated long before Helensburgh was ever dreamed of. One can see the raised beaches of Ardmore Point which are an enigma to geologists. Nobody really knows why the Point is there. One suggestion is that a large block of ice broke off from the Gareloch glacier and lodged itself, alternately melting a little and then refreezing over hundreds of years and gradually carving out the embayment.

It is endlessly fascinating to speculate upon why the land looks like it does. It is also wise 'to think of the rock from which you came, and the quarry from which you were dug'! ●

Stratigraphical Succession for the Helensburgh Area

AGE in million years	SYSTEM and PERIOD	FORMATION	LOCALITIES
up to 2	QUATERNARY	glacial deposits, raised beaches	Glen Fruin, Helensburgh, Rhu Spit, Ardmore
65	TERTIARY	volcanics, granites	Goat Fell and Holy Island on Arran
	Cretaceous,Jurassic and Triassic are not represented in the area		
280 - 350	CARBONIFEROUS	Clyde Plateau Lavas	Campsie Fells, Ben Bouie Dumbarton Rock, Renfrewshire Hills
350. - 400	DEVONIAN	Upper Old Red Sandstone	Helensburgh, Ben Bouie Inch Fad, Rosneath Point
		Lower Old Red Sandstone	Ardmore Point, Conic Hill
570	PRECAMBRIAN	Southern Highland Group	Argyll Hills, Ben Lomond

CHAPTER 9

The Natural History of Helensburgh

SANDY KERR

When I came to Helensburgh in 1975, I was immediately struck with the way in which the rhythms of nature were so obvious. Apart from the seasonal attire of the trees and the migrations of fish and birds, there was the daily movement of waders from moor to shore and the daily aerial display of the starlings going to roost. It came as something of a surprise when I started to research for this article that so little has been published to date. The West Dunbartonshire Natural History Society was formed in 1970 several years after the demise of the old County Society. It changed its name to The Helensburgh Natural History Society about three or four years ago. Meetings have an average attendance of between 50 and 60 and the membership of the Society stands at over 100. There is little in the way of an active fieldwork programme. In contemplating how to tackle a piece on the natural history of the area, it occurred to me that there are two major aspects. The first is the paucity of anything that could be described as 'natural or semi-natural' and the second is the great wealth of introduced species, particularly associated with well-loved and tended gardens.

Geology is well covered through the standard descriptive work of the Geological Survey. The town is situated on rocks of Old Red Sandstone age (220 to 320 million years old) and these vary from a very hard conglomerate to a softer sandstone. Ardmore Point is one of the two localities in the central valley of Scotland where the junction of the rocks of the Upper and Lower Red Sandstone is not at a fault line. Nonetheless, the junction is an unconformity. There is an inlier of Calciferous Sandstone series at the east end of the town. To the west at the boundary with Rhu there is the schistose grit lying to the north of the Highland Boundary fault. The top of Ben Bouie consists of basaltic tuff. Overlying the rocks there is a boulder clay, especially in and around the valleys of the main burns. The glacial history of the area is well researched because of the interest in the Loch Lomond Readvance – an increase in the size of the local glacier during the period between 10,500 and 11,700 years ago. The area was free of the ice sheet by about eight thousand years ago. The Spit at Rhu is an important,

Northern marsh orchid

Neil Macleod

internationally renowned locality for unravelling that story. As far as I can establish, the nearest locality to have been studied in relation to the succession of vegetation after the melting of the ice is that at the Dubh Lochan at Glasgow University Field Station at Rowardennan. The picture which emerges is broadly that of the standard initial spread of birch (10,300 to 9,600 years ago) followed by the incursion of pine and hazel and the appearance of oak (9,600 to 7,200 years ago), a sudden increase in peatland and then a resurgence of forests (7,200 to 5,000 years ago) prior to the arrival of man and the start of forest clearance.

The various Statistical Accounts give some interesting information but it is of course presented on a parish basis and hence it is seldom possible to tie it in with the Burgh of Helensburgh. However, in 1967 Macneur & Bryden published *Flora of Helensburgh and District*. This was the work of Robert R Mill a seventeen year-old pupil at Hermitage Academy. Robert went on to a career in botany and has published other works. At the time, he recorded 404 native flowering plants and ferns, 149 introduced species, 43 fungi, 33 bryophytes and 52 lichens. More recently, Ms Alison Rutherford has carried out intensive research into the flora of the area but her work has yet to be published. The general picture is one in which the development of the town has gradually encroached on the natural vegetation until the only refugia are to be found on the shore, in the wooded glens and on the open moor above the town. Over the last decade or so the spread of Dutch elm disease has destroyed many of the old elm trees in the woods and gardens of the town.

The most recent survey work appears to be that of the Scottish Wildlife Trust who have an unpublished report on the sites of most interest in and around Helensburgh. (*A Habitat Survey of Helensburgh and Ardmore Point* Keith Futter SWT 1991) This highlights the importance of the woodland habitats in Garrawy Glen and Inverlauren Wood. Duchess Woods suffered very badly from wartime felling and were then devastated by the 1968 hurricane, both of which led to the subsequent invasion of sycamore. Current management may assist a return to a more natural condition. Good wetland sites include the streamside parts of Garrawy Glen, Glenan Burn and the skating pond by the local reservoir. There are small but good quality examples of mire vegetation near Daligan farm and Dumfin and at Blackhill opposite the skating pond. At Craigendoran, there is a good example of marshy grassland with some interesting plants such as false fox sedge and northern marsh orchid. There and at several bays along the shore there are incipient patches of saltmarsh with all the usual constituents. I have found no records of marine algae.

Inevitably, the birds of the area have received most attention but none of this has yet been published. For many years there has been a very active members group of the Royal Society for the Protection of Birds. David Core was the mainstay of the group and has a long run of records. Many of these are testimony to the constant bird-watching effort in the town and hence to relatively rare casual visitors such as osprey at the local reservoir. In recent years there have been several occasions when northern migrants such as waxwing and redwing have appeared in town gardens.

Waxwing migrants may appear in local gardens in winter

The native mammals most likely to be seen around the town are hedgehog, woodmouse, short-tailed field vole and pipistrelle bat. The latter can frequently be seen hawking along the shore at dusk doing their civic duty of keeping down the number of midges. As far as I know, the separation into two species based on the frequency used for calling, has not been done locally. Roe deer frequent the larger gardens and stoat and weasel are present though not seen as frequently as the introduced grey squirrel, which is a regular garden pest or attraction according to your point of view. Otter is seen from time to time around the shore and may frequent the local streams. Badgers do not appear to be present in the town. Frogs and toads are common but newts and lizards much less so. The slow worm is still found occasionally in the larger gardens but there are no recent records of the adder.

An interest in fish and fishing is evident from the earliest days of the town through the existence of stone 'yairs' or tidal fish traps. These just look like lines of stones but, at one time, were actively managed and repaired in connection with local fisheries mainly for salmon. One can be seen across Ardmore West Bay, and the ruins of the yair-keeper's cottage stand just beside the Ardmore sewage works. Others can be seen clearly between Cardross and Dumbarton. Today the pier and shore are in frequent use by sea anglers throughout the year. The main species caught are eel, perch, herring, pollack, flounder, whiting and dab. A general account of the natural history of the Clyde Estuary was published by the Royal Society of Edinburgh in 1986.

There are few readily available records of insects. There is an abundance of moths and several less common hawk moths have been recorded. There is an important colony of the Common Blue butterfly at Craigendoran. This is dependent on the abundance of bird's foot trefoil along the railway line. A large colony of Green Hairstreak butterfly occurs at Blackhill, an area that is scheduled for development. Inverlauren wood hosts a colony of Purple Hairstreak.

The founding of the town and the influx of relatively wealthy people coincided with a period of intensive exploration for plants. William Hooker was professor of Botany at Glasgow University from 1821 until his departure in 1841 to take up the post of Director at Kew Botanic Gardens near London. His son Joseph was employed to scour India and Sikhim for new plants. William Hooker rented accommodation in Helensburgh over the summer for a period of years and was friendly with Andrew McGeorge who built Glenarn at Rhu. It is possible, if not likely, that Hooker supplied some of the new material to friends, including Mr McGeorge. Glenarn is open to the public and contains a magnificent collection of rhododendrons, magnolias and other interesting plants. It has been under restoration by the Thornley family since they purchased the house and grounds in 1983.

Certainly, the affluent residents appear to have been keen to follow the gardening trends of the day as can been seen from the many fine specimens of trees and shrubs in the gardens of the town. Many of these were species that were awarded medals by the Royal Horticultural Society. The Burgh Council came to demonstrate a matching interest. From 1910 onwards they undertook planting of street trees throughout the town and we are still able to enjoy the fruits of their labours today. The recent formation of a Tree Conservation Trust will help to ensure that this part of our heritage is maintained into the future. Argyll and Bute Council have a book which records all of the plantings with the plants identified to varietal level. The gardens of the town thus add considerably to the species richness of the area and they provide suitable habitat for many species of birds and insects in particular. Gardening has however produced an unwelcome addition to the fauna in recent years. Both the Australian and New Zealand species of flatworm have been recorded. These both prey on the common earthworm thus depriving gardeners of one of their best allies.

The seasonal and diurnal rhythms continue. Though the starling roost has changed, the aerobatics can still be seen in a different locale. The tides come and go and the passing geese still herald the coming of winter. Much remains to be done to produce a reasonable account of the natural history of the area – a task that the Natural History Society might be encouraged to undertake. •

CHAPTER 10

Origins of the Street Names

SANDY KERR

There are almost no street names for which we can be sure of an origin as the minutes of the Town Council and successor bodies simply record the decisions and not the reasons behind them. Therefore what follows has to be based on a combination of reasonable assumption and local folklore, as well as established fact provided by former councillors, and some speculative guesses. In some cases there are a number of perfectly possible justifications for the choice of a name. For example, many of the streets on the Churchill estate are those of famous seamen, but many of them are also the names of ships of the Royal Navy. The real joy of attempting to explain the origins of the names lies in the many unsuspected connections that turn up. Much remains to be done and I commend it as a very enjoyable and informative pastime. In the following text where a name appears in bold, the sentence gives the presumed origin of the street name. Hence, Sir James **Colquhoun** is shorthand for saying that Colquhoun Street derives its name from that family and possibly that individual. A list of those streets for which no satisfactory explanation has yet been found is given in the final section.

The Founder and His Family

Sir James **Colquhoun** of Colquhoun and Luss (1st Baronet of Great Britain, 24th of Colquhoun and 26th of Luss – throughout this chapter we follow the numbering explained in Chapter 3) married Lady Helen **Sutherland**, the daughter of William, Lord Strathnaver, son of the 16th Earl of Sutherland on 12th April 1740. Sir James's father had in fact been James **Grant** of Pluscarden in Moray, but he had changed his name to Colquhoun on marrying the heiress of Luss in 1702. Lady Helen's father died before he could succeed to the title and, after her nephew, the 18th Earl, died his daughter inherited the title. She married the second Marquess of **Stafford** who, six months before his death in 1833, became the first Duke of Sutherland. The infamous Sutherland Clearances took place during their lifetimes, and he is commemorated by the massive statue standing on the hill above Golspie.

Kenneth Crawford

The changing styles of street nameplates! From cast cement, through cast iron and pressed metal but all neglected by the auhorities and inhabitants whose walls they grace

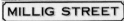

Argyll and Bute Council created this clearly visible style for 2001 and are trying to catch up with 20 years of neglect and loss

In 1772 Sir James commenced building **Rossdhu** House on the shores of Loch Lomond – it is now the clubhouse for Loch Lomond Golf Course and the name means black point or headland. Four years later he decided to initiate the development which ultimately became the town to be named after his wife, Helensburgh.

There is an argument over who named many of the town centre streets but it seems probably to have been Sir James's son, who was also called James. He in turn had three sons called **James, William** and **John,** while his Aunt Janet married General John **Campbell** of Barbreck in Argyll. The third Sir James married Janet **Sinclair**, daughter of the Rt Hon Sir John **Sinclair** of Ulbster in Caithness in 1799, and his mother-in-law was Sarah **Maitland**. Their son, yet another Sir James, married Jean **Abercromby** in 1843 (the second daughter of Sir Robert Abercromby of Birkenbog in Banffshire), and their daughter, yet another Helen, married John Page-Reade of Ipswich in 1829, her husband being Deputy Lieutenant of the County of **Suffolk**. The fifth and last Sir James married Charlotte **Munro** in 1877, while seven years later his nephew Alan (6th Baronet and 29th of Colquhoun) married Justine **Kennedy** of Underwood. Most recently in 1943 Sir Ivar Colquhoun married **Kathleen** Duncan.

However there are even earlier Colquhoun family connections. The link to the Dukes of **Athole** is via Margaret, third child of Sir John Colquhoun (9th chief of Colquhoun, 1439-78) by his first wife. Their eldest son was the ancestor of the Dukes of Athole and Earls of Tullibardine. The 12th chief of Colquhoun married Lady Catherine Graham, the eldest daughter of the first Earl of **Montrose** in 1537, while in 1620 the 16th chief of Colquhoun married Lady Lilias Graham, the eldest daughter of the 4th Earl of **Montrose**.

Some people wonder why there is so little to commemorate the founder of the town, and the answer lies partly in the fact that the family and its connections are enshrined in the names of the streets. At one time Colquhoun Street was Helensburgh's main street. However, by a decision of the town council in 1899 Sinclair Street was chosen to be the main north-south axis and the numbers of the houses in the east-west streets were changed to recognise this. For that reason, research into the history of houses in Helensburgh is fraught with difficulties.

Pre-existing Names

This section comprises two distinct categories. Firstly there are those names that existed before the conception of a new town of Helensburgh, and were used for streets. Secondly there are those streets named after features, houses, churches and so on, which were created after the foundation of Helensburgh but before the construction of the street. Some of these buildings have since been demolished. Councillor AT Anderson was responsible for the use of local place names for the streets in the Kirkmichael area.

Ardencaple Castle was the seat of the MacAulays (*qv*) from about 1350. For about a century prior to 1862 the Castle belonged to the Dukes of Argyll, and it is quite possible that **Duchess** Woods were named after the wife of one of the Dukes. Following demolition of the Castle in 1957, only the tower remains today.

Bannachra is the name of a house overlooking the lower reaches of Glen Fruin, and it was built beside the castle of the same name, the ruins of which can still be seen.

Ben Bouie (yellow hill) dominates the landscape to the East of the town; it is also spelled Ben Bowie.

Blackhill is the name loosely given to the land around the summit of the hill at the top of Sinclair Street. Usually the term 'black' refers to dark vegetation such as pine trees or heather.

Cairndhu (black cairn or black mound) is the name of a large house on West Clyde Street, now a nursing home. It was built in 1886 for Lord Strathclyde, then Provost of Glasgow.

Camsail is the name of a bay and wood at the south-east tip of the Rosneath Peninsula.

Cardross (point of the moorland ridge, or curved point) is the village between Helensburgh and Dumbarton.

Castle Avenue is named after Ardencaple Castle.

Chapelacre (land belonging to the church) was a large house demolished in the 1980s to make way for modern housing, although the lodgehouse still stands at 106c Sinclair Street. The chapel, dedicated to St Michael, is shown on early maps of the town.

Clyde is the estuary on the shores of which Helensburgh is built.

Columba (dove) Street presumably derives its name from the nearby St Columba Church.

Coulport Place and **Cove** Place are named after villages on the west side of the Rosneath Peninsula.

Craigendoran is Gaelic for rock of the otter.

Dalmore (big field) is the name of a large house, now flatted, and surrounded by modern houses.

Dennistoun was the name of the family which owned Camis Eskan House for over five hundred years.

Dhuhill is a hybrid Gaelic and English word meaning Blackhill.

Drumfork is the name of a farm with its steading situated at Colgrain, and Drumfork House still stands in Redgauntlet Road.

Drumgarve Court was built in the grounds of a house called Drumgarve which was donated to the town by the Anderson family, and which became better known as the Templeton Library. Drumgarve Court itself was initially provided for 'indigent gentlewomen'.

Easterhill was the name of a farm.

Faslane was once the seat of the Earls of Lennox, and now houses the Clyde Submarine Base.

Ferniegair (place of the alder trees) was the name of a large house, demolished in the 1960s, immediately to the east of Cairndhu. It was the home of the Kidston family, who at one time brought up a relative there, Andrew Bonar Law, who became Prime Minister in 1922-23.

Fruin (valley of the sheltered places) takes its name from the Glen behind the town.

Garrawy Glen lies immediately to the East of the Churchill Estate.

Glasgow (Gaelic for dear green place) Street is of course named after Scotland's largest city.

Glenan (or **Glennan**) is presumably derived from Gaelic,

meaning a glen, usually small.

Glenfinlas is a short steep sided glen on the west side of Loch Lomond above Rossdhu House. The burn has been dammed to form a reservoir.

Golfhill and **Golf** are right beside the local golf course.

Keil is the name of an estate near Southend on the Mull of Kintyre. A boarding school was established there and then it moved to Dumbarton, but was closed in 2000.

Kilbride (chapel of St Bridget) is named after an old chapel and farm in Glen Fruin.

Kirkmichael (Church of St Michael) Farm was situated at the top of Henry Bell Street at the junction with Old Luss Road. Churchill and Kirkmichael estates have been built on this farmland.

Lansdowne is the name of a house situated on the north side of Victoria Road at the junction with Sinclair Street. It serves as a boarding house for Lomond school, and houses have been built in the grounds.

Lennox (means either 'place abounding in trees' or 'field of the smooth stream') possibly has the same derivation as Lomond

Loch Drive surely derives its name from the Gareloch which is closeby.

Lomond refers to the Loch which was once known as Loch Leven. The only river flowing out of it still bears that name.

Luss (possibly Gaelic for a plant or

herb) is the name of a village on the west bank of Loch Lomond.

MacAulay is the name of the clan that held Ardencaple as the family seat.

MacAuslan was the name of the family and the farm that was situated up the Old Luss Road.

Mains (or Mains Park) was a farm shown on early maps well up the hillside roughly where Ardencaple Farm is today.

The **Middleton** family were at one point landowners in the the Craigendoran area.

Millerslea is named after a nursery which used to stand off South King Street.

Millig comes in a variety of spellings in old documents and maps. Early street directories referred to Milligs Street rather than Millig Street. There used to be a Mid Milligs and an East Milligs Farm. The latter was demolished in the 1960s and the farmhouse used to stand immediately to the east of where the Millig Burn flows under Maclachlan Road.

Monaebrook was a farm at Colgrain. It disappeared when the Lawrence development took place. The original farmhouse was situated close to the shore at the west end of the platforms at Craigendoran station. A later farmhouse was built to the north after the coming of the railway.

Mossend Nursery stood at 1 Cemetery Rd (later Old Luss Rd).

Norman Hurst was the name of a large mansion situated at 124 West King Street in the grounds of which the present set of flats known as Norman Hurst Court was built.

Nursery Street is probably named after Mossend Nursery (*qv*), although there were several nurseries in the South King Street area.

Park Lane is named after Hermitage Park, and not the street in London. Hermitage Park derives its name from the house which once stood in the grounds.

Queen's Court derives its name from the former Queen's Hotel, part of which has been incorporated into the development. This was previously known as the Baths Inn and was run by Henry Bell (*qv*) and his wife. It is located at 114 East Clyde Street.

Redcliffe was the former name of a house situated on the north side of Munro Drive East at the junction with Sinclair Street.

Rhu is the name of the village which predates Helensburgh and was the centre of the parish for many years. Previously the name was spelt Row, but a formal notice in 1927 indicated that it would henceforth be spelt Rhu, the name coming from the Gaelic 'rubha', meaning a headland. It is interesting to note that when it was spelt Row, it was still pronounced 'roo'.

Rosedale was the name of a nursery that until about 1980 occupied the ground on which

Rosedale Gardens now stand.

Rosneath (bare or unwooded promontory, or point of the sanctuary). This is the name of the peninsula, village and well on the west side of the Gareloch.

St Andrews Wynd is so named because it is built in the grounds of a house called St Andrews, situated at 13 East Abercromby Street.

St Columba Mews at 87 Sinclair Street is built in the shadow of St Columba Church.

St Michael has had two local chapels dedicated to him: Kirk-michael (*qv*) is named after one of these, while Chapelacre (*qv*) is named after the second.

Station Road in Craigendoran is self-explanatory.

Strathclyde was the name given to an ancient kingdom of the Britons, and its capital and principal stronghold was at Dumbarton Rock.

Stuckleckie is thought to derive its name from Murdoch of Leckie, son of Malcolm de Lecky, who was the elder son of Robert, Duke of Albany. There was a farmstead probably near the corner of Havelock Street and Upper Adelaide Street. In the past the name was sometimes shortened to **Stuck**.

Tower Place stands beside the tower of what was formerly the Old Parish Church. The rest of the building was demolished to make way for the development but the tower was preserved as a local landmark and is now the Tourist Information Centre.

Townhead was the name of a farm adjoining Drumfork (*qv*).

Woodend Farm is no longer surrounded by farmland, but the farmhouse itself still stands at 2 Duchess Drive. The wood referred to is presumably Duchess Woods.

Royal & Noble Connections

When the Helensburgh streets were being laid out it was customary to pay homage to the Royal family by naming streets after them. Most towns and cities have a King's Street and a Queen's Street and Helensburgh was not alone in having a **Princes** Street. In 1776 the King on the throne was **George** III so it is likely that **King** Street is named after him. He was the third monarch from the Royal House of **Hanover** in Germany. In 1761 he married Princess Charlotte of Mecklenburg-Strelitz and hence both **Queen** Street and **Charlotte** Street owe their names to her. There were fifteen children of the marriage, and the sons are presumably the Princes honoured by **Princes** Street. His son, William IV who reigned from 1830-37 married **Adelaide** of Saxe-Meiningen in 1818. Early versions of the Helensburgh Directory give the street names as King's and Queen's rather than the modern usage of King and Queen.

Queen **Victoria** came to the throne in 1837, and three years later she married Prince Albert of Saxe-Coburg-Gotha. While **Prince Albert** Terrace is named in his honour, Albert Drive and Albert Street probably have a different derivation. One of their daughters, Princess Louise, married the Marquis of **Lorne**, eldest son of the Duke of Argyll (or **Argyle**) in 1871 and went to live in Rosneath Castle.

There are two other possible royal connections. The first Earl of **Granville** fought at the Battle of Dettingen in 1743 alongside Sir James Colquhoun and King George II (at what proved to be the last occasion on which a British monarch actually led his army into battle). Secondly, Sir Henry **Havelock** was a distinguished soldier, particularly during the times of the Indian Mutiny (1857-58) – it is possible that the street was named after him as a national hero.

Sir Walter Scott and the Craigendoran Steamers

The first steamers built by the North British Steam Packet Company operated out of Helensburgh before the building of Craigendoran, and were given the names of characters from the works of Sir Walter Scott. Over the years this tradition scarcely varied, although there was the odd exception, and sometimes the name of a work rather than a character was used for the steamers.

The first time that this tradition was copied for a street name was when **Waverley** Avenue, **Kenilworth** Avenue and Ashton Drive (named after the Lucy **Ashton**) were built in the original Colgrain estate in the 1930s. The tradition has been continued with the use of the names **Marmion**, **Diana Vernon**, **Talisman**, **Guy Mannering**, **Jeanie Deans** and **Redgauntlet** (shown as **Red Gauntlet** on some street signs). Lastly, **Abbotsford** was for many years Sir Walter Scott's home near Melrose, and was the place where he died.

The Clyde Arran Estate

The Clyde Arran Estate has all of its streets named after places on the Isle of Arran. Provost Norman Glen suggested this because the mountain peaks on the island can easily be seen from many points within the estate. He also was responsible for the choice of names, and he informed me that most of them were simply names that he remembered from childhood holidays on the island. Thus we find **Brodick, Corrie, Drumadoon, Kildonan, Lamlash, Lochranza, Machrie, Pirnmill**, **Sannox** and **Shiskine**, while **Pladda** is a small island off the south coast of Arran.

The Navy Comes to Town

The earliest connection which the town had with the Royal Navy took the form of the training ships **Cumberland** and **Empress**. They lay off Kidston Park at the mouth of the Gareloch and were old 'man o' war' sailing ships. Besides the two streets near Kidston Park which are named after them, Cumberland Terrace in Rhu was built to house the ship's officers and a hospital. In 1889 the *Cumberland* was totally destroyed in a fire, perhaps started deliberately, but with no loss of life. It was replaced by the *Empress* which was eventually sold off and broken up in 1923.

During World War I the Navy took over Shandon Hydropathic Hotel for use as a hospital, and during World War II it was given over to the army who proceeded to establish hutted military camps in the area. Construction of Faslane port started in 1941 and during the 1950s the Gareloch was used extensively by the Royal Navy for laying up ships. It was not until 1957 that the Gareloch became the first permanent British submarine base. Consequently it was only latterly that married quarters for the families of the naval personnel were erected in the town. Understandably all of the street names are connected with famous sailors, Lords of the Admiralty, ships and naval battles – and just to complicate matters some of the ships were also named after famous sailors!

Naval property is largely concentrated in two areas: at Ardencaple and at Churchill. The latter is named after Sir **Winston** Edward Spencer **Churchill** (1874-1965) who was best-known as Prime Minister during and after World War II. He also served as First Sea Lord from 1911-15 and again from 1938-40.

The Earl of **Beatty** (born 1871) participated in the Battles of Heligoland and Jutland during World War I, in which he eventually became Commander in Chief of the Grand Fleet. He became First Sea Lord in 1919

Adam Duncan (1731-1804) was born in Angus. In 1797 he defeated a Dutch fleet off the village of **Camperdown** and at his retirement in 1800 he became the first Viscount Camperdown. The Duncan class of battle cruiser was named after him, as was HMS *Camperdown* which was launched in 1885.

Thomas **Cochrane** (1775-1860) was born in Lanarkshire and became the 10th Earl of Dundonald. After a successful career in the British Navy he served in the navies of Chile, Brazil and Greece. He was pardoned for various previous misdeeds in Britain in 1832 and appointed a Rear-Admiral. Battle cruisers were named after him: one for the British Navy and one for the Chilean, but the latter was sold to the British Navy before completion, and was eventually built as an aircraft carrier, HMS *Eagle*, in 1918.

Cuthbert **Collingwood** (1748-1810) was born in Newcastle upon Tyne and joined the Navy when eleven. His career was closely allied to that of Lord Nelson, whose second-in-command he was at the Battle of Trafalgar in 1805. A battle cruiser named after him was launched in 1882 and another in 1908.

John Arbuthnott **Fisher** (1841-1920) became the 1st Baron Fisher of Kilverstone. He was a Lord of the Admiralty from 1892-97 and became First Sea Lord in 1904. He coined the name 'destroyer' and over a period of about ten years was responsible for major steps to improve and enlarge the Navy.

Martin **Frobisher** (1535-94) was born near Wakefield and went to sea as a boy. In the 1570s he undertook three voyages in search of the North-West Passage to the East Indies, and in 1585 he was commander of one of the vessels that set out with Drake on an expedition to the West Indies. He died in action against the French near Brest.

James Robert George **Graham** (1792-1861) was born in Cumberland and was elected an MP in 1826. He served as First Lord of the Admiralty from 1830-34 and again from 1852-55, as well as being Home Secretary under Peel.

Thomas Masterman **Hardy** (1769-1839) was the flag captain aboard the *Victory* at the Battle of Trafalgar at the time of Lord Nelson's death in 1805. He became First Sea Lord in 1830.

Samuel **Hood** (1724-1816) was born in Dorset and served in the Navy off America and in the West Indies. He was elevated to the peerage in 1784 and made a Lord of the Admiralty the following year. Two ships have been named after him: the first was built in 1891 and the second in 1918. She was the largest and fastest ship of her era, but was sunk in combat with the *Bismarck* in 1941.

Sir Max Kennedy **Horton** (1883-1951) became Flag Officer for submarines in 1940, and as Commander in Chief of the Western Approaches from 1942 was responsible for convoys crossing the Atlantic.

John Rushworth **Jellicoe** was born in Southampton and served in the Royal Navy during the Egyptian

War of 1882. Eight years later he was severely wounded while Chief of Staff to an overland expedition to relieve Beijing (then Peking). He became Commander in Chief of the Grand Fleet on the outbreak of World War I, but was much criticised over the indecisive battle of Jutland. He became First Sea Lord in 1916 and from 1922-24 he served as Governor General of New Zealand, and was created Earl Jellicoe the following year.

John **Jervis** (1735-1823) was born in Staffordshire and served in the Navy with distinction in both the China Seas and the Mediterranean. In 1797 he defeated the combined French and Dutch navies off Cape St Vincent and subsequently became the Earl of St Vincent and a Lord of the Admiralty.

Jutland is the peninsula which separates the North Sea from the Baltic Sea and comprises mainland Denmark. In 1916 the only major engagement between the British and German fleets took place off the coast of Jutland – it was indecisive.

Kent does not appear to have been the name of an admiral or naval officer, unless it was one of the Dukes of Kent. However the Navy has had major dockyards in Kent along the Thames and Medway (eg at Chatham). The name of the county has also been used for a number of different classes of naval ship.

Sir Pulteney **Malcolm** (1768-1838) was a naval captain during the Napoleonic wars. A pair of ships have borne his name.

Horatio **Nelson** (1758-1805) was born at Burnham Thorpe in Norfolk and entered the Navy at the age of twelve. He became a national hero for his part in the battle of Cape St Vincent in 1797 and the following year he destroyed a French fleet in the Battle of the Nile. He died in the Battle of Trafalgar (off the Atlantic coast of southern Spain) in 1805, having chased a French fleet all the way from the Mediterranean to the West Indies and back to Europe. Two ships have been named after him.

George Brydges **Rodney** (1718-92) served against the French and Spanish in both European waters and off the West Indies. He was eventually created a peer for his services. As with Nelson, two ships have borne his name.

Local Worthies

It has long been the practice of local authorities to recognise the public service of Councillors, Provosts and others by naming streets after those who have made an outstanding contribution. Helensburgh has been no exception. Pride of place must go to Andrew **Bonar Law** who was prime minister in 1922-23. Additionally a number of Provosts of the Burgh have been commemorated in this way. During the period from 1802 to 1975 when Helensburgh was a Burgh it was served by thirty-three Provosts, but only eleven of them are commemorated in street names.

James **Bain** had two one-year terms as Provost, firstly in 1834 and then in 1839. He was born at Easterton Farm in Helensburgh in 1796. The farm must have been situated somewhere near the top of Glasgow Street because local lore has it that the venerable yew tree there was formerly known as 'the Provost's Tree' in recognition of his habit of sitting under it to read his books as a youngster.

Henry Bell was the first Provost of the town, holding that office from 1807 until 1809. What is now called Henry Bell Street appeared simply as Bell Street in the early Helensburgh Directories.

Provost Andrew 'Sweetie' **Buchanan** served from 1930 to 1936 and was a major benefactor to the town.

James **Douglas** Bonnar was Provost from 1912-18.

Jacob **Dixon** served as Provost from 1811-28; his service of seventeen years was the longest of all and he lived at Cairnsmore, 16 Queen Street.

Major John F **Duncan** VD served from 1918-27. He lived at Polkemmet (now Lynton), 6 Upper Colquhoun Street, and was very supportive of the Swimming Club.

Norman **Glen** TD was the last of the Provosts, and during his period in office he lived at Cawdor Lodge, 109 Sinclair Street. In typical fashion he chose one of the shorter streets in the town to bear his name!

According to anecdotal evidence another local worthy to do something similar was Bailie John Muir. His granddaughter Jenny Sanders informed me that the council suggested naming a street after him but he refused the honour. Given that this was at the time when the country was emerging from the depression of the 1920s, he suggested that the street be called **Hope** Street.

Richard **Kidston**, a merchant in Glasgow, was Provost in 1836 and then again from 1848-49.

William B **Lever** served as Provost from 1945-52.

John **Somerville** was Provost from 1941-44 and again in 1945.

J McLeod ('Cloudy') **Williamson** served from 1961-70. He was a builder in the town and also served as Convener of Dunbartonshire County Council for many years.

However the street which bears his name is spelt **MacLeod**!

After the Provosts come other prominent people who have had streets named after them. Thus Albert Drive is named after **Albert** Gordon who served on the town council. Bailie Lieutenant-Colonel **Barclay** Smith gifted houses in West King Street to the Abbeyfield Society. **Butt** was the middle name of the town clerk Edward Maclachlan. Alexander **Gillespie** was senior Bailie to Provost Norman Glen, James **Urquhart** was also a Bailie, and Councillor Ian **Johnson** served as convener of the housing committee. Dr J **Boston McEwan** was a very highly respected GP whose service to the town and whose popular esteem led to both of his names being given to streets on the Glade Estate. One family, father, son and grandson provided three town clerks. The father was George **Maclachlan** who served in the post for over fifty years; there is a portrait of him painted by Guthrie (one of the 'Glasgow Boys') hanging in the Municipal Chambers (see page 37). The son was called Edward and the grandson Ian. Unice **Moore** was councillor for Cardross and Alastair **Paterson** was a councillor and the only person to be made an Honorary Burgess (ie freeman) of the burgh. The firm of John **Lawrence** built several estates in the town and is commemorated in Lawrence Avenue in Colgrain.

Dr Harold **Scott** was a well known and respected GP in the town. He was the driving force behind the creation of the first combined medical centre at the junction of James Street and West Princes Street – Scott Court is named after him, but the old medical centre downstairs has been wrongly renamed Scotcourt House by Argyll and Bute Council!

Miscellany

The town recognised one of its most famous sons, John Logie **Baird**, inventor of television. Sir James George **Frazer**, author of *The Golden Bough*, is probably the man commemorated at Ardencaple – however this is not completely certain, because the name of Frazer Avenue shows up on maps spelt with an S instead of the Z which is on the road signs! Its location at Ardencaple suggests a Naval connection as a possible alternative, and Bruce Austin **Fraser** (1888-1981) occupied various senior posts during World War II, before becoming First Sea Lord (1948-51), and then Baron Fraser of North Cape.

However there was no local connection at all with the first three astronauts to travel to and land on the Moon in July 1969; Neil **Armstrong**, Buzz **Aldrin** and Michael **Collins** were all American!

The local building firm of J Allan Osborne Ltd put up three developments between 1981 and 1985, all of which contain a part of the Osborne name, namely **Glenborne** Court (at the corner of John Street and West King Street), **Millborne** Mews (at 91a Sinclair

Street), and **Westborne** Gardens (in Glasgow Street).

Possibly at the whim of the builder the houses in Courtrai Avenue were tiled with characteristic red roof tiles that are manufactured in the town of **Courtrai** in Belgium.

Unsolved

Possible explanations for the choice of the following names have not been forthcoming: **Beechgrove, Eastwood, Hillview and Rowallan**. The author would be interested to hear of any lines of enquiry as to their origins. •

Norman Glen (pictured shortly before his 90th birthday) was last Provost of Helensburgh and stands before the street that bears his name. Sadly he died just a few months later

Horse drawn taxi in East Princes Street outside the new Helensburgh Railway
Station in 1901. The coming of the railway to Helensburgh in 1858 was a major
factor in the growth of the town

The drawing (top) is from an 1858 timetable of the Glasgow, Dumbarton and
Helensburgh Railway Company

CHAPTER 11

Transport

STEWART NOBLE

At Sea

When Sir James Colquhoun placed his advertisement in the *Glasgow Journal* in 1776, Helensburgh was not an inviting place for travellers. The easiest way to get here was by sea. In fact in those days the sea was regarded as a highway rather than the barrier that it appears today. However anyone intending to sail to Helensburgh had to contend with various problems. Not only was the local shoreline shallow, but it was also dotted at random with large boulders. Furthermore the prevailing south-west wind blew onshore which could make a hasty departure by a sailing vessel difficult during an emergency.

In addition to the problems at Helensburgh itself, there were also difficulties on the journey. 'Fly-boats', vessels powered by sail or by oars or by both, made the journey from Glasgow, frequently taking more than twelve hours. Besides the problems associated with the wind and the tide, the River Clyde itself was also very shallow in those days and it was quite common for the fly-boats to run aground anywhere between Renfrew and Dumbarton. When that happened, it is reported, the crews were liable to scramble ashore and seek refreshment at the nearest hostelry, knowing that their passengers were safe for a few hours before the rising tide would float the boat off again!

However there were various ferries across the Firth, for example at Drumfork (just east of Craigendoran), at the foot of the Glenan Burn and across the Gareloch from Rhu spit. There was also a jetty which sailing cargo vessels could tie up alongside – a good example of this can be seen in the painting of Helensburgh seafront by an anonymous artist which is frequently on display in the Library.

All this started to change in 1812 with the arrival on the Clyde of Henry Bell's *Comet*, which is generally reckoned to be the first commercial steamship in Europe – a working replica of the *Comet* which sailed to Helensburgh was built in 1962 for the 150th anniversary and it can be seen today beside the main road in Port Glasgow very close to the spot where John Wood built the ship for Henry Bell. Other steam ships began to appear very rapidly and the *Comet* faced severe competition. Bell decided that he had to place his pioneering vessel on a new route from Glasgow to Fort William via the Crinan Canal and consequently he had her lengthened on the beach at Helensburgh. However on one of her journeys in 1819 she was washed ashore near Craignish in Argyll and sank because she broke in two where she had been lengthened. Apparently she had at least two sets of engines; one set is in the Science Museum at South Kensington in London, and a flywheel is on display in the Hermitage Park, along with the anvil on which the engines were made. It is planned to move them to the East Bay Esplanade in 2002.

The change from sail to steam was by no means instantaneous. It was only as the technology of steam engines, steering gear and metal hulls improved that steam gradually supplanted sail – thus the preserved sailing ship *Glenlee* which can be seen in Glasgow was built as late as 1896 by Anderson Rodger & Company in Port Glasgow. However the *Comet* brought the beginnings of many important changes: ships could now travel straight into the wind instead of having to zigzag in tacks; ships could now also travel straight into a tidal stream with reduced likelihood of being swept sideways; and shipping timetables became a bit less of a gamble. And, very importantly, travel became increasingly faster.

Initially the *Comet* sailed only between Glasgow and Port Glasgow, taking three and a half hours, but very shortly its journeys extended to Helensburgh because it enabled Henry Bell to attract custom to the Baths Hotel which he and his wife ran on the seafront at the corner of East Clyde Street and Hanover Street (where the Queen's Court flats are now). Indeed at low tide it is still possible to make out some large boulders at the foot of Hanover Street which are all that remain of an old pier. For Helensburgh the arrival of steam shipping at last gave an impetus to development of the town, and its importance cannot be exaggerated.

Henry Bell was rapidly followed by imitators and steamer services started to proliferate throughout the Firth. There was even a vessel called *Helensburgh* sailing on the Clyde by 1825. The Gareloch became a busy place and around 1850 six steamers a day sailed up the Gareloch in summer. This was largely because in Victorian times the road up the Lochside was in a deplorable state. Furthermore at one time there were no less than eight piers in the Gareloch. Indeed the steamer service to some of these piers lasted until 1942. In addition to the piers some places along Garelochside such as Rahane were also served by ferry. In the early days the paddle steamers sometimes towed an open boat behind them to be used to ferry the passengers ashore, but latterly the open ferries were based on the shore and came out to collect passengers from the steamers.

The ships carried not only passengers but also cargo and, as the

T Nelson & Sons (Chromo-view Guide Books) *The Scenery of the Clyde* (1880s)

The age of steam navigation dawned with the arrival in 1812 of Henry Bell's *Comet* and Clyde coast resorts came within easy reach of Glasgow's industrial working classes

Stewart Noble

The *Caledonia* and the *Waverley* lie alongside Craigendoran Pier on a summer evening in 1966

An LNER (London and North Eastern Railway) poster of about 1930 by Templeton advertising the delights of a visit to Helensburgh

HELENSBURGH

ATTRACTIVE CLYDE COAST RESORT

PLEASURE SAILINGS – TOURS – GOLF – TENNIS
Illustrated Folder from Secretary (Dept. P) Advertising Association and L·N·E·R Offices

The National Railway Museum/Science and Society Picture Library

years went on, more and more day-trippers. Not only was the Gareloch one of the shorter and hence cheaper journeys that could be made from the industrial towns, but it was also reckoned to be one of the most attractive lochs on the Firth. An interesting consequence of this took place in 1853 when Garelochhead became one of the first destinations for a steamer to visit on a Sunday. The *Emperor* had made her first ever Sabbath-breaking journey a few weeks earlier to Kilmun on 10th July, and she first sailed to Garelochhead on 1st August. Both these journeys passed off peacefully.

Meantime, Sir James Colquhoun, proprietor of the old and new piers at Garelochhead, decided that a second visit there should not take place. Consequently when the *Emperor* arrived at Garelochhead on 22nd August, not only was the pier barricaded, but Sir James acting in his capacity as Lord Lieutenant of the County had called out the local police and had also brought along twenty of his employees. While most of the good people of Garelochhead were sitting in Church, outside a pitched battle was taking place as the *Emperor* attempted to come alongside the pier. She succeeded partly thanks to a barrage of coals, bottles, potatoes and turnips, and a number of youths jumped from the steamer on to the pier and demolished the barricade. As a result of this a deckhand and a passenger were lodged in Dumbarton prison, but nothing seems to have come of the proceedings.

The *Emperor* visited Garelochhead again the following Sunday; both the piers were barricaded but her passengers were able to land peacefully. Sir James pursued the matter through the courts for several years, and Sunday steamers ceased to call at private piers (but not at others). Thus, the 'Battle of Garelochhead' marked one of the early signs of the non-observance of the Sabbath in this area.

In 1816 a rough stone quay was erected at the site of the present Helensburgh Pier. The press at the time described it as a frail 'ruckle of stanes'. It was lengthened in 1822 and taken over by the town council in 1834, but it was in such a bad state that a large cart had to be used if passengers were to come ashore without wet feet. It was even claimed that many travellers so disliked Helensburgh Pier that they preferred to take the steamer to Rhu Pier and then walk back to Helensburgh! Prior to a further reconstruction in 1859 it had been described as 'one of the most wretched in Scotland', and it was again improved in 1870.

However all was not plain sailing, and one of the worst shipping accidents on the Clyde occurred at Helensburgh on 21st March, 1842 when the paddle steamer *Telegraph* exploded when leaving the pier. The ship was only a few months old and had been advertised as being speedy and capable of making the passage from Glasgow to Greenock in 80 minutes – although owners were a little inclined to exaggerate such claims! The paddles had only just started to turn when the boiler exploded and the ship was simply blown to matchwood. The wreck of

Jeanie Deans reversing out of Craigendoran Pier in the summer of 1964

Stewart Noble

the boiler and engine were blown shorewards and fell a considerable distance from the water, fortunately without injuring anybody in the descent. At least eighteen people were killed outright and several others afterwards succumbed to their injuries, but so little was left of the ship that it was remarkable that any escaped with their lives. Naturally, for some time after this disaster the travelling public were inclined to be distrustful of any new vessel that was said to possess a much above average speed.

While the pier improvements had been taking place the railway line between Glasgow and Helensburgh was officially opened in 1858. This proved to be as momentous a development for the town as the introduction of the *Comet* had been forty-six years earlier. Initially the railways held no great advantage over the steamers in terms of speed, but their arrival meant that it was no longer necessary to travel on steamers down the particularly evil-smelling upper reaches of the river – people were not as concerned about the disposal of sewage and industrial waste then as they are nowadays!

The North British Railway Company was gaining experience of operating ships on the Solway Firth, and in 1866 they started a service from Helensburgh under the auspices of the North British Steam Packet Company, a separate but related business which was guaranteed against loss by the railway company. The North British thus became the first of the railway companies to operate a steamer fleet on the Clyde. However their initial plans were too ambitious: one of their ships provided a service to Rothesay and the other one went all the way to Ardrishaig. The loss that was incurred coincided with a financial crisis in the railway company and consequently the new shipping service was abandoned after just five months.

Three years later the North British tried again but with a much less ambitious service. This time they were much more successful and the fleet started to grow in numbers. After a while a tradition started of naming their ships from the works of Sir Walter Scott. The last survivor of this tradition is the *Waverley* (launched in 1946) which still calls at Helensburgh Pier. Many of the streets in Colgrain carried on this tradition when the housing was built there in the 1930s and again in the late 1960s .

Despite the *Telegraph* disaster, speed was becoming more and more important for the steamer passengers – the faster the ship, the greater the numbers who would travel on her. Races between paddle steamers took place and on occasion these could lead to accidents. Thus in 1884 the skippers of the *Athole* and the Craigendoran-based *Guy Mannering* appeared before the court in Glasgow charged with endangering their passengers when their enthusiasm carried them away and led to a collision by the former with Craigmore Pier beside Rothesay! All piers carried a signalling system in the form of black and white discs built into the front of the Pier House, and the Piermaster used this system to inform the captains which ship had won the race and hence was to be allowed alongside first – this mechanism can still be seen on Kilcreggan Pier. Over the years the fastest journey to the coast became increasingly important and so it was critical to be able to move passengers from train to ship with the minimum of delay. The North British were however at a disadvantage because their passengers had to walk from Helensburgh Central station through the town centre to the Pier, causing a delay lasting at least ten minutes. Clearly a remedy had to be found!

They proposed to extend the railway through the town centre to a considerably expanded Pier. Opinion in the town was evenly divided: one group, led by William Kidston did not want the centre of the town bisected by a railway line, and one end of the promenade transformed into 'a dirty coaling place'; another group believed that the proposal

would lead to increased numbers travelling through the town and hence to greater prosperity. The North British failed to get Parliamentary approval for their scheme, and eventually decided to build their station in the sea at Craigendoran. Although all the building work was not complete, the new terminal was opened for business on 15th May 1882.

Craigendoran pier itself was U-shaped, so that four steamers could berth alongside it at any one time – latterly the company fleet reached a maximum of six. In winter time vessels not in use would lie in Bowling harbour, which was much more sheltered than Craigendoran.

Besides the two platforms on the main railway line, a third platform was built leading directly to the Pierhead; special excursion trains would go right down this platform, while those regular Helensburgh-Glasgow trains connecting with the steamer services would go straight through the mainline station, and then reverse down the pier platform – this practice continued for many years after the introduction of the electric trains. In addition sidings were built on to the pier for the supply of coal and latterly oil to the ships.

The sandy bottom in the vicinity of Craigendoran and the proximity of a shallow sandbank just off the pier meant that every single steamer built for service at Craigendoran by the North British and its successor, the London and North Eastern Railway, was a paddler. Furthermore, perhaps to give a new identity to its operations, in 1883 the North British repainted all their ships, and we can still see a very similar colour scheme today on the *Waverley*, with its predominantly red funnel with black top and a narrow white band about three-quarters of the way up. This is particularly fitting as the *Waverley* was the last steamer to be built for service at Craigendoran, coming into operation in 1947.

It is hard to imagine today just how popular steamer services actually were. Not only were they an important form of communication, but day trips were also very well patronised – at Craigendoran it was not uncommon to find buses parked all the way up Station Road, awaiting the return of their passengers from a steamer trip. There were also regular transatlantic liner sailings from the Clyde and, because there was at that time nowhere in the Firth for the liners to come alongside, the steamers also acted as tenders to the liners.

Furthermore, many West of Scotland people took their summer holidays in various resorts along the Firth of Clyde and they and all their luggage had to be transported to such places as Dunoon, Rothesay and Millport. Cars could also be carried on some of the steamers, but they had to be driven on board over a couple of precarious planks – and of course the tide had to be at the right height at the piers at both ends! However by the 1970s increasing car ownership and the growth and availability of overseas holidays largely put paid to this way of life

During both World Wars Craigendoran steamers (and indeed many other Clyde steamers) played their parts. It was found that paddlers were particularly good for mine-sweeping because of their manoeuvrability. Consequently several were requisitioned and some never returned, perhaps the best known example of this being the previous *Waverley* which was sunk by German dive-bombers at the evacuation of Dunkirk in 1940. Meantime, only the well-known *Lucy Ashton* (built in 1888) was left to carry on regular services from Craigendoran during World War II. When she was eventually withdrawn in 1949 after sixty one years service, she was purchased by the British Shipbuilding Research Association who removed her superstructure and paddles and then carried out research into water resistance by installing jet engines – in this guise she shattered the peace of the Gareloch for a further two years before being scrapped!

Meanwhile, what of Helensburgh Pier? In 1895 the trustees of the late Charles Kidston made a gift of £2,600 for the removal of a bond on the pier, thus enabling people to use the pier free of any pier dues. The generosity of the Kidstons was once more much appreciated, but the *Helensburgh & Gareloch Times* reported 'that there is no credit due to the Colquhoun Trustees, for they have exacted even more than their pound of flesh'. After all the legal procedures were completed the pier became free in 1896, and the *Helensburgh & Gareloch Times* recorded that 'the event was celebrated by a cake and wine banquet in the Council Chambers, and at night there was a brilliant display of fireworks'.

The opening of Craigendoran Pier naturally led to a significant decline in passenger numbers at Helensburgh Pier. This together with the tendency of the sea bottom off Helensburgh to silt up meant that eventually Helensburgh Pier was closed to regular steamer services in 1952. However, smaller ferries continued to serve Helensburgh. For many years these were provided by Roy Ritchie of Gourock with the *Granny Kempock*. Today Clyde Marine Motoring of Greenock continue to operate a service with the *Kenilworth* throughout the year. Briefly

Clyde Hover Ferries Ltd also provided a hovercraft service in 1965 calling at both Helensburgh and Craigendoran, while in 1976 Western Ferries using a high-speed catamaran called the *Highland Seabird* made regular sailings from Helensburgh.

There were however other users for the pier. In July 1933 Clyde Flying Boats Ltd offered pleasure flights from the beach immediately to the west of the pier at a cost of ten shillings (50p) and longer trips to see Loch Lomond for £1. The sea plane belonged to Tom Guthrie, the son of Sir James Guthrie, the 'Glasgow Boy' artist. The 1939 guide *Helensburgh and Environs* (Macneur & Bryden) shows a photograph of a fishing fleet operating from the pier, while puffers would use it on occasion too. In common with most other Clyde resorts rowing boats were available for hire, and in the 1950s and 1960s Helensburgh Sailing Club occupied the building on the pier. After World War II a rocket range was established at Benbecula in the Outer Hebrides and a station to track the rockets was set up on the island of Hirta in the St Kilda group. The army decided to service Benbecula and St Kilda with a fleet of tank landing craft and in the 1950s and 1960s these used Helensburgh Pier as their base, before moving for a few years to the Rhu Hangars.

While Helensburgh Pier survived the withdrawal of regular steamer services, Craigendoran was not to be so lucky. Throughout the 1950s and 1960s there was a dramatic decline in the numbers using the steamers, and this finally led to the withdrawal of steamer services from Craigendoran Pier in 1972. Over the next couple of years another use was occasionally found for it. Oil rigs were being built at Clydebank, but were too tall to pass under the Erskine Bridge in their finished state. Consequently a couple of them were fitted out alongside Craigendoran Pier. Since then the pier has changed hands a few times and various schemes have been mooted for it, but none has come to fruition. The pier itself has become increasingly derelict and the timber section is now almost non-existent, while the station buildings with their glazed canopies down to the Pier were long ago demolished.

The *Waverley* continued in the service of the Caledonian Steam Packet Company until, in 1974, she was sold for the princely sum of £1 to the Paddle Steamer Preservation Society which set up a separate company, the Waverley Steam Navigation Company Ltd, to run her. She is now advertised as the last sea-going paddle steamer in the world. In 2000 the *Waverley* returned to service after an extensive renovation. She spends part of each summer on the Clyde, but also travels round the British coast, and in 1990 she actually made the trip to the spot at Dunkirk where her predecessor had been sunk fifty years earlier. For a while the *Waverley's* nearest calling point to Helensburgh was Kilcreggan, but in 1979 Strathclyde Regional Council dredged the approaches to Helensburgh Pier, and the *Waverley* now regularly calls at the town every

On 1st June 1963 a special double-headed steam train called *The Jacobite* went to Fort William. It was scheduled as the last steam train on the West Highland line. Here the pilot engine, *Glen Douglas,* restored to North British Railway Company livery, sits with *The Jacobite* at Helensburgh Upper. In fact, steam trains returned 21 years later

Stewart Noble

200 YEARS OF HELENSBURGH

summer. Calls have also been made by the *Waverley's* two motor-ship consorts: firstly, the ill-fated *Prince Ivanhoe* (which was wrecked off South Wales in 1981) and subsequently by the *Balmoral* (which was built for Bristol Channel services in 1949 and acquired by the Waverley Steam Navigation Company in 1986).

Thus the old traditions continue, but the sea today is largely used for pleasure by the many yachts and sailing dinghies in the area, although from time to time proposals are put forward to use the Clyde once more as a commuter route.

On and Off The Rails

The first railway in this area, between Bowling and Balloch, was built in 1850 – thirty-eight years after Henry Bell's *Comet*. This very fact gives us some idea of the pre-eminence of shipping and in particular of the steam ship. In fact travellers from Glasgow were meant to reach Bowling by ship and then, having arrived at Balloch by train, were meant to proceed up Loch Lomond by ship.

The Glasgow, Dumbarton and Helensburgh Railway Company had other ideas. They believed that it was feasible to travel all the way by train, and set about the construction of a new railway line with its western terminus in Helensburgh. Starting from a junction with the Edinburgh and Glasgow Railway at Eastfield near Cowlairs, the new line joined up with the existing route at Bowling. Because of the alignment of the existing route to Balloch, the new route made an awkward junction at Dalreoch which still slows trains down to this day. Travellers to Helensburgh in those days followed exactly the same route out of Glasgow as the West Highland line does today.

The new line was built by the end of 1857 and it opened for goods traffic on 28 May 1858 and the first passenger train ran three days later. However by today's standards travelling conditions were somewhat primitive. The *Dumbarton Herald* for 17 June 1858 says of the new railway:

> Arrangements are generally satisfactory, though there are complaints about the 'stand ups' and complaints about the uncomfortableness of some of the 'third class with seats' are not infrequent. The 'stand ups' are, we fear, a necessary though disagreeable consequence of the low fares.

The new line had an immediate impact on the town, which can be seen by the way in which population expanded. The 1851 Census gives Helensburgh's population as 2,895; ten years later it was 4,613 and twenty years later 5,975, while the 1881 Census shows 7,693 – an increase of about 170% in thirty years. Previously Helensburgh had been a backwater, on the route to nowhere – this is why the first railway in the area ran to Balloch which was on the route to the West Highlands.

Communication between Glasgow and Helensburgh became much easier. The prevailing west wind meant that the smoke and fumes of the city were blown away from Helensburgh, and because commuting became possible merchants increasingly started to build their homes here. Day-trippers too found it easy to visit the town. We also often forget that in the early days of the railways carrying goods tended to be more important than carrying passengers, largely because competition from the roads at that time was much less than now, and Helensburgh would be no exception to this.

In 1862 the Glasgow, Dumbarton and Helensburgh Railway was taken over by the Edinburgh and Glasgow Railway Company, and then three years later it in turn was taken over by the North British Railway Company. Events in Helensburgh took place almost as rapidly. The original railway station for the town was at George Street but in 1863 a new station was built on its present site in East Princes Street next to the Municipal Buildings after only five years. Beside the station a large area was laid out at the corner of Sinclair Street and East King Street for sidings, a goods yard, a goods shed and an engine shed. Today the site is occupied by the Co-op supermarket, its associated car parking and the medical centre. Latterly there was also a siding diagonally across East Princes Street for taking coal into the gas works. Indeed about the only remnant in the area of the original railway is the station building at Cardross. In the late 1870s tank engines with local names were introduced on the line. However when these were transferred to Fife in 1879 *Helensburgh* and *Craigendoran* became *Kirkcaldy* and *Lochee*.

From 1869 the North British Railway Company very rapidly became involved in shipping services, and then tried to extend the railway line through the town centre on to Helensburgh Pier in order to speed up combined journey times. There was much opposition to this, and the eventual failure of the proposal led to the construction of Craigendoran Pier and Station in 1882. After passing Craigendoran Bay the railway line had previously cut straight across inland, but building the new pier meant a minor diversion of the line round the shore. Indeed a bridge of the old line can still be seen today over the Drumfork Burn at 2 Marmion Avenue beside the entrance to Colgrain Bowling Club.

When the Edinburgh and Glasgow Railway had been built the engineers were very uncertain as to how steep a gradient the trains could tackle. Consequently the line was built almost exactly level, but with one very important exception – the Cowlairs incline in Glasgow. This had a very steep gradient and because of concerns about the possibility of runaway trains into the terminus at Queen Street station, all trains were hauled between Queen Street and Cowlairs by cable. Naturally, this added time to the journey. Furthermore, travellers to Helensburgh spent the first few miles of their journey to the Eastfield junction travelling eastwards instead of in a north-westerly direction.

Mr RD Campbell

Engine no 67460
pushing the northbound
'Wee Arrochar' at
Craigendoran Junction
signalbox in May 1958

Additionally Queen Street station was becoming increasingly crowded. Clearly something had to be done.

The answer was the construction of Queen Street low-level station in 1886. This gave a much more direct route to Helensburgh and the Cowlairs incline was avoided. Over the years the remaining sections of single track, such as at Dalreoch tunnel, were gradually replaced by double track. All in all, services to Helensburgh were much improved.

However the impact of the railways was not yet at an end. A few years later the construction of the West Highland Railway commenced from a new junction at Craigendoran, and it finally opened to traffic in 1894 as far as Fort William. (The extension to Mallaig came only in 1901, while Oban trains travelled via Callander and only occasionally used the West Highland Railway before 1965). Visually the West Highland had a much more dramatic impact on the town than the coming of the railway to Helensburgh Central – a massive embankment was constructed up from Craigendoran towards Kirkmichael, and a very deep cutting was excavated to the east of Helensburgh Upper station. An upper station was also built at Craigendoran and further stations were built at Rhu, Shandon and Garelochhead. With the exception of Rhu, the stations were all constructed to look like Swiss chalets, but of the local stations only Garelochhead retains its original buildings today.

Many of the residents of upper Helensburgh were not at all happy at the idea of a railway invading their privacy and they tried to persuade the West Highland Railway to build special walls to preserve this, and to keep anything as unpleasant as trains from their gaze – they were unsuccessful, although three years later the railway gave them £110 and told them to arrange the work themselves! It is amusing to contrast this with the welcome given nowadays to steam trains on their occasional trips up and down the West Highland line, a particularly good example being the double-headed special steam train which celebrated the centenary of the West Highland Railway in 1994.

Besides the through trains from Glasgow and sleeper trains from London to Fort William, there was also a local service known as the *Wee Arrochar* several times a day between Craigendoran and Arrochar & Tarbet station. For many years this was performed by a 'push and pull' train – two carriages with a tank engine always at the Craigendoran-bound end. It pushed the train up to Arrochar & Tarbet and pulled it back down to Craigendoran. The West Highland stations also had their own goods yards, and the one at Helensburgh Upper functioned as a coal yard with the wagons being dropped off regularly by a local goods train.

The nineteenth century ended with the building of a new station at Helensburgh Central in 1899. Following a major renovation in 2000, this building is still very much with us. However after nearly fifty years of hectic activity, very little happened to local railways during the first fifty years of the twentieth century. The North British Rail Company (including the West Highland Railway) was merged into the London and North Eastern Railway in 1923.

After the outbreak of World War II the Government was extremely worried at the vulnerability of English ports to German bombers. Consequently it was decided to build a port at Faslane, and a very steep double-track branch line was constructed down to Faslane from Stuckenduff between Rhu and Shandon. Additional sidings were also constructed in the area, particularly at Craigendoran and Stuckenduff. After the war much of Faslane port was taken over by Metal Industries Ltd for shipbreaking, and nearly every day a trainload of cut-up steel was sent to Lanarkshire for re-use. The business was later named Ship-breaking Industries Ltd (a division of Metal Industries), and it carried on until 1980.

In the 1950s the decision was taken to electrify the Glasgow North suburban lines through Queen Street low-level station – in fact these were the first passenger routes in Scotland to be electrified (apart from Glasgow Underground). This meant major construction works. Not only did the overhead electric gantries have to be erected, but many bridges also had to be raised. About this time the general manager of the Scottish Southern Area of British Rail, Sir Stanley Raymond, came to live at Craigendoran. And about this time the fastest express of the day which had previously run non-stop from Helensburgh Central to Partickhill started to call at Craigendoran – was this merely coincidence!

Electric train services started in 1959. On the whole 'the blue trains' (as they were originally known because of their colour) were faster, and they also ran at regular intervals – in the days of the steam trains, for example, there was very little movement on the line in the early afternoon. However despite these improvements not everyone was happy. The coaches of the steam trains had all had separate compartments, while each electric train coach was open-plan – it was no longer as easy to travel every day in the same bit of carriage with your friends as it had been previously! Even worse, the steam trains had had first and second class compartments, whereas the electric carriages were all one class; many of the bowler-hatted commuters who travelled to Glasgow were very unhappy about this, and there were mutterings of a boycott! British Rail agreed to a review after a year.

However in the first few months of the electric trains a major problem became apparent – explosions! Before they had even been a year in service the electric trains were all withdrawn and the steam trains reappeared. It transpired that the cause of the explosions was the fact that the trains ran at 25,000 volts on most of the line, but at 6,250 volts in the tunnel between Partickhill station (the remains of which can still be seen on the opposite side of Dumbarton Road from the modern Partick station) and High Street station. The equipment on board the trains was occasionally unable to cope with this change,

Stewart Noble

The 'Wee Arrochar' passing Helensburgh Upper goods yard in 1964. The Maclachlan Road flats now occupy the site

In September 1938 Helensburgh Central won first prize for the Best Kept Station. The siding to the gasworks curves round behind the footbridge

Helensburgh Library

hence the explosions. It was just over a year before the electric trains returned to service in September 1961 – however in the meantime the return to the grimy steam trains had killed off the revolt about the lack of first class accommodation on the electric trains! It is also interesting to note that most of the original electric trains are still in service today, more than forty years after they were built – in the years before World War II it was reckoned that rolling stock should be renewed every fifteen years! Furthermore trains also became shorter – seven or eight carriages had been the norm for the steam trains as opposed to three or six with the electrics.

The Beeching Report on the future of the railways produced in 1963 had quite a marked local impact. Amidst great ceremony the last steam train on the West Highland ran that summer. It was hauled by two locomotives, one being the preserved *Glen Douglas*, resplendent in North British livery. *The Wee Arrochar* (latterly a diesel railbus) disappeared the following summer and consequently the stations at Craigendoran (Upper), Rhu, Shandon, Whistlefield and Glen Douglas were all closed. Local goods services on the West Highland also disappeared, as did more and more of the goods traffic into Helensburgh Central station. Consequently the goods yards and sidings at the Central station were gradually closed down, until eventually the supermarket and the medical centre were built on the site in 1985 and 1996. Helensburgh Upper station continues in service, but during the 1970s one of the tracks was removed so that passing was no longer possible. In 1984 the Upper station also lost its attractive buildings.

The last major piece of engineering in the area was the singling of the track from the east end of Craigendoran Bay westwards into Helensburgh Central station in 1984. This took place partly because Craigendoran Bay had always been a problem area for the electric trains. Helensburgh-bound trains previously ran right along the sea wall, but consequently the overhead electric wires could easily be brought down in a gale – the engineers now moved the track inland where it was more sheltered.

On the West Highland line the clock has been turned backwards. In 1984 steam trains started to run again on a daily basis in summer between Fort William and Mallaig. This has been very successful, and hence the operators realised that they were missing out on an opportunity by running the steam engines without a train up to Fort William at the start of the season and back down again at the end. Consequently special steam trains are to be seen passing through Helensburgh several times a year.

The title of this section is On and Off The Rails, and so we have to say a little about railway accidents. Fortunately there is not much to say. In 1894 a West Highland train was derailed at Woodend Farm Crossing because a fourteen-year old servant girl had placed a stone on the line.

Although the engine and two coaches ended up in a cornfield, there were no injuries, but the girl was was sent to prison.

The second accident occurred at the same place, just above Woodend Farm. During World War II in 1940 a troop of soldiers were manhandling a heavy anti-aircraft gun across the railway to the battery just above it. Unfortunately it got stuck on the level crossing and a train ran into the gun which was quite badly damaged. As there were only twenty-four such guns to defend the whole Clyde Estuary, the incident was hushed up to prevent the Germans learning of it. Thanks to Norman Glen (last Provost of Helensburgh and an author of this book) who was in the same regiment, the incident is revealed in print for the first time here!

Roads and Road Transport

In the early days there was no road travel worth mentioning to Helensburgh. Of course drove roads existed as a means of taking cattle – the small black Highland cattle – down through the glens to the markets of the Lowlands, principally Crieff and Falkirk. However the drove roads were not really roads as we would know them today – they were more tracks, and were not designed for wheeled traffic. Along the way there were special drovers' inns with pens for the cattle and later sheep. The best example of a drove road locally is the Highlandman's Road, now a public footpath, running from Glen Fruin over the side of the hill to Rhu. It has been suggested that Drumfork House in Red Gauntlet Road was originally a drovers' inn. The drove roads were often linked up with ferries, but of course it should be remembered that in those days very few people travelled at all – the difficulties of travelling led to a lack of travellers, while the lack of travellers meant little incentive to improve travelling conditions!

The Jacobite rebellion of 1715 gave the government a major fright and they decided that the only way to control the Highlands was by the construction of forts (notably Fort William, Fort Augustus and Fort George – the last being then in Inverness) and of roads to link up these forts. General Caulfeild (*sic*) had just started work on a road from Dumbarton up Loch Lomond to Inveraray when the Jacobite rebellion of 1745 broke out. The defeat of Bonnie Prince Charlie at Culloden the next year considerably speeded up the building of proper roads as we know them today. Many of the landowners who fought on the losing side at Culloden had their lands confiscated, and from the money which these forfeited estates provided, the government employed the army to build military roads. Thus by 1762 there must have been some form of road in Milligs, because in that year Lord Frederick Campbell (whose family held Ardencaple Castle) was petitioning the Commissioners of Supply for bridges to be provided where the highway crossed the burns at Millig, Glenan and Ardencaple. When Sir James Colquhoun placed

Ardencaple Hotel was a coaching inn with its own stables to cater for road transport in the early nineteenth century

Neil Macleod

his advertisement for the New Town in 1776 there was only one road classified as a highway, namely from Dumbarton to Rhu and up the Gareloch to Portincaple.

Around this time the Duke of Argyll, who owned both Ardencaple and Rosneath Castles, started on a substantial programme of road building and improvement. Thus the road from Portincaple was extended to Arrochar, and at the same time his castle at Rosneath was linked by a new road along the west bank of the Gareloch. An ancient path from the Drumfork ferry across the hills to Duchlage, just south of Luss, was upgraded.

These roads then permitted horse-drawn coaches to appear for the first time, and an early record of a coach service to Helensburgh dates from 1809 when, prior to constructing the *Comet,* Henry Bell ran a stagecoach service known as 'Bell's Buses' between Glasgow and Helensburgh, with his brother Thomas as driver. He had two coaches – the *Lady Charlotte Sociable* and the *Mermaid,* a six-seater – but the service only operated in summer, was not pleasant and took six hours.

A number of coaching inns with their accompanying stables began to appear, and the Ardencaple Hotel and the Tontine Hotel (now the Imperial Hotel at 12 West Clyde Street) are examples of this, both dating from the early nineteenth century. By around 1820 the coach service founded by Adam Waldie in Helensburgh was being established, running the Royal Mail stagecoach to Fort William with a six-in-hand. The journey lasted twelve hours, with four changes of horse en route. In due course the firm came to operate an omnibus service between

Helensburgh and Dumbarton as well. Once built, roads then had to be maintained. In the early part of the eighteenth century there was a system of statute labour whereby local people had to provide free labour on the roads for up to six days a year – naturally this was bitterly resented, and in many places came to be replaced by a form of local tax on house-holders. This system was abolished in 1786 and replaced by turnpikes, where users of the roads had to pay a toll at various toll houses, such as the Old Toll House on the north-west side of the road at the top of Sinclair Street – this serviced the new road built across the Blackhill in 1832.

Old Toll House, at the top of Sinclair Street (1962)

Stewart Noble

County Acts of Parliament in 1807 and 1816 led to the introduction of turnpikes between Dumbarton and Arrochar through Helensburgh, and on the Duke's Road (later known as the Old Luss Road). Toll bars and toll houses were also erected at Drumfork (from 1816) and at Ardencaple (from 1857). The turnpike system lasted in Dunbartonshire until 1883.

However these improvements were by no means an answer to all the problems. In 1864 Battrum's *Guide to Helensburgh and Neighbourhood* gave a very scathing description of the state of at least one road locally.

> A narrow and indifferently kept road, notwithstanding the number of turnpikes on it, runs from Row Point to Garelochhead. At many points two carriages can hardly pass abreast, and when it rises above the level of the beach, wall or fence often insufficiently interposes to protect the incautious driver from being precipitated on the stones beneath. It is badly drained, and there is no footpath for humble pedestrians, and in wet weather is generally submerged in mud to a depth varying from two to five or six inches.

Is it any wonder that, with 5 to 15 cm of mud on the roads, the steamer services up the Gareloch were so popular?

Meanwhile, what of the roads within Helensburgh itself? As one can imagine, their condition was very similar to that of the turnpike and consequently causeways of large stones were provided at popular crossing places, but even so stout footwear would certainly be recommended. On the other hand, dry weather brought its own problems, in particular with the large quantity of dust sent up by wheeled vehicles, and consequently watering carts were a common sight on the streets in summer – and an army of small boys enjoyed a dousing with water as a refreshing way of cooling down!

The opening of the railway in 1858 made that the obvious means of travel between Helensburgh and Glasgow, but for more local travel the steamer and the stagecoach were both used in the latter half of the nineteenth century. Likewise, horses had to be used to pull delivery carts and vans of various sorts around the town. One of the better known centres for this later became Waldie's Garage which was entered through a pend at 32-34 Sinclair Street in order to reach the stabling.

However the invention of the internal combustion engine heralded the age of the motor car in 1885, and it is believed that the first car in Helensburgh actually belonged to the future Prime Minister, Bonar Law. In today's era of the motor car we tend to forget how large the population of working horses once was, and how great was the number of people who had to look after them and provide for them. It is also a mistake to think that the use of horses vanished overnight – thus for example Waldie's continued to use horse-drawn cabs outside Helensburgh Central Station until 1939, and the last working horse in the town was 'Peggy', who was used to haul A&R Spy's coal cart until 1963.

The hardships posed by mud and dust on the roads disappeared in the early 1920s when tarmac was put on the surface of most roads throughout Dunbartonshire, although some remained untarred until later. This of course gave a boost to bus services, partly at the expense of other forms of transport, an example being the decline in the numbers using the steamer services up the Gareloch throughout the 1930s. However long before that, in 1906, McFarlane's started operating Gareloch Motor Services, one of the earliest motor coach services in Scotland, providing a service to Clynder from the old granary at the south-west corner of Sinclair Street and West Clyde Street. Local bus services were also provided for many years by Waldie's, initially using blue-painted charabancs (a form of motor wagon with rows of benches facing forwards) and then buses between Helensburgh Central station and Rhu until the early 1950s. Brown's of Garelochhead also had a mixed batch of rather ancient Albion single-deckers, from which the road below was clearly visible through the floorboards! After World War II this business was taken over by the Foy family and became Garelochhead Coach Services. Nowadays local services within Helensburgh and around the Rosneath Peninsula are provided by a combination of Wilson's of Rhu and Garelochhead Minibuses. There is even a service twice a day to Carrick Castle on Loch Goil, and many coaches are also used locally to transport children from the outlying districts to school in the town, and to carry workers from outside the town to the submarine bases at Faslane and Coulport. In fact during the day when their passengers are at work the great bulk of these coaches lie in the pier car park.

Besides local bus services, there were also services direct to Glasgow and from 1936 those were provided by the recently formed Central

SMT (Scottish Motor Traction). By 1938 there was a bus service every twenty minutes from Helensburgh to Glasgow. Glasgow-bound buses were not allowed to pick up passengers between the city boundary at Dalmuir and their final destination of Waterloo Street in the city. Similarly on the journey back to Helensburgh passengers were only allowed to leave the bus after Dalmuir. Despite this the buses could easily be held up by the Glasgow trams which ran all the way up the middle of the road from the city centre to Dalmuir. The departure point for those Glasgow-bound services was at the foot of Glasgow Street, and the service continued until about 1980 after which point it became necessary to change at either Dumbarton or Old Kilpatrick. However it was reintroduced in 2001 on a trial basis.

It is often forgotten that there was a second longer distance bus service through the town provided by Alexander's Bluebird buses which ran en route to Oban from Glasgow, and this continued until about 1970. Helensburgh was also a destination for many tourist buses, and many of them were frequently to be seen at Craigendoran waiting for their passengers to disembark from a steamer trip.

For those who did not want to travel on the buses or whose destinations did not lie along a bus route, there was the option of taking a taxi – and what an option it was! Prior to World War II Waldie's motor taxis consisted of Rolls-Royces! Nowadays a fleet of somewhat less luxurious vehicles await the traveller outside the Central station or in West Clyde Street opposite the pier car park. The introduction of stricter laws against driving while under the influence of alcohol has led to an increased demand for taxi services, while driving a taxi can provide a welcome extra source of income for submariners during their longer periods ashore.

World War II meant that Garelochside and the Rosneath Peninsula were a restricted area, and travel there was only permitted if one had a pass. Because of petrol rationing and very low levels of private car ownership public transport during and after the War was vitally important.

The only bit of totally new local road construction in the last twenty years has been the Haul Road through Glen Fruin. This was intended to be a temporary road for the use of construction traffic during the expansion of the submarine base at Faslane to take Trident submarines. The road was built in 1987, but when the time for its demolition came a few years later pressure was successfully put on Luss Estates and the Ministry of Defence to allow Strathclyde Region to adopt the road as a public highway.

Since the reform of local government in 1997 the roads in the area have come under the care of Argyll and Bute Council. However given the fact that the Council recently stated that they only had enough money in their budget to resurface the side roads within the town every one hundred and twenty years, perhaps 'care' is not the appropriate term to use!

Ironically the success of the motor car has brought increasing problems in its wake, and for Helensburgh one particular problem has been where to accommodate these cars during the daytime when they are not in use. Increasing traffic congestion in the town centre led to the introduction of 'pay and display' ticket machines for off-street parking in 1999 – because there were no meters on the streets the result was that the off-street car parks became almost completely empty and parking took place in the streets around the town centre instead! Simultaneously increasing pressure is being put on the Council to consider pedestrianisation of more of the town centre, the only example to date being the southern half of Colquhoun Square.

More and more people are beginning to appreciate the pleasure to be had from travelling through the countryside more slowly. Consequently Helensburgh Community Council opened the Upland Footpath from the back of Rhu to the top of Sinclair Street in 1992. One could almost say that the clock has been turned back several hundred years because much of the route follows the old drove road of the Highlandman's Road. Likewise in 2000 it was announced that the national network of cycle paths would be extended to Helensburgh. Consequently for the first time there would be a range of roads and paths available to meet all kinds of traffic from the pedestrian to the heavy goods vehicle – although their adequacy is open to question! ●

CHAPTER 12

Sport and Leisure

PATRICK McCANN AND BETTY STANTON

Exactly what Sir James Colquhoun intended for Helensburgh when he founded the town in 1776 is anyone's guess. It may be that he wished the place to prosper as an industrial centre, similar to Glasgow and other towns on the Clyde. However given the close proximity of Helensburgh to the Firth of Clyde, and acknowledged by many as an ideal base from which to explore the central Highlands, it is little wonder that the town quickly developed into a popular seaside resort.

This reputation grew with the advent of steam navigation in the early nineteenth century, pioneered by the town's first Provost, Henry Bell and his steamer, the *Comet*, in 1812. The development of steam navigation made Helensburgh easily accessible to those in the city (communication by land was virtually non-existent) and as a result the town became a popular holiday resort and place of residence for many Glasgow merchants. Helensburgh with her clean air and peaceful way of life was seen as the perfect escape from the pollution, stress and strain of the nineteenth century industrial city. This reputation was further enhanced by improvements in land transportation, especially the opening of the railway in 1858. Indeed the railway ensured that even greater numbers would take the opportunity to visit the town.

Helensburgh has never had any real trade to rely on, despite early attempts to establish the town as a textile centre. Her great natural beauty ensured that Helensburgh prospered from her infant years as a tourist attraction. The town can boast of grand public parks, seafront esplanades and streets adorned with cherry blossom trees. Many of the town's mansions and villas also keep well-maintained gardens, and this led to Helensburgh being known as the 'Garden Town of the Firth of Clyde'.

Helensburgh's tradition of fine gardens and keen gardeners led to the formation of the Helensburgh Horticultural Society (currently known as the Helensburgh &

D Small's painting of Helensburgh pre-1900

Gareloch Horticultural Society) in 1850 or possibly even earlier. The annual horticultural show organised by the society was noted for the fierce competition among the gardeners. The annual show is still as competitive as it was in the early years, however with the growth of smaller housing and decline of professional gardeners, competition is now open to enthusiastic amateurs. Despite the fact that the society has recently celebrated its one hundred and fiftieth anniversary, the annual show has stood the test of time, running from 1850 to the present day. The only years in which a show was not organised were 1940 to 1942 during World War II. However the shows of 1943 and 1944 raised a large sum of money for the Red Cross and general war effort.

The town's horticultural tradition has also been enhanced by the activities of the Helensburgh Flower Club, founded in 1957 and the gift to the town of the first cherry blossom trees by Dr J Ewing Hunter just before World War I. These trees, which bloom in spring, were planted to commemorate Dr Hunter's service with Helensburgh Town Council. More were added at later dates.

With the steady growth of Helensburgh's population in the nineteenth century came the need for greater recreational facilities. Public concern was growing at the number of games and sports being played on the streets, especially the game of shinty! As a result of this public anxiety Sir James Colquhoun and other prominent locals gifted land at East King Street to the town in the 1860s. East King Street Park was initially used for cricket but it is now mainly a venue for amateur and juvenile football and the occasional gala.

Not long after this came Cairndow Park, established in 1877 by a local consortium headed by William Kidston of Ferniegair and Sir James Colquhoun. The land for this park belonged to the Duke of Argyll who intended to build houses on it. However he was persuaded to part with it for the sum of £650. Cairndow Park could boast of a bandstand and jetty, built for the benefit of the boys from the training ship, *Empress*, whose band assembled at the bandstand before marching through the town. Known locally as 'Neddy's Point', after a fisherman-cum-ferryman who lived nearby, the park was renamed Kidston Park in the late 1880s after the death of William Kidston. A sum of £1000 was left by Kidston in his will for the general upkeep and maintenance of the park on the condition that it was renamed in his honour. This appears to have been contrary to the wishes of the consortium, especially Sir James Colquhoun, who felt that the park should not be named after any of the original contributors.

Another member of the Kidston family would donate land to the Town Council in 1907 for the purpose of public recreation. Adrian Kidston gifted an area of land at James Street, formerly known as 'The Barracks' or 'Fugie's Yard' and owned by the railway company to house their labourers or navvies. In keeping with similar working class dwellings, 'The Barracks' featured regularly in the local crime reports. Eventually the Council decided to demolish the houses in the 1890s due to their poor physical condition. The recreation ground at James Street is currently enjoyed as a children's play area and after local parents petitioned Argyll & Bute Council to improve facilities, the Council provided funding in 1999 to upgrade the park and improve safety features. The new playground was officially opened by ex-Celtic and Dumbarton international footballer, Murdo McLeod.

Probably the most popular park in Helensburgh is Hermitage Park, created when the Town Council purchased the grounds of the Cramb family in 1911 for the sum of £3,750. Originally known as Cramb Park, the main feature was Hermitage House, the Cramb family home. After the purchase of the grounds Hermitage House served many purposes. During World War I it was used as an auxiliary hospital and after the war it became an annexe to Hermitage

Helensburgh Lawn Tennis Club prizegiving 1910

Model yachts on skating pond – this stopped in the mid 1950s

School, built in the grounds in 1880. When a new Hermitage Primary School was built in 1926, the Council used Hermitage House as a workshop and store for its Parks Department. This continued until 1963 when the house was finally demolished and today a stone and timber shelter stands on its former site. Hermitage Park is home to the town's War Memorial built by local architect Alexander Paterson and inspired by 'Glasgow Boy' artist James Whitelaw Hamilton. Also the flywheel from Henry Bell's *Comet* steamboat was located within the grounds until 2002. In bygone days the park had a fine bandstand which played host to many Sunday afternoon concerts, supported well by both locals and tourists. Sadly the bandstand literally fell apart and was never replaced. Legend also decreed that a hermit lived in the park and 'Hermit's Well', with its copper ladle, granted a wish to those who drank from it. Today the park, with entrances at Sinclair Street, Victoria Road and Grant Street, offers the public the opportunity to enjoy bowls, tennis (perhaps to be replaced by skateboarding) and putting as well as the chance to walk around the park and appreciate the gardens. At the Sinclair Street entrance stand the Victoria Halls, built in 1887 and still at the heart of the town's social life. Over the years many concerts, dances, performances, exhibitions and other events have been enjoyed in the Halls and surely will continue to be in years to come.

Pierhead bandstand (c1910) Built as a memorial in 1902, the bandstand, now no longer there, was once a popular meeting place. The granary is immediately behind it, and the tower of the Old Parish Church

Apart from the attraction of its parks and fine gardens, Helensburgh's other natural treasure is the seafront esplanades on Clyde Street (east and west). Land was reclaimed in 1880 to construct the esplanades and the costs involved were split with three-quarters coming from public subscription, and a quarter being taken up by the Trustees of Sir James Colquhoun. Work was completed in 1888 and the esplanade on West Clyde Street was, and still is, the busier due to its close proximity to the town centre and railway station. Prominent features on the West Clyde Street esplanade include the Henry Bell Monument and the John Logie Baird Bust. The granite obelisk erected in 1872 to commemorate the memory of Henry Bell was the gift of Sir James Colquhoun and Robert Napier. The bust of John Logie Baird was originally placed in Hermitage Park. It was later moved to the seafront.

Sadly some features have disappeared from the esplanades over the years, the most distinguished being the bandstand, built as a memorial to ex-Provost Alexander Breingan in 1902. Before it made way for the car park at the front of Helensburgh Swimming Pool, 'Breingan's Bandstand' was a popular meeting place for local courting couples (although one must assume that they would have to snuggle up closely on cold winter nights). A look at photographs past and present of the seafront clearly demonstrates the popularity of Helensburgh in the summer months. Past visitors to the town could enjoy donkey rides on the sand (sadly today the sand has all but disappeared), hire boats from the seafront or take in a pleasure flight which included the scenery of Loch Lomond. Sandcastle competitions were also common, the second annual competition in 1915 attracting 220 entrants. Today the only organised activity on the seafront is the putting green, opened in 1925 by Provost John Duncan. During World War II it was excavated for the purpose of building an air raid shelter. The fact that the shelter was never used owed more to sea water penetration than lack of German

Pony rides on
Helensburgh beach
c1970s

bombs. The War was also responsible for the removal of iron railings
which adorned the esplanades and Kidston Park. These were removed
in 1940 to aid the war effort and unfortunately never replaced.

The month of June brings the annual Faslane Fair to Helensburgh
Pier and with it five to ten thousand visitors. The Faslane Fair is
organised by the Royal Navy and dates back to the Navy presence on
the Clyde from about the mid-1960s. Early Fairs were held in Rhu
(unfortunately they could not be held in the Faslane Naval Base for
security reasons) and as the event grew in popularity, the decision was
taken in 1988 to move it to Helensburgh Pier. The 2001 Fair was
organised to coincide with the Royal Navy's Submarine Centenary
celebrations, which were presided over by HRH Princess Anne. This
prestigious event at Faslane attracted the largest gathering of
international submarines in the world and resulted in huge crowds at
Helensburgh Pier for the Faslane Fair. The Fair offers the Ministry of
Defence, as the largest employer in the area, the opportunity to promote
its activities to the general public. More importantly however is the
opportunity for the Fair to raise money for charity. Many good causes
have benefited through the years including, Vale of Leven Hospital
Special Baby Unit, Loch Lomond Mountain Rescue Service, The British
Red Cross and Erskine Hospital to name but a few. It is not uncommon
for sums in the region of £25,000 to be raised.

In common with other towns across the country Helensburgh had
a number of cinemas to cater for the demand to see the latest movies,
or for the children to enjoy the Saturday matinees. Films were first
shown in the town's Mission Hall, 35 West King Street, in 1911 before
the move to 23 John Street and the Picture Palace. In 1913 ownership
of the Picture Palace changed hands and it became known as the Cine
Electric Picture House, closing in 1927 due to competition from other
cinemas. The building reopened as the Plaza Ballroom, a popular venue

for British and American servicemen during the war and known locally as the 'Honky Tonk'. Eventually the Town Council bought the land and in 1970 flats were built on the site.

Around the time that the Cine House opened another cinema appeared in the town. La Scala opened in 1913 at 8 James Street and was the first local picture house to use tip-up seats. It would show movies for the next seventy years before closing as a cinema in 1984. In fact the owners of La Scala applied to Dumbarton District Council in the early 1980s for a licence to use it as a combined cinema, snooker hall and leisure complex. The building continued to be used as an amusement arcade for a number of years after the cinema closed and currently it lies unoccupied and in a poor physical state. Interest had been shown in converting it to a public house but this fell through and the possibility of converting it into a heritage centre has been raised.

The last cinema to be opened in Helensburgh was The Tower in 1927. Situated at 5 Colquhoun Square (where the Oxfam shop now stands), it was opened by the former manager of the Cine House when it closed and was seen by many to be direct competition for the popular La Scala. The Tower was equipped to show 'talkies' in 1930 and further improvements in 1955 brought it the benefits of cinemascope. Despite its popularity The Tower closed after bad storm damage in 1968 and was eventually demolished in 1973. Sadly Helensburgh no longer has a cinema, this being the result of a number of modern day factors, such as the growth of large cinema complexes like the UCI in Clydebank, and the growth in demand for films in video format and for satellite TV movie channels.

Helensburgh has long been associated with a fine musical tradition. Over the years concerts have been held, several in the Victoria Halls, for the enjoyment of many. In 1957 the Helensburgh Orchestral Society was formed and its membership grew in the 1960s due to the influx of navy families into the area. To commemorate their fortieth anniversary in 1997, the society commissioned a new work by John Maxwell Geddes on the theme of The Hill House. This was undertaken with the help of a Scottish Arts Council grant and the first performance of the work was given on 31st March 2001.

In addition to the Orchestral Society, the Helensburgh Oratorio Choir was established in 1963 by Arthur Brocklebank of St Michael's Church and has its origins in the many local church choirs. The choir's first concert was held in Park Church. Past Musical Directors include Walter Blair who had strong connections with the Royal Scottish Academy of Music and Drama and BBC Scotland. In fact both these organisations would provide ad-hoc orchestras for many of the choir's performances. Another local choir of note is the long established Helensburgh Dorian Choir. The Dorian singers perform a wide variety of material from Bach to The Beatles and organise two main concerts per year, one in the summer and the other at Christmas.

Other local musical groups of note include the Helensburgh & Lomond Fiddlers (formed in 1988 as the Helensburgh Fiddle Society), and the Lomond and Clyde Pipe Band, formerly known as the Helensburgh & District Pipe Band (and before that as the Helensburgh & Clan Colquhoun Pipe Band). The fiddlers play as a dance group at many local venues, the most prestigious being the gathering of the Clans at the Tarbet Hotel. Lomond and Clyde Pipe Band came about as a result of the amalgamation of Helensburgh & District Pipe Band with Loch Lomond Pipers and a Cardross piping class in 2000. Apart from entering competitions, the pipe band organise piping classes at Lomond School in Helensburgh. In their first season they won the Champions of Champions title. The Helensburgh & District Pipe Band have an illustrious past, being invited to play at the opening and close of the Empire Exhibition of 1938 at Bellahouston Park, Glasgow. The invitation probably came about due to the fact that Sir Ian Colquhoun was on the exhibition committee.

In addition to a strong musical background, Helensburgh has a long association with the performing arts. For many years the Helensburgh Amateur Dramatic Society performed plays produced by Miss AT Anderson MBE in the 1920s and 30s. The society also sponsored visiting theatre groups and raised money for many good causes. This work is carried forward by the Helensburgh Theatre Arts Club, who in 1967 won the prestigious Stirling Trophy in the tenth annual finals of the Scottish Community Drama Association Play Festival. Today the performing arts are staged locally by the Helensburgh Savoy, formed in 1983. The fundraising traditions of their predecessors are upheld by the Helensburgh Savoy, whose musical shows have raised significant amounts for charities such as Enable, Childline and the Royal National Lifeboat Institution.

The youth of Helensburgh have long made a valuable contribution to the social life of the town through their involvement in local clubs and activities. Many organisations exist solely for the benefit of young people, whether in the form of informal youth clubs or the more structured and uniform associations such as the Boys Brigade, Scouts and Guides. The oldest uniformed youth organisation in the town is the Helensburgh Boys Brigade Company, initially founded in 1889 and reformed in 1916 after two lapses. Shortly afterwards the 1st Craigendoran Scout Group was formed by Mr DG Lyall in 1911. The Scouts cater for boys aged six and upwards and over the years have expanded to take in groups such as the Wolf Cubs, Beavers and Venture Scouts. The formation of a Boy Scout movement led to demands for a similar association for girls. An early Girl Guide movement existed at the time of World War I. They were formed by Miss Browne and referred to as her 'Maids of Honour'. In 1921 Miss AT Anderson MBE formed a

Brownie Pack for younger girls, naming them the 2nd Helensburgh Brownie Pack in recognition of the existence of the earlier Girl Guide movement. In addition to these uniformed organisations various 'pre-service' movements such as the Army Cadets, Sea Cadets and Air Training Corps appeared at the start of World War II. All strive to instil a sense of purpose and discipline to the lives of young people.

An integral part of community life in any town is a good library service. Helensburgh has had a public library since 1950 when Drumgarve House was presented to the town in 1946 by the same Miss AT Anderson MBE, a former Town Councillor (and supporter of the arts) whose father had served as Provost. Her aunts and uncles, the Templetons, lived in Drumgarve at 51 John Street and on the death of the last of them, Miss Anderson and her brothers and sisters gave Drumgarve to the town, in order that it be used as a public library. The library was named Templeton Library and served the town well in that capacity for nearly fifty years. Templeton Library finally closed to the public in September 1998 in preparation for the move to a new library building in West King Street. Modern developments within the library service, coupled with the need to provide easy access for all to the building, meant that the service had outgrown Templeton Library. Dumbarton District Council built the shell of the new library in the mid-1990s and Argyll & Bute Council finished the job at the cost of approximately £560,000.

The new Helensburgh Library opened to the public on 5th October 1998 and currently has around 9,000 registered members. Library users can now enjoy facilities which were not available in the Templeton Library, including access to open learning and the internet. The library also hosts many displays and exhibitions. It is home to the Anderson Trust paintings, bequeathed to the town by Miss Anderson before her death in 1980, with the wish that they be displayed locally, and the *Unknown John Logie Baird* exhibition which was commissioned by the Helensburgh Heritage Trust. Another attraction within the library is the Helensburgh & District Quilters' wall-hanging, designed to commemorate the millennium, and on permanent loan to the library. The 3 x 2 metres quilt, depicting the pictorial history of the town and surrounding area, won 2nd prize at the Scottish Championships 2000 and took the Quilters twelve months to complete.

These are an indication of how highly the library is regarded by the Helensburgh community. In addition to the duties carried out by the library service, Helensburgh's literary tradition is also upheld by the Helensburgh & District Writers' Workshop, founded in 1972 to assist budding local authors. All forms of writing are covered and author visits are organised to encourage the exchange of ideas and techniques.

Sporting activity accounts for a very large part of how we currently spend our leisure time. Helensburgh can boast of many sporting clubs

A 1959 scene from a schools' gala at the outdoor swimming pool

(below) Water polo and other water sport from the 1930s

Scots Magazine February 1993

and interests, a tradition stretching back to the early days of the town. One of the first organised sporting clubs to appear was the Helensburgh Curling Club, founded in 1847 and admitted to the Royal Caledonian Curling Club in 1856. Curling was first played at a site between East King Street and Henry Bell Street, moving in 1896 to a new site at the east end of Havelock Street. This location was constructed at a cost of £200 and could accommodate twelve rinks. Both these early curling venues disappeared as land was feued for housing, however the club moved to the skating pond at the top of Sinclair Street where curling continued well into the 1980s. As outdoor curling relied heavily on 'good' frosty winters, the milder modern winters hit the sport hard. Indoor curling was the way forward and it began to grow in popularity after World War I. Helensburgh Curling Club competed at the indoor rink at Crossmyloof, Glasgow and when facilities there deteriorated in the 1980s the club moved to a rink at Finnieston, Glasgow. Finnieston closed in 1998 and since then Helensburgh Curling Club has used the indoor rink at Braehead Shopping Centre, Renfrew.

Around the time that curling was starting to make an impact locally, another winter pastime was growing in popularity. Street

James Russell

James Russell

Street tobogganning lasted in Helensburgh until the 1950s. Here, around 1910, children of all ages are heading down the stretch of Colquhoun Street below Queen Street

tobogganing was ideally suited to Helensburgh where the steep hills made for exciting, if dangerous, rides. In fact one of the co-authors of this chapter, Betty Stanton, recalls as a child racing down one of the hills and passing straight under a horse with Hansom cab travelling across her path. This type of incident caused much anxiety locally and calls were made for tobogganing to be banned from the streets. The Town Council Minutes of January 1895 record an attempt by a member of the public to appeal to the Secretary of State and Lord Advocate to investigate the 'neglect' of the local Police and Magistrates with regard to curbing this activity. When the County Procurator Fiscal proposed to investigate this allegation the Town Council objected in the strongest terms that the Procurator Fiscal was overstepping the mark. The steady increase in road traffic during the twentieth century would gradually resolve the problem as it finally brought to an end street tobogganing in the 1950s.

Another early sporting club is the Helensburgh Bowling Club, founded in 1861 and opened for bowling in 1863. The club is situated at the junction of Sinclair Street and East Abercromby Street and is known locally as the 'High Green'. Sir James Colquhoun made available the land at a cost, initially, of 10 shillings (50p) per year and a clubhouse was finally built in 1875 for the sum of £250. The clubhouse was replaced in 1965 and the new facility opened by Honorary President, J Arnold Fleming OBE. An extension was added in 1990. No-one can accuse Helensburgh Bowling Club of lacking innovation throughout their history. In 1919 they experimented with a tennis court in the upper green before changing it to a 9-hole putting green in 1921. Also the early years saw many weird and wonderful suggestions for improving the quality of the bowling greens, all recorded for posterity in official club records. These include the use of nitrate of soda, washing soda, soot, manure and cow wash to promote the growth of a better quality grass. The advent of World War I led to the club offering the use of its facilities to convalescing war wounded, who mixed well with members and were easily distinguishable by their uniform of blue shirts and red ties. The sport of bowls grew in popularity locally and public agitation led to the opening of a public bowling green in Hermitage Park, known as Hermitage Bowling Club, in 1926. This did not adversely affect membership figures at Helensburgh Bowling Club, which continued to rise steadily.

The publicly run Hermitage Bowling Club also attracted many members, but facilities eventually began to deteriorate. Shortly after World War II attempts were made to raise funds to improve facilities. In 1947 a group of bowlers decided to break away and made a bid for land at the corner of West Princes Street and Suffolk Street; this failed, as did a bid to purchase land from Craighelen Tennis Club. Finally land was secured at Monaebrook (now Colgrain) in 1948 for the sum of £100 and construction of facilities went ahead in 1950 at the cost of around £1,500. Insufficient funds meant that the early clubhouse was a large Nissen hut, used previously as part of a Prisoner of War camp at Shandon. The membership took the decision to disband as Hermitage Bowling Club in January 1951 and reconvene as Colgrain Bowling Club. The new club and facilities were declared open by the Club's Honorary Vice-President, future Provost J McLeod Williamson in April 1951. Argyll & Bute Council still provide a bowling green in the Hermitage Park.

Water sports are a main feature of life in Helensburgh which is not surprising considering the town's coastal location. Both swimming and sailing have been favourite pastimes through the centuries. In 1891 Helensburgh Amateur Swimming Club was formed and for the first thirty-eight years used the waters off Helensburgh Pier for club activities, although female swimmers had to use Drumfork Pier as mixed bathing was forbidden. When the outdoor pool was opened in 1929 this became home to both male and female sections of the club, although usage was restricted to eighteen weeks in the year due to the local climate. Since its inception the club has organised swimming and diving competitions, life-saving lessons, galas and much more. The galas in particular were great public occasions, attracting massive crowds when held between the months of June and September. Local swimmers could also compete for a number of club trophies as part of the galas. Local woman, Doris Gentles, recalls other notable gala events, especially her father's tales about a one-legged swimmer and others who swam with lighted candles. Unbelievably these stories are true. The gala of 1914 witnessed a display of 'trick and ornamental swimming' by David Hutcheson, a one-legged swimmer from the Govan YMCA Club. In addition, swimmers dressed in night attire attempted to swim while holding lighted candles. These feats are an example of what made the local swimming galas events not to be missed.

In 1912 the Scottish Amateur Swimming Association (Western Division) decided to hold its first long distance Championship of Scotland swim in the waters off Helensburgh. The race involved contestants swimming from the CTS *Empress* in Rhu Bay to Helensburgh Pier and was won by William Kirkwood of Paisley in fifty minutes. Helensburgh would become a regular venue for this swim over the years. Open water swimming started to decline with the opening of the outdoor pool, however one open water event would soon become an established feature in the local swimming calendar after World War II. The Craigendoran-Helensburgh swim first took place in August 1949 and was held religiously every year until it disappeared sometime in the 1970s (a one-off swim was organised in 1991 to commemorate the centenary of the club). The swim was between both piers and involved rowing boats, with qualified life-savers, accompanying each swimmer. Those who completed the swim could look forward to a piping hot mug of soup at the end. Another distance event was the Rosneath-Helensburgh swim, between Rosneath Caravan Park and Kidston Park, and this first took place in 1970.

Helensburgh Amateur Swimming Club was also responsible for establishing the now traditional Ne'erday Swim – not recommended for those with a weak constitution. For years this dip in the Clyde on 1st January took place off Helensburgh Pier. However it moved to Rhu Marina after concerns were raised over the safety of the Pier steps. It must be pointed out though that superior facilities exist at Rhu Marina.

Sadly open water swimming is now almost a thing of the past due to public health issues concerning water pollution. Helensburgh Amateur Swimming Club is still an active club, competing in regular league fixtures and friendly galas. Unfortunately the days of large crowds watching swimming events from the town's pier (or outdoor pool) and shoreline are long gone and consigned to history. It would appear that swimming today is only a healthy activity if undertaken in an indoor pool.

The outdoor pool was a gift to the town by Bailie Andrew Buchanan (later to become Provost Buchanan) and cost in excess of £6,000. Using filtered seawater, the pool held regular swimming galas and floodlit bathing sessions, as well as accommodating those wishing to sunbathe. Its popularity can be gauged by looking through old photographs of Helensburgh. One amusing incident concerning the pool occurred in 1975 when a set of false teeth were found at the bottom of the pool after it was drained for cleaning. The teeth belonged to a Glasgow man who had lost them when he dived into the water. The gentleman in question, although very embarrassed, was most grateful to be reunited with his teeth and this prompted the pool manager to declare that the individual concerned was '. . . now back on solid food' (*Helensburgh Advertiser*, 22nd August 1975). Sadly the outdoor pool closed about a year after the indoor pool was opened and after demolition in 1996, the site was converted into a children's play area.

The indoor pool was officially opened in March 1977, four years after the decision to start building was taken by the former Helensburgh Town Council. This decision was only reached after a public referendum had shown demand for such a facility and the financing of the project had been settled. In addition to the swimming pool, the facility offers users the opportunity to use the fitness suite, sauna and steamroom. Helensburgh Amateur Swimming Club currently use the pool and therefore it is fitting that the Trail family and business, long associated with the swimming club, built the pool.

Sailing in the waters off Helensburgh is as old as the town itself, which is why it is strange that Helensburgh was the only Clyde coast town in the late nineteenth century not to have an organised regatta. This was remedied in September 1891 when a 'mongrel fleet' took part in the town's first regatta. Annual regattas continued until 1903 when the organisers, the Royal Western Yacht Club, switched venues to Hunters Quay by Dunoon. This did not deter sailors in Helensburgh, and in 1951 the Helensburgh Sailing Club was formed. The sailing club honour Henry Bell, father of steam navigation, by featuring the flywheel from the engine of the *Comet* on their club crest. In 1962 they took part in the 150th anniversary celebrations of Bell's famous steamboat, when a regatta was organised between Greenock and Helensburgh. The club eventually moved from their original home at Helensburgh Pier to a site west of Kidston Park, before switching to a clubhouse at Ardencaple, built in 1968. In their short history the club have had to overcome some unexpected difficulties. These have included freak weather storms which caused much damage to yachts, and the occasional interference, in the late 1960s, from Royal Navy submarines during club races.

Helensburgh can also proudly claim to have introduced a future Olympic gold medallist to sailing. Mike McIntyre, who was brought up and educated in the town, won gold for Great Britain at the Seoul Olympics in 1988, partnering Bryn Vaile in the two-handed Star keelboat class. Mike developed an interest in the sport at the early age of eleven when he began sailing at Helensburgh Sailing Club. Currently living in England, he was awarded the MBE for services to sailing.

Helensburgh Golf Club was founded in 1893 and play took place originally on a 9-hole course designed by a former Open Champion, 'Old' Tom Morris. Situated just west of the Old Luss Road, the clubhouse relocated to Abercromby Street (near to the West Highland Railway line) in 1900 and the course was upgraded to 18-holes in 1905. Further redesign of the course was carried out in 1923 by another former Open Champion, James Braid. Helensburgh Golf Club can lay claim to having a very famous committee member in its early years. Andrew Bonar

Law served the club before moving on to serve the nation in a greater capacity as Prime Minister in 1923. His diplomatic skills would have come in handy when in 1926 the club introduced Sunday golfing. An article appeared in the *Helensburgh & Gareloch Times* criticising the local clergy and town officials for not denouncing the breaking of the Sabbath. Despite the controversy, Sunday golf survived and is enjoyed by many today. Ironically the first winner of the club championship was Rev JW Walker in 1924, presumably winning on a day other than a Sunday.

The club championship is the source of an interesting story concerning the trophy. Shortly after the championships began the trophy was renamed the Hood Trophy in honour of the officers of HMS *Hood* who had presented a trophy to the club in appreciation of the welcome they always received from officials and members alike. HMS *Hood* would later become famous as the ship which was sunk by the German warship, *Bismarck*, in 1941 during World War II.

Over the years the Golf Club has produced many fine golfers including former Scottish Amateur Champions, J Morton Dykes (1951) and Colin Dalgleish (1981). Garry Orr, the English-based tournament professional, was accorded Honorary Membership of Helensburgh Golf Club, his home club, in 2000. This was in recognition of his achievements in winning the Algarve Portuguese Open and the Victor Chandler British Masters in that year. On a lighter note the club decided to keep a suggestions book in the clubhouse for members to register comments and opinions. A glance at some of these entries shows that at times members used the book for recording personal complaints and grievances. One particular example occurred late on the evening of 31st December 1977 when a member made the entry suggesting that the entire committee resign en-masse. The next comment entered was early on the morning of 2nd January 1978 and called for the remarks of Hogmanay evening to be withdrawn, and an apology given to all on the committee. Time for sober reflection, perhaps.

Besides golf, the other major national sports include football, rugby, cricket and tennis. Helensburgh has a fine tradition in all. Football is currently played in the town at a variety of youth levels. Helensburgh did at one time have a senior side, Helensburgh Football Club, who played for three seasons in the Scottish League Division 3 between 1923 and 1926. Founded in 1886, Helensburgh FC played their home matches at Ardencaple Park. During their three seasons in senior league football the 'dark blues' scored 171 goals, conceding 179. In their last season they finished a very credible third place with 34 points, however within a year they had sadly folded.

Today the professional game is enjoyed by many in the town, whether it involves watching the 'local' team, Dumbarton FC, or travelling further afield to support either Celtic or Rangers. At least three coaches leave the town on a regular basis to watch the 'Old Firm' clubs.

Helensburgh may not have a senior football team any longer but the town has well-run, and very successful, cricket and rugby clubs. Organised cricket has a long association with Helensburgh. The origins of cricket in the town can be traced back to the late 1850s and Sir James Colquhoun's attempt to gift land to the community for recreational purposes. Many early cricket clubs existed in the 1860s but most had disappeared by the following decade. One such example was Ardencaple Cricket Club, founded in 1874, which played in the west end of the town and was disbanded in 1877. The current club, Helensburgh Cricket Club, was formed in 1882 and played matches at East King Street Park (gifted by Sir James Colquhoun). Dissatisfaction with facilities resulted in a move to Kirkmichael Park (part of the farm) in 1883 before the decision was taken to move once again, this time to a more spacious location. In 1886 the club moved to Ardencaple, their current home, sharing facilities with Helensburgh Football Club.

The theme of ground-sharing would once again visit Helensburgh Cricket Club in the early 1970s. A steady decline in cricketing standards during the 1960s resulted in relegation to a lower division and almost finished the club. To compound matters further a fire destroyed the club pavilion in 1970. This event led to calls for the club to merge with Helensburgh Rugby Club, as it was felt by all concerned that the maintenance of a new pavilion would be better shared. The amalgamation of cricket and rugby clubs in 1972 (to form Helensburgh Cricket and Rugby Club) seemed to strengthen both and Helensburgh Cricket Club quickly returned to the top division, becoming champions for the first time in 1978.

Helensburgh Rugby Club has a much shorter history than their cricketing counterparts. Formed in 1963 by local enthusiasts who enjoyed rugby at Hermitage Academy, the Helensburgh club found themselves without a pitch and accepting an offer to fulfil the fixtures of Shawlands 3rd XV. This state of affairs continued until the club amalgamated with the local cricket club in 1972. The rugby club fortunes have fluctuated throughout their short existence with the early seasons spent in the lower district leagues, before promotion was won to the National League for the first time in season 1976/77. Relegation again followed and the club went back to competing in the Glasgow & District League until promotion was once again secured to the National League (Division 7) in the mid-1990s. The past decade has been without doubt the club's most productive and currently the first team are playing rugby in Division 4 of the National League.

The success of both rugby and cricket sections within the club is reflected in the pavilion which both have shared since 1973. Major refurbishment in 1998 has made the clubhouse one of the best in the country, a facility of which Helensburgh Cricket and Rugby Club can be rightly proud. The redevelopment of the clubhouse was made possible by a grant of £140,000 from the Scottish Sports Council Lottery Fund. The club matched this sum with funding secured from other sources. The new improved clubhouse facility was officially opened in October 1998.

Like cricket, local participation in tennis has its origins in the 1880s. Presently there are two clubs in the town, the older being Helensburgh Lawn Tennis Club, founded in 1884. Their ground at Suffolk Street was donated by ex-Provost Breingan and included a wooden clubhouse lit by gas. Today they can be proud of a two storey structure with modern facilities, surrounded by seven floodlit artificial grass courts. This was made possible by joint funding between the club and the Sports Lottery Fund in 1997.

The other local club is the Craighelen Lawn Tennis and Squash Club, formed in the early 1920s (probably between 1922 and 1925). Like its neighbour, the Craighelen Club started life with antiquated facilities before attracting funding to make the necessary improvements, including floodlighting. Craighelen was also one of the first tennis clubs in the West of Scotland to introduce artificial grass courts and when the new clubhouse was built in 1957, the club played host to many Open Championships. Two squash courts were added to take account of the growth in popularity of the sport during the 1970s. Costing £20,000 this project was made possible with the help of a Scottish Sports Council grant.

A third local tennis club was in existence during the inter-war years. Ardencaple Tennis Club was formed shortly after the outbreak of World War I and according to scant information available, folded sometime after the end of World War II. Sadly not much more is known about this club.

The clubs referred to in this chapter are by no means the definitive list. Many more exist, but pressure of space means that their various contributions to community life must go unrecorded. What is abundantly clear is that Helensburgh is fortunate to benefit from a wide diversity of recreational interests.

At the time of the town's bicentenary, Argyll & Bute Council are considering a planning application which would result in the current swimming pool being replaced by a supermarket, and a new purpose-built sports centre erected beside the Clyde Community Education Centre as compensation for losing the pool (and as a planning 'gain' for the supermarket). This issue has split opinion within the town with many people opposed to the plan, claiming that it will diminish the natural beauty of Helensburgh's seafront and pier. Others take the view that a seafront supermarket is a small price to pay for a much needed modern sports facility.

Concern regarding the well-being of Helensburgh's natural assets is not a new phenomenon. From Helensburgh's early days it has always been accepted that prosperity relied heavily on the town maintaining its tourist attractions. This message was driven home by Macneur & Bryden in their book, *Helensburgh and Environs*, published in the late 1930s. It reads,

> The natural beauty of Helensburgh and its salubrity have been the keystone to its prosperity, and the powers that be realise that upon the maintenance of these characteristics will depend its future welfare.

This warning holds true today as it did then.

Sport and leisure can be taken seriously - Helensburgh Rugby Club on an outing to Cardiff Arms Park in 1990 with captain Robbie Price leading the charge

Scotsman Publications Ltd

During World War I, 214 Helensburgh service personnel were killed (there are also separate memorials at Rhu, Shandon and Cardross). This was more than one in five of the 18 to 35 age group. Another 100 names were added after World War II

Lennox Herald 8th November 1981

Chapter 13

War and Peace

Stewart Noble

Few other influences have had as big an impact on Helensburgh as the wars of the twentieth century and the national defence policy which was pursued after those wars. The impact has been visual and has led to population growth.

At the same time as the burgh centenary was being celebrated in 1902 the Boer War in South Africa had come to an end after three years of fighting, and the forty four local men who served in it are commemorated by a plaque inside the municipal buildings. This was the first time that the Volunteer Rifles of Helensburgh had seen action. Their history goes right back to the 1800s when each parish had its own detachment in what became known as the 1st Dunbartonshire Volunteer Rifle Corps. The remains of the rifle range can be seen on the moors to the north of the Blackhill Plantation.

Sadly however a much more important conflict for the world and for the town was only a few years away. By the time that World War I broke out in 1914, the Volunteer Rifles were known as (A) Company of the 9th (Dunbartonshire) Princess Louise Battalion Argyll and Sutherland Highlanders. They left for France from their Drill Hall which can still be seen at 75 East Princes Street, only to be caught in one of the worst gas attacks of the war at Ypres, suffering many casualities. When the ceasefire in 1918 came into effect on the 11th hour of the 11th day of the 11th month an immense slaughter had taken place. Those who lived through it felt that this bloody war should never be forgotten. Consequently each November on the Sunday nearest to the 11th day of November a memorial service takes place at the War Memorial in Hermitage Park.

It is truly horrifying to contemplate just how many names are actually on the war memorial. For Helensburgh there are 214 (of which only one is definitely of a woman) and it must be remembered that there are also war memorials in Rhu, Shandon and Cardross. Helensburgh was of course a much smaller town at that time and its total population in 1911 was 8,529. If we assume that half of this population were male and if we assume that men between the ages of

The names of forty four local men who served in the Boer War are commemorated on a plaque in the Municipal Buildings

Kenneth Crawford

18 and 35 made up about a quarter of the male population, then the arithmetic says that there were 1,066 males of that age in Helensburgh of whom 213 died – in other words more than one in five of that age group. Sadly Helensburgh was not alone in losing such a large proportion of its young men.

When the War was declared in 1914 a mood of national euphoria had swept the country and young men were encouraged to volunteer to join the ranks. It was soon discovered that a surprisingly large percentage of them were not fit enough to pass the initial medical examination, and the blame for this was placed to a large extent on inadequate housing. Consequently towards the end of the war the Government made the pledge that it would build 'homes fit for heroes'. Helensburgh was not alone in complying with this and the first council housing in Helensburgh was provided at Ardencaple Quadrant in 1919.

By the time World War II broke out in 1939 the Volunteer Rifles had again been reformed. The men of Helensburgh were now known as 162 Company of the 54th Light Anti-Aircraft Artillery. As in 1914, watched by their families and friends, the men of Helensburgh's 162 Company left for France and, after the fall of that country, assisted for a time with the defence of Gibraltar. Back home the men were involved in protecting such targets as the ICI factory in Manchester from air attack, before participating in the D-Day landings in France, and ultimately serving with the Field Security Police in Germany after the end of the War.

While World War I had a major effect on the people of Helensburgh it failed to have a direct impact on the town itself. The same could not be said about World War II. An immediate worry of the Government after war was declared in September 1939 was the vulnerability of southern English ports to German bombers, and consequently the establishment of new ports in the West of Scotland was a priority, and added impetus was given to this when the Americans joined in the War in 1941. A branch line was built from the West Highland Railway between Rhu and Shandon down to Faslane where a major harbour known as Military Port No. 1 was established – this was a much more intrusive operation than the actual building of the line more than forty years earlier, but was undertaken without the fuss that there had been originally! The Rosneath area became a major American naval base and a flying boat base was established in Rhu Bay – two large hangars were built almost opposite the Ardencaple Hotel and a newer one is still there today. The whole of Garelochside and the Rosneath peninsula became a restricted area and travel permits were required to go there. Huge convoys of ships assembled at the Tail of the Bank off Helensburgh and the Admiralty Hydro-Ballistic Research Establishment was built in Glen Fruin – the buildings now serve as part of the Army's Garelochhead Training Camp.

Helensburgh itself was extremely lucky in that it suffered no bombing damage whatsoever, although a land mine did explode just off the beach at the foot of Maitland Street. This was in stark contrast to Greenock and particularly Clydebank with their shipyards. Even Cardross suffered from bombing damage and visible evidence of this today is the ruin of the Old Parish Church on the Main Road. However Helensburgh played its part in trying to reduce this bombing damage and anti-aircraft batteries were established in various locations round the town – one example was above the West Highland Railway at Woodend, while another was tucked between the main railway and the beach between Craigendoran and Ardmore.

However, in common with the rest of Britain, the death toll from World War II was much lower than for World War I. Nevertheless the war memorial in Hermitage Park carries one hundred names.

Three major buildings which were taken over by the armed forces during World War II were left in such bad repair that they did not long survive and had to be demolished. Rosneath Castle, home of Queen Victoria's daughter, Princess Louise, later Duchess of Argyll, was demolished in 1961 and Rosneath Castle Caravan Park occupies the site. Robert Napier's magnificent former home at West Shandon was returned to civilian use in 1951 and for a few years was run again as Shandon Hydropathic Hotel. However the proximity of the naval base spoiled the view, and the growth in private car ownership meant that people could travel further for their holidays. Consequently it was closed and demolished in 1957. Even nearer home Ardencaple Castle remained in the hands of the armed forces until it was finally demolished in 1957-59. Only its tower was left standing and navigation lights for vessels travelling to Faslane were attached to it.

After the War Faslane was split in two. Towards the end of 1945 the southern section of the military port was handed over to the Royal Navy, who then used it as a base for the Reserve Fleet, sometimes including submarines. In August 1946 the rest of the port was handed over to Metal Industries Ltd for breaking up ships. Many famous vessels ended their days there, including the last four-funnelled liner, the *Aquitania*, the Royal Yacht *Victoria and Albert*, and the *Vanguard* which was the last battleship built for the British Navy and which was broken up in 1960 without ever having fired a shot in anger. World politics had an impact on the shipbreaking workers, as the failed revolution against the Communist government of Hungary in 1956 brought a number of refugees to work at Faslane. There they joined Poles who had decided not to return home to life under the Communists after the War.

During the War a net known as the boom was slung across the Clyde from the Cloch Lighthouse to Dunoon to prevent enemy submarines coming into the Firth. After the War the boom was taken ashore and stored beside the railway just to the west of Ardmore near where the sewage works are today. It lay there for several years and was ultimately taken away and broken up; the storage area was used in the 1960s for burning the carriages of the old steam trains, the remaining metal then being sold for scrap.

Although the huge wartime shipping convoys had disappeared, laid-up naval and merchant ships could frequently be seen – for example the battleship *King George V* lay for many years in Rhu Bay, and the Gareloch itself was full of shipping. In 1957 the Royal Navy closed its base in Rothesay Bay and consequently the submarine depot ship HMS *Adamant* was transferred to Faslane and the Reserve Fleet Headquarters moved away to Rosyth. Six years later the British government decided to buy its seaborne nuclear weapons from the United States and to base them at Faslane – a decision which had a substantial impact on Helensburgh and the surrounding area.

At Faslane itself considerable work took place and the main road was replaced with a bypass around the northern edge of the much expanded base, which utilised much of the site of Shandon Hydro. However Metal Industries continued breaking up ships and even some steam locomotives until 1980. The road between Rhu and Faslane was substantially widened, and Shandon Pier (which used to be immediately opposite the Church) was demolished. A dredger widened Rhu Narrows considerably so that the much larger Polaris submarines could pass through at sufficient speed to maintain steerage against the strong tides. The construction of an underground NATO nuclear weapons store was started in Glen Douglas in 1963.

New housing was also built for the naval personnel at the Churchill and Ardencaple estates in Helensburgh, the Smugglers Way estate in Rhu and round the Rosneath Peninsula. The Old Parish Church had been closed in 1956 and the building was converted into a hostel where Navy men could stay the night. It continued in this role until 1968 when with the exception of the tower the building was demolished and replaced by the flats now called Tower Place. The retained tower became the Tourist Information Centre.

While this substantial naval expansion brought job security and prosperity to the area, many were appalled by the whole concept of nuclear weapons and decided that it was their duty to protest against their presence in the Helensburgh area. Consequently the Peace Camp was established at Faslane in 1982 and its residents, often accompanied by other demonstrators from far and wide, have made frequent protests over the years, many of which have resulted in their appearance in local courts, and some of which have led to spells in prison.

In the early 1980s the Government decided that the Polaris nuclear deterrent represented outdated technology and that it should be replaced by something more modern. It consequently bought Trident

'In humble thanksgiving to God,' runs the inscription, 'for the safe return from the War of 1914-18 of their sons Leonard Harper Captain QORG Yeomanry and John Wesley Harper Lieutenant Scots Guards this window is placed here AD 1924 by Leonard Gow and Mabel Harper Gow.' Originally in St Bride's Church these windows are now on display in Helensburgh Library, having been restored by Helensburgh Heritage Trust

Painting by AN Paterson *The Clyde in Wartime 1943* (Watercolour 28 x 53 cm) shows ships preparing to cross the Atlantic in convoy, while a flying boat, probably from Rhu Hangars, crosses overhead

nuclear weapons from the United States. Work started in 1985 and this resulted again in great upheaval for the area. At Faslane itself a substantial shiplift was built to replace the old floating dock, and a dredger made Rhu Narrows even wider because the Trident submarines were considerably bigger than the Polaris ones.

Trident had less of an impact on Helensburgh than Polaris, but outside the town big changes took place. A major depot was built at Coulport which resulted in the Ministry of Defence taking over virtually the whole of the north end of the Rosneath Peninsula. At that time Faslane and its surroundings were probably the biggest construction site in Europe and to cope with this a haul road was built through Glen Fruin and along the north of the Rosneath Peninsula.

With the end of the Cold War in 1989 the Ministry of Defence started to cut back on servicemen and civilian employees. Besides the

The target area of the old rifle range now provides a good shelter for sheep. The first reservoir is visible and Ben Bouie is in the distance

Donald Fullarton

impact on employment and house prices, a major effect on Helensburgh was that some of the housing in the Churchill estate became surplus to requirement. Initially the Ministry of Defence decided that the houses should be demolished, but after local protest it was decided in 2000 to transfer ownership of some into private hands, and of others to the Dunbritton Housing Association to provide rented accommodation for local people, but some were demolished.

The impact which those developments have had on the growth of the town is well illustrated by the Census figures. Thus in 1911 the population of the town was 8,529, but by 1951 this had only risen to 8,760. However another forty years later the population was 15,852. This considerable expansion has had an impact in many other ways. Employment has been provided both directly and indirectly and of course there has been increased demand for various services such as medical facilities and road provision. Most would agree that the economic impact has been beneficial. Many would argue that the presence of these weapons of mass destruction on our doorstep has been too high a price to pay for the economic benefits.

Of one thing we can be certain. If the wars of the twentieth century had not happened, and if the nuclear deterrent had not been placed here, the Helensburgh of 2002 would have been a very different town.

Helensburgh Quay as depicted by an unknown artist, thought to have been painted around 1830. It shows the overlapping ages of sail and steam (Oil on panel 55 x 82 cm)

Steamboat on the Clyde, near Dumbarton (Engraving and Aquatint 23 x 30 cm) by William Daniell

East Clyde Street
(Watercolour
51 x 74cm)
by John Carlaw

CHAPTER 14

Art and Artists – the Early Art Scene

DORIS GENTLES

Although the town cannot claim a 'Helensburgh School' of painters, many artists chose to live and work here for at least part of their careers. Some of them had great influence on the development of Scottish painting, some are of international renown.

There has been a lively interest in the arts from the early days of the town. Fortunately there have also been collectors who have been generous in donating works of art and consequently we have a 'Helensburgh Collection', gifted by individuals and the Anderson Collection. This was originally formed by Miss Nance Anderson OBE who wished the collection to be retained after her death. A Trust was formed and the Chairman is her nephew WFT Anderson. The Trust paintings, which are of local interest, can be seen in the Helensburgh Library from time to time, as also can the Helensburgh Collection.

One of the earliest works in the Anderson Collection is an aquatint by William Daniell (1769-1837) *Steamboat on the Clyde, near Dumbarton* which was an illustration in his *Voyage Round Great Britain* published in 1817, and was a recording of Henry Bell's *Comet* even though only the tall funnel is recognisable! The very fine painting *Helensburgh Pier* c1835 is by an unknown artist. It is an evocation of an earlier age when river traffic was the main means of transport. Sail predominates, exemplified by a large coal gabbard and several smaller fishing boats, but the future is anticipated in the paddle steamer coming into the pier. Henry Bell's *Comet* of 1812 had proved that steam navigation was possible. It is interesting to compare this painting with the lithograph by William 'Crimean' Simpson (1823-1899), (he was a war correspondent in the Crimean War), *Helensburgh 1848*, showing the town as it was then emerging as a sea-bathing resort with a bathing hut in the foreground.

Among the early, new residents of the town about 1857 were artists J Milne Donald (1819 – 1866) and Alexander Kellock Brown ARSA RSW (1849-1922) who lived at Helenslee, 21 Suffolk Street and Duncan MacLaurin RSW (1849-1921) who lived at Broomfield, 33 Lomond Street. The painting *Old Helensburgh Postman on his Round by Kirkmichael* (Anderson Trust) is a social record of early days in Helensburgh.

•

Colin Hunter (1841-1904) who grew up in Helensburgh, son of the postmaster, became very successful outside Scotland. He painted first with Milne Donald and had a studio in Edinburgh, then he moved to London and became an eminently successful marine painter. It is said that his love of the sea was born in Helensburgh where he had spent much of his time sailing. He painted the sea as 'a wonderful, quivering mirror'.[1] Glasgow bought his *Goodbye to Skye* for £500 in 1896. He returned to Scotland every year to paint. He visited America where he was commissioned to paint *Niagara*, which was a great success. His wealth enabled him to live at Holland Park, London, where he entertained many of the leading artists of the day. His hospitality, which included capercailzie, black grouse and salmon from Oban, became legendary.

His son, John Young Hunter (1874-1955), grew up surrounded by artists such as John Millais RA and John Singer Sargent RA. with whom he studied. He became a friend of the Duke of Argyll and his Duchess, the Princess Louise, daughter of Queen Victoria, who was a fine artist herself. The Duchess became a friend of the artist's wife Mary, who was also an artist. A watercolour by the Duchess, *The Avenue, Rosneath Castle* is in the Helensburgh Collection.

The Young Hunters stayed at the castle when they were painting watercolours to illustrate the beautiful book *The Clyde* (1907) by Neil Munro. There are views of the Italianate Rosneath Castle, the Rose Garden, and the training ships *Cumberland* and *Empress* to mention a few of the beautiful illustrations of this area in the book. There is also *Helensburgh from the Golf Links*, an oil study by John Young Hunter in the Anderson Collection.

They both went to America with a

Helensburgh from the Golf Links (Oil 14 x 15cm) by John Young Hunter. On his death in 1955 the *Helensburgh & Gareloch Times* noted that 'he was considered easily America's greatest living artist'

letter of introduction from the Duke to the American Indians. John Young Hunter is remembered for his unique record of the vanished frontier lifestyle of that race. In 1932 he won the Members' Gold Medal for the best picture in the Annual Exhibition of the Allied Artists of America.

•

One of the most interesting of the early visiting artists was William Leighton Leitch (1804 – 1883) who taught Queen Victoria and her daughter Princess Louise. The Helensburgh Collection boasts four delightful watercolour sketches of the *East* and *West Esplanades* painted in 1869 and 1872. The open aspect of the seafront of the Victorian town is captured in harmonious colours. Andrew MacGeorge who lived at Glenarn, Rhu, wrote a book on William Leighton Leitch, and also a manuscript autobiography[2] in which he mentions meeting with Leitch at a station in Glasgow forty years later. They then journeyed together to Helensburgh where Leitch was going to visit a relative, Mrs Smellie at Ellangowan, at (possibly 90) Colquhoun Street. MacGeorge was able to explain why he had missed earlier lessons from the artist due to illness and Leitch, being a kindhearted man, offered to make up for the lost lessons even though he was now retired. (The Smellie Collection in Glasgow Art Gallery contains some beautiful watercolours by Leitch).

In 1882 a branch of the Glasgow School of Art and Haldane Academy opened in Helensburgh and day and evening classes were held. In September of that year Helensburgh held its own Fine Art Exhibition. Many fine works were lent, including those of Corot, McCulloch and MacTaggart. Over three thousand people attended. John Murray, later better known as J Reid Murray (1861-1906) was the only local contributor connected with the Glasgow School of Art. He was the son of Donald Murray, a joiner in Helensburgh who was also on the Town Council. He studied in Glasgow, Edinburgh and later in Antwerp and became a friend of Edward Atkinson Hornel who had also been to Antwerp. The influence of that artist is evident in his *Landscape with Goats* (Glasgow Art Gallery) with its bold colour and handling of impasto (a brush laden with paint and used in a sweeping gesture created this effect). An earlier painting by him *Portincaple, Loch Long* (Anderson Trust) is dark and is more conventional in approach. Reid Murray was a fringe member of the Glasgow School.

•

The Glasgow Boys is the collective name for loosely formed groups of friends who painted together at different locations from about 1880. For example, at this time the early group of James Guthrie (1859-1930), Joseph Crawhall (1861-1913) and John Lavery (1856-1941) were working in this area, at Rosneath, while John Lavery and J Whitelaw Hamilton had exhibited paintings at the Dumbarton Art Club from 1881.

The Boys admired the work of the French Realist painters, such as Bastien Lepage (1848-1884) whose painting *Poor Fauvette* (Glasgow Art Gallery) influenced them greatly. They wanted to paint in this direct, realistic way, with broad brushstrokes, with a recognition of tonal values, and a decorative strain, 'en plein air'. Those elements were already in the work of William York Macgregor (1855-1923) and James Paterson (1854-1923), and the young artists joined them.

The younger artists saw the works acceptable to the Academy as sentimental and anecdotal, overlaid with Victorian morality; they called the Academicians 'Gluepots'! The Boys' innovative style of painting was in direct contrast to the style that was acceptable to the Academy. They did not see themselves as a group – the title 'Glasgow School' was bestowed upon their work at a London exhibition in 1890.

James Guthrie became the leader of the group. His friend JG Whyte, a Glasgow dentist who lived in Helensburgh, was himself a talented amateur watercolourist and collector. He had a studio at his home, Eastwood, 221 East Clyde Street which he lent to Guthrie to complete his *Funeral Service in the Highlands* (Glasgow Art Gallery). Dark and atmospheric, it reflects the artist's profound sadness at the tragedy of a young

Royal Scottish Academy (Diploma Collection)

Midsummer (1892)
(Oil on canvas,
99 x 124.5 cm)
by James Guthrie

boy who had died by drowning. He finished the painting in Helensburgh using local men as models for the mourners and Robert Whyte as the young boy.

The following year saw *To Pastures New* (Aberdeen Art Gallery) finished. This was a key painting in the Boys' work. It was sketched at Crowland, in Lincolnshire and completed in Whyte's studio. The Whyte family were most accommodating, Mrs Whyte allowing a goose to join her hens and her young daughter Christina posed for the goose girl, a task she found very boring. This painting is the antithesis to the Funeral painting.

It is in full sunlight and painted in bright colours. The Funeral seems to fix a still, frozen moment in time, but this picture celebrates an on-going procession, from one side of the picture to the other as the little girl herds her geese to pastures new. When John Lavery saw this painting in the Glasgow Institute in 1885 he decided not to return to Paris. He said that it was better than anything he had seen abroad.

Much of Guthrie's early innovative work was done in Helensburgh. His diploma painting *Midsummer* (1892) was painted in the town. It was executed in a radically free

Victoria Road 1883
(Watercolour, 33.6 x
51.4)
by EA Walton

style in the garden of Thornton
Lodge, 107 Sinclair Street, the
Hamilton home. Maggie Hamilton, her sister Mary Ann and one
of the Walton sisters, probably
Hannah, are taking tea on a lovely
sunny day and it is easy to imagine
the scene with the dappled sunlight shining through the trees
casting cool shadows on the dresses
of the three young ladies. This
picture was given to the Royal
Scottish Academy when Guthrie
was made a full Academician. He
also painted two portraits of
Maggie Hamilton. The one in the
Glasgow Art Gallery, *Maggie
Hamilton,* shows a stylishly dressed
and confident young lady. Also in
the gallery is his portrait of
Whitelaw Hamilton's son *Lt A Leslie
Hamilton* who was killed in the last
days of World War I.

1900 was a momentous year for
the Boys as they were recognized
in London and Munich. James
Guthrie stayed in Helensburgh
with his mother that year while his
studio in Glasgow was being
prepared for him. This was when
he painted a series of lovely
pastels. Christina Whyte sat at the
dining table at Eastwood with Mrs
Guthrie for the beautiful *Causerie*
(Hunterian Art Gallery, University
of Glasgow). Christina Whyte's
family and friends were the models
for the pastels. *Stormy Twilight*
(Anderson Trust) depicts a view
from the East Esplanade. It is
interesting to compare this night
scene with John Carlaw's painting
of the area.[3] Fifty of these paintings
were shown in Glasgow and every
one was sold.

Another Helensburgh resident is

En Plain Air (1885)
(Watercolour 44.5 x 59.7)
by EA Walton

captured in paint in a later work, reflecting the influence of James Whistler (1834-1903). *Christina Wilson, Mrs Thomas Steven,* by the now Sir James Guthrie PRSA, was painted in Edinburgh, and hangs in the Scottish National Gallery. The sitter was the wife of Provost Thomas Steven (1867-1877). They lived at Ardlui, 1 East Montrose Street.

•

Edward Arthur Walton (1860-1922), J Whitelaw Hamilton and James Guthrie were great friends as well as fellow artists who painted together sharing ideals and ideas. Walton spent his winters at Thornton Lodge and it is he who has left the most memorable records of life at Helensburgh in his lovely watercolours. It was here in 1883 that he began his innovative series of townscapes recording the genteel urban lifestyle of the wealthy residents of the town. His friends modelled for him and he recorded them with a background of the Victorian town exemplified in *Victoria Road* (Private Collection). This composition with its concentric curves of the road and footpath, its strong vertical line in the trees creating a pleasing pattern, and the figure of the young girl in the foreground walking towards the viewer, gives a feeling of movement. The beautiful colours and autumn tones make this a delightful picture. His *En Plein Air* (Private Collection) depicts two elegant young ladies leisurely approaching Thornton Lodge, probably his sisters or the Hamilton girls. The figures are placed near the front of the picture, against a rising background and moving towards the viewer. The sense of movement is even more marked by the contrast of the speed of the horse careering downhill. Other Glasgow School motifs such as strong verticals, in figures and telegraph poles, combined with the strong horizontal and diagonal lines of the streets, create a pleasing sense of pattern. The colours are delicate and, with the inclusion of the parasols and the green of the trees in full bloom, is an evocation of summer. His *At Helensburgh* (Hunterian Gallery, University of Glasgow) shows the West Esplanade. The esplanade was built in the early years of the 1880s so was a novel feature of the town. Unusually for the time these paintings were not commissioned, but with their clear colours and images and sheer decorative sense they were quickly sold. Later another important picture, Walton's very different and extremely large exhibition painting *Daydreams* (Scottish National Gallery), with its complicated spatial composition, had been started at Cockburnspath in 1885 and completed in Helensburgh.

EA Walton was one of a gifted family and other members had links with the town. George Walton (1867-1933) designed the fireplaces and wallpaper at Thornton Lodge; fireplaces for The Long Croft, West Rossdhu Drive; furniture and stencil decorations[4] for Baillie Scott in The White House, 15 Upper Colquhoun Street; in 1898 he designed a mosaic[5] for the overmantel at the Ferry Inn, Rosneath. His sisters Helen and Hannah were visiting teachers of ceramics, first of all at the Helensburgh Art School and later at St Brides School for Girls. They were also friends of Maggie Hamilton.

•

James Whitelaw Hamilton (1860-1932) who lived all his life in Helensburgh, was at one time thought to be a Glasgow Boy but though he worked in their bold and vigorous manner he is now considered to be a fringe member. He was certainly a friend of James Guthrie, and with his sister Maggie had joined the Boys at Cockburnspath. Their family home was Thornton Lodge, and after his marriage he lived at the Grange, 23 Suffolk Street a house that had a fine studio designed by Alexander Nisbet Paterson (1862-1947) who had become his brother-in-law in 1897. The style of *Evening on the Gareloch* (Anderson Trust) is reminiscent of Whistler's *Nocturne* series. It shows the old sailing ship *Empress* anchored in the Gareloch. Another work *Ebb Tide* (Anderson Trust) painted in 1886 shows the seafront just west of the pier. The stretch of sand now seems exaggerated, but the scene is still recognisable as is the Bank of Scotland building at 34/36 West Clyde Street as it was

then with a hansom cab and patient horse standing outside. The original bank premises now house 'The Cat's Pyjamas' and the former manager's drawing room is a dental surgery. *Common Ground between Granary and Pier* (Helensburgh Collection) shows land gifted to the town by the then Sir James Colquhoun. The Granary, 1 West Clyde Street, (now demolished) had been a feature of the town from its earliest days; a pub called *Clockworxs* now occupies the site

Whitelaw Hamilton's interest in art extended to his civic duties as a Town Councillor. He encouraged AN Paterson to enter the design competition for the War Memorial in Hermitage Park and as a result we have a splendid Memorial in

the old walled garden of the previous estate. Hamilton was instrumental also in obtaining Sir James Guthrie as the artist to paint the portrait *George Maclachlan*. This picture was commissioned by the Town Council to commemorate the sixty years service of this gentleman as the Town Clerk. Hamilton even posed for the hands as the sitter was apt to nap. This picture usually hangs in the Municipal Buildings. (see p37)

●

Several members of the Paterson family were also connected with Helensburgh. James Paterson (1854-1932) frequently visited his parents at Hapland, 48 Charlotte Street, and his *View of Helensburgh* (Anderson Trust) is possibly painted from there or from above

The Skating Pond 1940
(Watercolour,
27 x 38cm)
by AN Paterson

the railway. His *Above Rosneath*, also in the collection, is a lovely landscape in watercolour showing the hills and the Gareloch, including the training ship anchored in the loch. Paterson was an important early member of the Glasgow Boys together with William York Macgregor (1855-1923). After his marriage in 1884 he lived for many years, and brought up his family, at Moniaive in Dumfriesshire. *The Last Turning* (Glasgow Art Gallery) is a typical Moniaive painting. His younger brother Alexander Nisbet Paterson was an architect and also trained in Paris. A sketch of AN Paterson by James is in the Anderson Collection.

Alexander Nisbet Paterson was a fine watercolourist, he was elected a member of the Royal Scottish Watercolourists in 1916. The Anderson Trust has two watercolours by him painted during World War II. *The Skating Pond, 1940* is an evocation of a winter sports scene in one of the coldest spells of weather in the war years. Some of the skaters are in uniform. The painting also evokes memories for the older generation of earlier times when skaters would have enjoyed musical entertainment by the boys from the training ship *Cumberland* and as darkness fell flares would have illuminated the scene to allow the fun to continue in the evening. *The Clyde in Wartime 1943* (see p151) painted from above Woodend, where there was a gun site as shown in the picture, depicts the naval presence in the

Above Rosneath
(Watercolour,
14 x 29cm)
by James Paterson

river rekindling memories of a dreadful time. The liner *Queen Elizabeth* seen here came to the Clyde every fortnight, alternately with the *Queen Mary*. The liners were used as troopships and after 1941 brought American servicemen to Britain. Many of them went to Rosneath Castle to be deployed elsewhere.

AN Paterson had married Maggie Hamilton, sister of Whitelaw Hamilton in 1897. They lived at the Turret, now Ard Rhu at 22 Millig Street, and later at The Long Croft, West Rossdhu Drive, both designed by Paterson. Maggie Hamilton was also an expert needlewoman and above the fireplace in the drawingroom is a delightful embroidery by her in the Arts and Crafts tradition.

●

Maggie Hamilton (1867-1952) was a talented painter as well. In 1883 she had gone with her brother to Cockburnspath to help Mrs Guthrie to keep house for the Glasgow Boys, including Arthur Melville and George Henry who joined them at times. As far as is known she did not study at the Glasgow School of Art, but she certainly attended classes run by Mary Park and Madge Ross at the 'Studio' at 8 then 3 Prince Albert Terrace. (Stephen Conroy, the artist, was born at number 3 in 1964) These enterprising women had met while studying in Paris. The classes continued from 1890 until 1906 when Mary Park returned to New Zealand and Madge Ross went to Glasgow. They asked

In the Shade of the Old Yew Tree (Watercolour, 39 x 60cm) by John Carlaw

Alexander Roche and John Lavery to come as visiting tutors. Exhibitions were held in the gallery of Macneur and Bryden, Stationers, 7 East Princes Street and at their later home at Greenburn, 26 East Clyde Street where a four-day exhibition was held in 1895. The last exhibition was held in 1906 in the Good Templars' Hall, 28 West Princes Street (behind the Co-op Store). The *Helensburgh & Gareloch Times* in 1893 noted 'so we have at our doors an atelier conducted on the identical lines of the Paris studios' and in 1895 that they had 'done so much within recent years to educate the artistic taste'.

•

Rosa Templeton (c1868-1936) was also a student; in the 1885 exhibition her work had been considered 'commendable' by the local paper's critic. Her *Old Pier, Craigendoran* (Anderson Collection) depicts the old pier that served the area before the railway pier was built in 1882. It also contrasts the peaceful scene of children playing by the pier and no traffic around with the smoke-filled sky above Greenock on the opposite side of the River Clyde. Her *View of the River Clyde* is also in the Anderson Collection.

•

The Carlaw brothers, William (1847-1889), and John (1850-1934) had family connections with the town. John came here on his retirement as a designer with the Saracen Foundry c1895. With his sisters Effie and Lizzie, who also painted, he lived at Seacliffe, 112 East Clyde Street, a house incor-

porated originally into the Baths Hotel, now Queen's Court. William was a well-known painter of marine subjects. *East Clyde Street, Helensburgh* (Anderson Trust) is a delightful watercolour by John Carlaw depicting the East Esplanade on a summer's day with a brilliant blue sky. The steamers at the pier recall a period of great prosperity for the seaside town. The people in the picture, mainly women and children, and some animals, appear to be enjoying the lovely day. His painting *In the Shade of the Old Yew Tree* (Anderson Trust) shows another aspect of the town. In contrasting colour it is an attractive watercolour depicting the old tree that has been a feature of the town for many years and is still growing at the top of Glasgow Street. John

is better known as a painter of animals and the goats add interest to the picture. James Bain, tutor to Lord John Campbell of Ardencaple and later twice Provost, studied under this old tree.

●

Charles Blatherwick RSA (d1895), who lived in Rhu, was a doctor who was also a talented watercolourist, writer and President of the Glasgow Art Club. He and his daughter, Lily, were founder members of the Royal Society of Watercolourists. His *The Clyde from the Old Duntocher Road* and other views of the River Clyde are in the Anderson Collection. The Glasgow Boys were included among his many artist friends.

●

Lily Blatherwick SWA (1854-1934) was the talented daughter of a gifted painter father, Dr Charles Blatherwick, who influenced her work. Lily's speciality was flowers, insects and small creatures, exemplified in her *Flowers and Berries*.[6] She exhibited at the Glasgow Institute in 1876 and continued to send work to Scotland after she left Rhu in 1896 when she married AS Hartrick. She also created beautiful lithographs. In his autobiography her husband wrote 'she painted the spirit and feeling of flowers in a way that was unique'.

•

Archibald Standish Hartrick (1864-1950) trained in London and the Academie Julian in Paris. He had met Gauguin in 1886 in Brittany, where he painted a picture of the artist's house. Hartrick was greatly influenced by developments in the art scene in France. He was an accomplished illustrator and excellent lithographer. In his fascinating book *A Painter's Pilgrimage through Fifty Years* (1936) he includes an account of his sketching trip to Cockburnspath with Dr Blatherwick (who was both his stepfather and father-in-law), where he was introduced to James Guthrie and subsequently became a friend of the Glasgow Boys.

•

Alexander Frew (d 1908) was a doctor who gave up medicine to follow a profession in painting and as a keen yachtsman to enjoy sailing. He came to live in Helensburgh at 'Glendevon', 45 William Street, a property that included a small cottage he used as his studio. He sailed round the coast painting fishing villages and harbour scenes 'en plein air'. His technique was to use deep tones and rich impasto. He exhibited at the Glasgow Institute of Fine Art and sent works abroad. He was also a talented photographer. One of his photographs of his garden[7] includes the figure of the girl he was to marry in 1899, Bessie McNicol, the only Glasgow Boy who was a girl; such was the prejudice of the day that she was admired because she painted like a man! She proclaims her profession by holding a palette. Bessie painted a portrait of Alexander Frew in 1898.[8]

•

A later student at 'The Studio' was Norah Neilson Gray (1882-1931). She was born in Helensburgh at Carisbrooke, 108 West King Street, the daughter of a Glasgow shipowner. She attended Miss Murdoch's School in the town. The family went to live in Glasgow after her father died, where she attended the Glasgow School of Art under Fra Newbury. She taught fashion and design at St Columba School for Girls at Kilmacolm for a time, where she was named 'Purple Patch' because she advised her pupils to look for colour in shadows. By 1910 she had her own studio in Bath Street, and had her first exhibition in Glasgow. She excelled in portraiture especially with children with whom she had a wonderful rapport, although a very reserved person herself. Two portraits are in the Glasgow Art Gallery, *Boy with Oranges* and *Little*

Brother – she kept the latter in her studio as an example of her work. She painted important works during World War I. *The Belgian Refugee* (Glasgow Art Gallery) is a sympathetic portrayal of a man who had to leave his home in Liege. In 1918 she went as a Voluntary Aid Detachment nurse to the Scottish Women's Hospital at the Abbaye de Royaumont near Paris. In her free time she was able to paint the reception of wounded in this old vaulted abbey, *Hôpital Auxiliaire d'Armée 30 – Abbaye Royaumont 1918* (Helensburgh Collection) which is on semi-permanent display at the Helensburgh Library. She was then commissioned to paint the staff and patients for the Imperial War Museum. Another important painting was of a mother and child *The Country's Charge* (Royal Free Hospital, London) used as a rallying cry to the nation to defend the family. After the war she returned to painting portraits, and was especially successful at the Salon in Paris, becoming better known abroad than at home. She was the first woman to be elected to the 'hanging committee' of the Royal Glasgow Institute in the company of local artist John Whitelaw Hamilton. She died of cancer at the height of her career aged forty-nine.

•

Evelyn Carslaw (1881-1968) also studied at the Glasgow School of Art and Paris. She illustrated a book by her husband *Leaves from*

Hôpital Auxiliaire d'Armée 30 – Abbaye Royaumont 1918 (Oil, 71 x 99cm) by Norah Neilson Gray

Rowan's Logs (1944) about a family cruise on the West Coast. She was a friend of Norah Neilson Gray who painted a portrait of her and her daughter Mary (Private Collection and *Helensburgh Advertiser*, 10 May 2001).

•

Another woman who trained at Glasgow School of Art was Louisa Perman (1854-1921) who specialised in painting roses. *White Roses* was bought by the Luxembourg Gallery in Paris and another example of her work is *Red Rose and White Rose* (Glasgow Art Gallery). She came to live at The Glen, 22 Queen Street, in 1912 when she married James Torrance, yet another Glasgow Boy.

•

Portraits of *Mr and Mrs Younger*, painted by two Glasgow Boys, James Torrance (1859-1916) and George Henry (1858-1943) respectively, hang in The Hill House. The portraits are of the parents of Mrs Blackie, wife of the original owner of the house.

•

Hilary Stair (1884-1960) painted portraits of *Mr and Mrs Walter Blackie*, which hang in the dining room of The Hill House. This artist trained at the Glasgow School of Art and in Germany.

•

James Gordon Burgess (1865-1950) was a Helensburgh man and a talented watercolourist who studied at the Dumbarton School of Art under Mr Strongman, and later taught there himself. James

Burgess exhibited at the Glasgow Institute and the Royal Scottish Academy. He also taught at his studio Rosevale, 2 Campbell Street. Later he became the first teacher of Art at Hermitage School. He established a firm of interior decorators which still trades under his grandson Gordon Burgess.

•

Sir William Russell Flint (1880-1969) stayed in Helensburgh when he was Admiralty Assistant Airships at Inchinnan in 1918 and 1919. His watercolour *View of the Gareloch* (Anderson Trust) is of a wintry scene of snow and mountain, the antithesis of his better known exotic scenes with beautiful women. He was greatly influenced by the 'wet' technique of Arthur Melville, a Glasgow Boy. While he was in Helensburgh Russell Flint painted two portraits of young girls he had met at The Long Croft, the cousins Viola Paterson and Hilda Hamilton (the latter became Mrs Murray Purvis).

•

Viola Paterson (1899-1981) inherited her parents' talent and studied at the Glasgow School of Art principally under Maurice Greiffenhagen. She then went to the studio of André L'Hôte in Paris She loved Paris and the Mediterranean countries and painted in Malta and Venice. She stayed on in France in World War II taking the last boat home from Vichy France. She worked for the Admiralty in Oxford for the rest of the war and only came to live at The Long Croft in the 1950s. Her colourful

oil paintings and innovative woodtype prints, a technique of printing in watercolours from woodcut blocks, will ensure her future recognition. Her *View from The Long Croft* is in the Anderson Collection. She also designed stained glass windows, including those from the former St Bride's Church which are now preserved.

•

Gregor Ian Smith (1907-1985) was a talented local artist who has left us a legacy of evocative images of the town. He was President of the Helensburgh and District Art Club for many years and a Trustee of the Anderson Trust. He later lived in Glen Fruin and was associated with its history. He was instrumental in erecting a cairn to the Battle of Glen Fruin at the north-west end of the Glen. *The Parish Church, Helensburgh 1954* shows the church that was built in 1847 which became the Parish Church in 1862. Now only the steeple and clock and the porch erected in 1923 by Robert Wemyss remain, housing the Tourist Information Centre. *Lower Colquhoun Street, Helensburgh* is viewed from the north and shows Colquhoun Square, the original centre of the town and at the bottom of Colquhoun Street at the entrance to the pier is the handsome red-sandstone arch designed by Robert Wemyss in 1898.

•

Old Cottage, Drumfork was the ferry cottage from where cattle and goods were transported across the river. In the great gale of 1882 the elderly couple who lived there

John Logie Baird
(Oil, 102 x 77cm)
by Stephen Conroy

artist. The artist was born at 3 Prince Albert Terrace, Victoria Road, Helensburgh. He studied at the Glasgow School of Art. This painting is typical of his work; it shows an unsmiling, formally dressed figure of a professional man who is also introverted, in this case a scientist, the inventor of television. There is a bust of Baird by Donald Gilbert on the West Esplanade at the foot of William Street, gifted by his friend Arnold Fleming.

•

There are many more paintings of local interest depicting the past which are in the Collections and available for viewing, too many to mention here. There is also the later art scene, to be recounted elsewhere.   •

escaped when they were flooded out and the gable fell in. *Old Ferry Cottage by the West Burn* was situated at the mouth of the Glenan Burn at the bottom of William Street, in the little fishing village of Milligs, which became the New Town, then Helensburgh. This burn marked the west boundary of the nascent town.

•

The portrait in the Helensburgh Collection by Stephen Conroy (b1964) of *John Logie Baird*, the town's most famous son, is too important to leave out hence the inclusion in this chapter of a living

References
(see bibliography)

1 Caw, page 325
2 Mike and Sue Thornley ms
3 Described on p165 and illustrated on dustjacket and on p153
4 Moon, photo 146
5 *ibid*, photo 122
6 Burkhauser, photo 302
7 Tanner 'Bessie McNicol' plate 32
8 *ibid* plate 44

CHAPTER 15

Some Architectural Gems
& their Architects

DORIS GENTLES

The Victorian architecture of Helensburgh reflects the social structure of the time. It is interesting to walk up Sinclair Street from Clyde Street viewing the buildings. The tenements and terraces with the resultant high density of population give way, above Argyle Street, to ever more splendid houses and spacious gardens.

Neil Macleod

Morar House,
17 Upper Colqhuoun Street

Helensburgh developed on the site of the village of Milligs after 1776, in a strict grid pattern according to Sir James Colquhoun's diktat and this is still obvious today. Charles Ross of Greenlaw, Sir James's factor, is credited with the execution of this plan. Lady Colquhoun was said to be very house-proud and meticulous in everything she did. She had recently moved into her new home, the Palladian mansion, Rossdhu House, Luss, built in 1773 by John Baxter who had been an assistant to Robert Adam. The order and proportions of the New Town, which became Helensburgh in her honour, would be much to her taste one imagines. The squares and broad streets of sixty feet (18m) instead of the usual thirty feet, is a feature that we still enjoy today. A further embellishment was the gift, by Dr Ewing Hunter, just before World War I, of cherry and hawthorn trees that were planted on the grass verges. Combined with the abundance of trees in the long-established gardens of the wealthy Victorian owners, such as magnolia and laburnum, whose blooms are truly magnificent, Helensburgh earned the title of The Brighton of Scotland.[1] When the blossom is at its best in May Helensburgh is something worth seeing; an echo of that splendid golden age seems to permeate the town.

Helensburgh has been especially fortunate to have had three resident architects, William Leiper (1839-1916), who was the most prolific and influential; Alistair Nisbet Paterson (1862-1947) and Robert Wemyss (d 1955). The west and upper part of Helensburgh, where there is a concentration of their work, has been designated a Conservation Area. In spite of this safeguard the intrusion of modern architecture is also unfortunately obvious. This consists mostly of houses

The Victoria Halls like many other buildings had their railings removed for the war effort around 1940. Neil Macleod produced this picture as part of the fund-rasing appeal to have them reinstated in 2002, thus enhancing this fine Victorian building

built in the gardens of these handsome homes. There are also many unimaginative and unsightly conversions of villas; or blocks of flats built of brick that appear incongruous between the buildings of stone or harling, materials which gave upper Helensburgh a homogeneous appearance.

William Spence (1806-1883) had already left his mark on the town when these young architects came to live here. There are also examples of buildings by such eminent architects as Alexander 'Greek' Thomson, Baillie Scott, Charles Rennie Mackintosh and the largest Art Deco house by John Boyd, the only such house in Scotland, to ensure an exciting visit for the lover of architecture. Influences of the Arts and Crafts Movement including that of Charles Voysey (1857-1941) and Richard Norman Shaw (1831-1912), for example, are also to be found as well as fine work of modern architects.

However, the emerging town was small with the boundary to the west at the Glenan Burn at William Street. It is claimed that 'one of the first houses to be built was a red-tiled building at the foot of William Street'.[2] *Flowerbank,* 1 William Street and 95-97 West Clyde Street, is an example of early vernacular building of the time and this is now a listed building.

Before the town achieved burgh status the east boundary was at

Maitland Street, beside the Milligs Burn. Mr McAulay, a fisherman, thought that 'the oldest house in Helensburgh was a red-tiled one at the foot of Maitland Street, occupied by John Gray'.[3] (The cooper who later became a Bailie?) In the lower, east side of the street, carved on a stone in the wall there is the date 1778 and the cooper's coat-of-arms, the letters P G M D G, a pair of compasses and some implements. There was a cooperage near the shore end that had been washed away in a storm. A Street Report of 1845 states that 'nettles and rubbish, no footpaths',[4] were features of the lower end of the street. On the opposite side of the road at numbers 7-9 and continuing round the corner to 16 East Clyde Street is one of the earliest feued sites [5] (1797) and an example of the simple vernacular style of early architecture. This low building now houses *Mission for Men*, a hairdressing business.

In 1804 Lady Augusta Clavering had a small estate beside the Glenan Burn at 82/3 West Clyde Street. The house and grounds were described thus, 'This is a plain, substantial house with a grass plot in

The early town developed along the flat areas by the river, to both the east and west. In 1803 Sir James Colquhoun employed Peter Fleming of Glasgow to draw up a plan of eighty two feuing lots, rectangular or square, of two acres (0.8 hectares) with two or four houses on each acre, except on the front street, reinforcing the grid pattern.

Kenneth Crawford

Helensburgh's most famous names commemorated in stone.

(above) The handsome obelisk to Henry Bell terminates the view down James Street. It was erected in 1872, 42 years after Bell's death at the instigation of Robert Napier of West Shandon, the shipbuilder

(opposite) John Logie Baird's bust by Donald Gilbert was moved from Hermitage Park to the West Esplanade in 1994. Unfortunately vandals have broken off his spectacles

front and a strong iron railing next the street'.[6] By 1897 the house had been divided into two flats. The tenants must have been of a certain social standing as one, Miss McDonald, left £100 each to the Infirmary and Fever Hospital in 1907. The original house, built by Dr Gardiner, still stands, behind *Augusta Lodge Cafe*, West Clyde Street.

There was little building beyond the front street in the early days, while seven farms surrounded the town. From the west were *Woodend*, (the farmhouse still stands in the housing estate) and *Easterton* (James Bain, a future Provost of Helensburgh (1834-35 and 1839-1840) was born at Easterton Farm c1796). He evidently studied 'under the shade of a venerable yew tree, which stands in Glasgow Street at Yew Bank House'.[7] The tree still survives. Glenan, Milligs, (the Hermitage Park now occupies the adjacent site), Stuck, Townhead and Kirkmichael were farms with ancient names that are still prevalent today. There was a small farm at *Hopewell Cottage* 23 Lomond Street and shore farms at *Brandon Grove*, 119 West Princes Street (mentioned in a report in 1760) and *Cromalt*, East Clyde Street.

The early houses were demolished to build tenements with shops below. However, one of the earlier buildings to survive was the Tontine, c1830, a Coaching Inn, that had a daily service to Luss, whose address was once East Clyde Street when the numbers started at Colquhoun Street. It was later renamed the George and is now the *Imperial Hotel*, 12 West Clyde Street. A handsome building, it has a string-course and long and short quoins in black against contrasting cream-coloured walls to commend it.

A pleasing bull-faced snecked red-sandstone building at *18 West Clyde Street*, 1909, built by T&L Low, of Greenock, for JR Marten, is a Glasgow-style tenement with Art Nouveau details, and shops below. Above the entrance is a cartouche with the number of the tenement. Above the centre of the façade is an attractive detail of a date stone.

Woolworths, (1933) at 20-23, is cheek by jowl with the above, in the Art Deco style of a later date. This building appears to squat between the two adjacent tall buildings.

At *24 West Clyde Street*, built for the National Bank of Scotland in 1928 by AN Paterson & Stoddart, is a striking cream sandstone corner building curving round to Colquhoun Street, with two almost symmetrical facades. These sport quoins and a string course, with urns on the Clyde Street elevation. There are flats above with a tripartite window in the centre of the first floor that has an attractive wrought-iron balcony, while the higher level window has a wrought-iron window guard. The asymmetrical doorway has a coat-of-arms to tympanum.

36 West Clyde Street, built for the Bank of Scotland (1876) by William Petrie is an example of Scots Baronial exuberance, complete with crow-steps and corbels, the irregular crow-stepped gables create an interesting skyline. The entrance has a half-glazed vestibule door and an encaustic tiled porch. A *Dental Surgery* now occupies the drawing room of the former Bank Manager's house and the original bank houses *The Cat's Pyjamas*.

At the foot of James Street is the *Henry Bell Monument* (1872). Carved from a single piece of polished red Aberdeen granite this handsome obelisk, gifted by Robert Napier and Sir James Colquhoun, 4th Baronet, commemorates the achievements of this gifted inventor and Provost. Further along the *West Esplanade*, 1880s, is *a bust* of a son of the town, the genius *John Logie Baird*, inventor of television, gifted by his friend J Arnold Fleming and unveiled by his sister and his son, Malcolm. It is inscribed 'They need no candle'.

Kenneth Crawford

EAST END

On the Milligs-Cardoss boundary was *Camis Eskan,* Colgrain (1648) seat of the Dennistoun family of Colgrain for over five hundred years until sold to Colin Campbell of Breadalbane who made many additions to the house. A gracious house, it was remodelled by David Hamilton (1768-1843) in 1840 and later by AN Paterson in 1915. The main elevation has an impressive porch and bay windows with Gibbs surrounds, the whole crowned with urns; varied fenestration including an unusual elongated window on a gable, and a pedimented attic dormer are a few of the details that adorn this handsome building. It has seen many uses, for example, as a sanitarium, then a geriatric hospital before regaining its

prestige as six luxury flats in 1979. The estate had two lodges *Camis Eskan East Lodge* and *Camis Eskan West Lodge*, the latter, 1840 is probably by David Hamilton. These attractive houses marked the boundary of this splendid estate and reflected the prestige of the wealthy owner.

Drumfork House, Red Gauntlet Road (1748-1760), is also older than Helensburgh. This house is an unpretentious building on the old drove road from Loch Lomond to Drumfork Ferry from where the cattle were shipped across to Greenock. Painted a dazzling white with quoins in contrasting black it proudly defies the encroaching suburbia. It has been suggested that it was once a Drovers' Inn.

(Colonel G de CE Findlay VC lived there at one time).

There was little development in the early town until Henry Bell (1767-1830) launched his steamship *Comet* in 1812, making possible steam navigation and as a consequence faster travel. Thereafter the town extended first to the east, where the mansions of the rich had already been built, as early as pre-1802 on the site of a riverside farm with a date in the byre of 1711. In 1806 Henry Bell built his handsome, castellated Baths Inn, at 114 East Clyde Street. As symmetrical as the grid pattern of the streets, this square building with neat fenestration was a spa for a time and renowned as the best hotel in the west, its success exemplified by the addition in 1810. Apart from being a spa and hiring coaches, it enticed visitors such as Harriet Beecher Stow, author of *Uncle Tom's Cabin* and Jane Welch Carlyle, diarist and wife of the philosopher Thomas Carlyle, to visit Mrs Bell in 1853 (her husband died in 1830). James Smith of Jordanhill, a future Provost of Helensburgh, and Sir Joseph Hooker of Kew, (who lived at Burnside House, 38 Campbell Street, a Georgian house and now a listed building) played in the hotel as boys (after 1831). Hooker recalls 'our games in the conservatory at the Baths where Bell's steam engine lay' were happy days.[8] When it became the Queen's Hotel (already mentioned in 1877) its reputation was enhanced. Although the original castellations were removed a distinctive

Victorian glass and timber porch was added, this combined with dazzling white stucco walls ensured that the building was distinctive. In 1984, a development by Baxter Clark and Paul demolished the porch and overwhelmed the original building by the addition of flats. The exterior is now of a dull ochre. It is known as *Queen's Court*. Two Provost's lamps, with stained glass lanterns depicting the Helensburgh coat-of-arms, now grace the entrance to the development. These are modern lamps reminding us that the original building was once the home of the first Provost of the town, Henry Bell (1807-09) and until the year 2000, home of the last Provost, Norman Glen (1970-75).

Rockland, 150 East Clyde Street (1854) is an Alexander 'Greek' Thomson (1817-1875) villa with the proportions, pilasters and pediments one expects of his classical style. The entrance has an entablature with patera decoration to the frieze and an inner doorway with anthemion and palmette frieze, echoing some of the classical motifs of the interior decoration. This house is of importance as 'the first villa where Thomson clearly broke from the Italian Romanesque and cottage ornee styles'.[9] The hall and grand stairwell continue the temple style. The first floor drawing room has an outstanding ornate ceiling. Uniquely for 1854 the house is designed for seascapes, with almost half the seaward two storeys as windows in groups of 2-7. Ronald McFadzean claims the stone porch with Thomson's Greek motifs was added later.

Cromalt, East Clyde Street (1700). The aforementioned farmhouse is engulfed in this house and serves as the kitchen area. This elegant two-storey, classically designed house, with its pedimented porch dated 1802 was extensively altered by David Hamilton, by adding single-storey wings that incorporate pedimented pavilions with bow-ends. The west wing included a handsome billiard room. Neil Munro (1864-1930) the novelist lived here beside his beloved River Clyde and renamed the house *Cromalt*. *Cromalt Stable Block*, coach house and stables with attractive arched entrances is to the east of the house; interestingly there are many accoutrements of the stables intact. The original granary part was topped with a domed cupola, (replaced 1991 after a storm) and a weathervane finial. At the bottom of the garden is the original castellated stone bathing hut.

Tigh-na-Mara, 152 East Clyde Street, (once Rockbank then Tarandoun) contains an earlier house and has its own well. William Leiper's alterations of 1905 comprise eighty per cent of the present house. The additions are recognizable by the use of many of his favourite motifs such as rosemary tiles, protruding bays, Chinese caps and turrets. There is also a handsome doorway with Moorish decoration. ('Greek' Thomson was a lifelong friend of

Helensburgh Library

Leiper). The original house was overwhelmed by the later additions – it is now the kitchen and play area of the present house. James Bridie (1888-1951) (pseudonym of OH Mavor, the novelist), briefly lived in the house from 1949. Jimmy Logan OBE the actor later lived in part of the house, then named *Tarandoun*.

Rockfort, 154 East Clyde Street (1849) is the antitheses of Rockland. It is a Gothic building with tall chimneys, headmoulds and decorative bargeboarded gables. It stands at the end of the promontory, proudly displaying its polygonal chimneys of groups of three and four, making it easily recognizable from the river. It has an attractive Tudor-arched doorway and fanlight. It is claimed that the *Folly* associated with the house was used as a resting-place for coffins that were brought by boat on their journey to Helensburgh cemetery. (The house has been extensively renovated and the spacious grounds now house modern homes). The sweep of the

Rockland, one of many fine villas, and one of Alexander 'Greek' Thomson's buildings stands at 150 East Clyde Street (photo c1975)

bay and these handsome buildings can be viewed to great advantage from the East Esplanade.

Victoria Infirmary (1895), 93 East King Street by William Leiper is a delightful cottage hospital incorporating many features of his work including an asymmetrical doorway with twin bell-capped bays with elongated finials. The main building of red sandstone has two storeys, a mansard roof and turreted rooms giving a pyramidal shape in the centre. The top storey held the private wards of the original hospital. The long wings housed the public wards, operating theatre, matron's office and doctors' consulting rooms. Public subscription made it possible to build the hospital and inside are handsome plaques of light oak bearing the names, in gilt, of the subscribers. The names of the many workers who had money deducted from their wages every week on a voluntary basis are not mentioned. The building is now part of the National Health Service Trust.

To rehouse the tenants of old tenements such as those in Maitland Street and Grant Street that were scheduled for demolition in the 1930s, an early council-build scheme was started at *Kirkmichael Road,* (1935) north of the Infirmary. These blocks were built reflecting the philosophy of the day that better living conditions meant healthy living. To make as much fresh air and sunshine as possible available to the tenants, concrete balconies were included

in the design. These were embellished with ironwork. Other features included dormers and gablets and glass blocks to stairhead windows. Later developments included tenements at *Ben Bouie Drive* with red-tiled mansards and dormers.

Helensburgh Cemetery is also in this area. William Leiper used Celtic crosses in much of his work including memorials. Examples of the intricate designs and delicate carvings he used can be seen here.

Further along East King Street to the *Eastend Park*, (gifted by Sir James Colquhoun and conveyed on the 7th March 1862, to 'promote the comfort and morality of the working classes' [10]) the grid plan of the streets is breached on the north side of the park at Kings Crescent (originally to be called North King Street), restarting at George Street and East Montrose Street. At 15 Kings Crescent is *Towerville Lodge* (1858), John Honeyman, Gothic in style as is the main house, Towerville, which it served. In 1888 Peat and Duncan added bay windows to this attractive house.

Towerville, 46 George Street (1858) by John Honeyman (1831-1914) is a large, impressive Gothic villa in Scots Baronial Style with castellations, hoodmoulds, buttressed bay windows and quatrefoils to mention a few of the fascinating details of this house. The interior is as impressive as the exterior, including stained glass, such as the vestibule window with the figure of a knight by Oscar Paterson (1862–

1934),[11] fine woodwork and plaster work. The area has a homogenous appearance as a result of a number of the houses being sympathetically extended by local architects, Leiper, Paterson and Wemyss. The addition to *Rossland,* at 19 East Montrose Street, 1893 by Leiper is a good example of this cooperation.

Moorgate, 4 Albert Street (1903) is by AN Paterson. In Scots vernacular with Arts and Crafts details, this red-roofed, harled villa has the expected motifs of the architect's eclectic style, including scrolled skew-putts, crowsteps, flush dormers and thistle-style tops to flues. The entrance to the north has an asymmetrical doorway with an unusual Venetian window and keystone inscribed WL 1903, the initials of the owner William Lewis.

Redcote, 23 Henry Bell Street (1881), TL Watson. This attractive villa shows the Norman Shaw and Old English Arts and Crafts influence. Its early mock half-timbered style is a precursor to the style so favoured by Leiper.

North of this area is *Bowhouse,* 33 East Argyle Street (1981), Tony Vogt. This is an eye-catching modern house with a timber-clad prow. It resembles a ship apparently straining at its ropes to be launched.

Greenpark, at the top of Charlotte Street (1935), John S Boyd. This is the only house he is known to have designed. Built for his brother-in-law RS McNicol it 'is immediately recognized as a mid-thirties *moderne* house – but also essentially

Mr & Mrs J McNeil

Greenpark is probably the largest Art Deco house in Scotland and stands at the top of Charlotte Street

Scottish'.[12] The house is built on the site of *Balvaird* an 1880s mansion that was burned down in 1932. The couple who bought the site in 1934 wanted a large modern Art Deco style house and got probably the largest Art Deco house in Scotland. It is an angular building with sweeping curves befitting the thirties' ideal, with a large flat roof and a balcony for sunbathing true to the obsession of the time for the tenets of healthy living. The staircase tower has a large studio-type window. Surprisingly the metal window frames are original. There are magnificent wood features in the interior. The craftsmen employed had worked on the state rooms of the luxury liner *Queen Mary*. Floors of American oak, 'doors with cherry wood frames with panels of walnut on the ground floor and oak upstairs'.[13] The original cut glass panels in the doors, designed by Charles Baillie, (1903-c1960) (who had designed the interior of the *Queen Mary* including a beautiful, illuminated glass panel in green with a fish motif)[14] remain including one depicting a sun god in Greek style. Baillie was also commissioned to paint a mural over the living-room fireplace that remains, but is hidden. 'The kitchen, butler's pantry and bathrooms were fully tiled from floor to ceiling in Vitrolite glass tiles'[15] (reconstructed to date with tiles from the kitchen). To enter this delightful house is to step back in time, a wonderful experience not to be missed when the house is open to the public on 'Doors Open Day' each September. Much of the original garden remains, the two 150-year-old, 85 feet (26m) high, spectacular Monterey Cypresses still dominate the lawn. The original Coach House of Balvaird survived the fire of 1932. It has a splendid cupola topped with a golden weathervane by AN Paterson (1910). The weather-vane, gilded by Robert Sills, is in the shape of a stylised arrow with forked ends and the initials (probably) PW with the date 1910. The building was sold resulting in 'the loss of a Fives court in Scotland',[16] fives being a sport akin to squash. Robert Sills redesigned it as his residence and architect's office. It has now been resold and is a private house called *The Fives Court*, standing round the corner in East Rossdhu Drive.

It is the extension at *Arden*, 46 Charlotte Street that is unusual with its flat roof, ashlar walling and stone mullioned and leaded windows in a flat central bay, features suggesting the influence of Sir Edwin Lutyens (1869-1944).

Downhill and heading west to 15 Charlotte Street, *Park Church* (1862) where another John Honeyman building stands. Built to accommodate the growing congregation of the Free Church in the square, on a site gifted by Richard Kidston, it is in the Gothic style with 3-stage tower with broach-spire and open belfry topped with a weather-vane. There is a large rose window with quatrefoil tracery over the entrance and the gable is crowned with a stone cross. William Leiper remodelled the interior in 1888. Rectangular in plan the five bay pointed-arch arcades have columns of Peterhead granite dividing the three aisles. Gothic style reredos grace the west end of the church. The octagonal marble pulpit is in the same style. The font is also octagonal.

At the next corner at 39 Lomond Street and East King Street is the *Roman Catholic Church of St Joseph* (1911), CJ Menart, (architect of St Aloysius Church in Glasgow). Built of red sandstone from Closeburn Quarry in Dumfries-shire in neo-Gothic style it is without a steeple. It is of cruciform plan with side aisles and gabled stair towers flanking the twin entrances on Lomond Street. In the centre above the doors is a figure of St Joseph. On the next level is the rose window with its attractive stylized bar tracery. A Celtic Cross tops the east elevation. In the interior are octagonal pillars of Auchenheath stone. The supporting block of the marble Table Altar depicts a pelican feeding its young with its own blood, an image inspired by St Thomas Aquinas. The Crucifix above the tabernacle, the plaque on the St Joseph Altar and the Byzantine-style painting of the Madonna and Child on the Lady Altar is the work of Frank Tritschler. The paintings around the walls depict the Stations of the Cross.

Round the corner at *Alma Place* at the corner of East King Street and Grant Street (1936) Stewart and Paterson, is another example of the high standard of house building demanded by the Burgh Council of the day. These are three blocks of thirty five houses with attractively decorated staircase bays and lunette windows over-looking a courtyard that is linked with entrance arches.

On the opposite side of the road at number 7 East King Street, set off the street, is the small, neat *Baptist Church* (1886), David A Crombie (1802-1889), with its sturdy finiall-ed spire. This Gothic church with pointed-arch windows and hood moulds with floreate label-stops has also many lancet windows. The interior is attractive with gothic decoration to the reredos and a stained glass west window of 1906 depicting the foundation of the Zenana Mission in India by the Reverend John Sale. Two Comm-union cups dated 1859 survive from the early church of 1833. At the ceremony of the laying of the Memorial Stone a jar containing the history of the church, current coins and local and district papers were placed beneath the stone.

SINCLAIR STREET

At 81 Sinclair Street is the *United Presbyterian Church of St Columba* (1861), William Spence. This is a no-nonsense building relieved by a very tall Gothic tower topped with an Italianate balustrade. The pale stained glass of the Gothic windows was originally contrasted with the beautifully coloured stained glass window that once graced the west gable. This is now almost hidden on the north wall of the organ recess as a result of the west gable being broached in 1877 by Duncan MacNaughton (1845-1912) to house the splendid 'Lewis' organ, the first such organ to be installed in a Helensburgh church and the second in Scotland. The design of the interior is eclectic. Classical pillars with Corinthian capitals contrast with the Gothic arches of the choir screen and the motifs on the balcony echo the design on the tower. At the meeting of column and vaulting ribs are placed shields with various emblems of the faith. The redecoration of 1895, under the direction of AN Paterson, included the plain frosted glass being replaced by 'clear muffled glass with borders and traceried heads of green and richer points of venetian'.[17] The marble Christening font is particularly fine, with angel figures supporting the bowl. (St Columba was added to the name in 1900).

Round the corner at 2 West King Street, adjacent to the church is the original Seceeders' Church, built in 1845, probably by William Spence, known as the *'Wee Kirk'*. (It is from this church that St Columba

Church evolved). Steps lead up to a Tudor-arch doorway and into a space which once housed a church with an added gallery in 1851 (demolished 1961) for a growing congregation of the now United Presbyterian Church. Soon it was too small to hold the worshippers and the larger church was built in 1861. The Bible that was presented by the Reverend Hugh Somerville on March 27th 1844 is now in the Helensburgh Library. That was the day they became a congregation in the Old Courthouse in Sinclair Street (on the site of the Municipal Buildings). Until the Town Hall was built the Wee Kirk served as a Public Hall and housed meetings, religious and secular, including those of the Suffragettes! It is now used as the church hall.

Across the road is the delightful red-sandstone former *Rhu Parish Council Chambers*, (1890) 25-27 West King Street, by Robert Wemyss with its name inscribed over the doorway. This building now houses a well-appointed *Wedding Room*, administered by Argyll and Bute Council.

Continuing uphill on the east side of Sinclair Street is the site of one of the earliest and most important amenities of the early village and later town, the *Malig Mill* by the side of the *Milligs Burn*. A *Grindstone* and *Roundel* mark the site of the mill that was once owned by the prominent McNeilage family.

The *Victoria Halls* (1887), J and RS Ingram occupy the adjacent site.

This handsome building was funded by public subscription to commemorate Queen Victoria's Diamond Jubilee. It has crowsteps, castellations, tourlettes and mansard-style tower. Above the main entrance is a large balustraded balcony supported on sturdy console brackets, with ball finials and a medallion of Queen Victoria in the centre. The lady looks down disapprovingly. The arrangement of tripartite and tall, single windows enhance the façade. Alterations and additions were carried out by AN Paterson in 1899.

Adjacent is the *Hermitage Park*, bought by the Council for £3,750 from the Cramb family (who had already gifted land for Hermitage Primary School and playground), to create a public park. It has many amenities, bowling greens, tennis courts and putting green, swings and playground and a modern shelter. With the Milligs Burn snaking through it and an abundance of rare plants and bushes, with many lovely walks to be enjoyed, this is almost a secret garden. Until 2002 here was to be found the fly-wheel of the *Comet* along with the anvil used in the smiddy, (probably at 77 East Clyde Street or the adjoining property) of John McMurrich, the blacksmith who worked with Henry Bell. These items were gifted in 1912 by the grandsons of John McMurrich. The splendid *War Memorial* (1923) by AN Paterson was executed to his winning design in the competition that was run for this memorial.

Councillor J Whitelaw Hamilton, who was also an artist and an associate of the Glasgow Boys, suggested that the memorial should be sited in the old walled garden of the original estate. The square base with its four sides lists the names of the Fallen in two World Wars. The graceful arcaded rotunda has urns with flaming torches in every second bay and the whole is topped with a gilded dome. The rectangular pond in front, designed to reflect the structure, once contained water lilies and golden carp but is now empty and dirty, however an echo of its grandeur and reverence still lingers in this oasis of peace. Once the grassy surrounds contained rows of rose trees with red roses, the colour symbolic of sacrifice. These were replaced with green shrubs some years ago. The cast-iron ornamental gates with thistle wreath and palm leaf decoration are of fine quality.

The most northerly part of the park that was once the site of the popular allotments and source of many prize-winning entries at the Horticultural Show, is now occupied by the Bield Housing Association's *Sheltered Housing* of 1991, designed by McGurn, Logan, Duncan and Opfer. Behind the park is the tall building of *Prince Albert Terrace* (about late 1870s) William Tait, for the Cramb family, which it is said, is of such a height on the orders of the owners to obscure the view of the river from a neighbour's garden. The Helensburgh Art 'Studio' (1890-

Donald Fullarton

1906) operated from numbers three and eight. AJ Cronin (1896-1981) the novelist lived here at some time and Stephen Conroy the artist was born at number three in 1964.

Thornton Lodge, 107 Sinclair Street (1857), Boucher and Cousland. Designed for James Hislop it is an Italianate villa in cream sandstone with a pilaster porch with entablature and parapet. Later owners were the artistic Hamilton family and it became a meeting place for the Glasgow Boys. George Walton designed fireplaces and wallpaper for the Hamiltons. James Guthrie painted 'Midsummer' in the garden. (see p157)

'Rhu Parish Council Chambers' is inscribed over the doorway at 25-27 West King Street. However as it was built in 1890 to a design by Robert Wemyss, it is possible to see where the inscription has been changed from Row to Rhu

CENTRAL HELENSBURGH

The attractive focal centre of the town is Colquhoun Square, with its *Celtic Cross* of unpolished pinkish granite on a stepped base. The inscription reads 'Centenary memorial 1802 Henry Bell Provost, 1902 Samuel Bryden Provost' (although there is no record now of who was Provost between 1802 and 1807) and at the back 'Presented by Sir James Colquhoun 12th Baronet of Luss 1903'. Colquhoun Street leads south from the square to the entrance to the Pier. The entrance was once graced by an elegant Victorian red sandstone arch designed by Robert Wemyss in 1898 and captured in an architectural sketch by the architect, 'Entrance to Pier Buildings' now in the Helensburgh Collection in the Helensburgh Library (see title page). The early pier was constantly referred to disparagingly as a dyke; however it was improved and became the centre of attraction on the seafront. With rowing boats for hire and with paddle steamers' passengers embarking and disembarking there was always much to see.

West Kirk (so named since 1981) 23 Colquhoun Street, is on the northwest corner of the square, on the site of the first Presbyterian church of 1825. JW & J Hay of Liverpool based it on a prize-winning design at the Great Exhibition of 1851 and it was built in 1853. A buttressed broached spire dominates the south side of the building, a trademark of the architects as was the distinctive half-timbered ceiling. Gutted by fire in 1924 the church was sympathetically restored by local architect Robert Wemyss in 1924. William Leiper was commissioned to add a handsome crocketted porch to the main entrance on Colquhoun Street in 1892 in memory of the Reverend Alexander Anderson, a former minister of the church. The decoration includes amusing carved animals, one of which appears to be eating the stonework! Part of the rich ornamentation in the interior of the porch is the oak panelling of the reredos from the demolished St Bride's Church, designed by AN Paterson and installed in the porch in 1990. There is also the finely carved War Memorial plaque from St Bride's in place. The World War II Memorial gates from the Old Parish Church were installed across the path at the southwest corner of the church. The interior of the church is splendid. The fine stained glass windows delight the eye and lift the spirits. In the east gallery there is a magnificent 5-light commemorative window to Andrew Bonar Law, (Prime Minister 1922-23) his wife, Annie, and their two sons who were killed in World War I.[18] The narrative content is of the labourers in the vineyard with Christ in the central light, an appropriate choice considering that Bonar Law was brought up in the church and later became a member and a Sunday School teacher. The window was unveiled by the then Prime Minister Stanley Baldwin in 1929. The three windows in the Choir depict the twelve Apostles, with Paul replacing Judas. Both works are by Oscar Paterson. Most other windows are by the eminent decorative artist Gordon Webster (1909-1987). In the nave a two-light window has the theme of treating others as you would wish yourself to be treated, narrated with heavy symbolism. Others represent the Calling of the Disciples with Christ and the appropriate symbolism of nets and fish; another of Christ crucified with the pelican, the symbol of sacrifice; one of the Saints Columba, Francis and Giles with attributes (objects associated with a particular person). In 1988 a window in the modern style was dedicated to commemorate the centenary of John Logie Baird's birth. His widow Margaret unveiled it. The three lights depict St Bride's Church, (his father was the first minister of that church), the young Baird, and the third lists some of the benefits resulting from the inventor's work. The artist was Artur Spiers. The baptismal font of 1968 is of Portland stone and dedicated to the memory of a former minister of Old and St Andrew's Church, the Reverend John Henry Dutch.

To the east of the West Kirk and facing Colquhoun Square No 26 is the former *Union Bank* (1861), probably by John Burnet (snr); it currently stands empty and its owners, the Bank of Scotland, have put it up for sale. This square classical building has cill courses, cornice, parapet and rusticated quoins as details of interest. The main entrance, facing the square, has the classical motifs of pilasters supporting the entablature and a round-arched architraved door with floreated keystone. A sympathetic single storey extension by David Morgan in 1983 is to the north and it is this new part that is now the *Bank of Scotland*.

In the south west quadrant the *General Post Office* (1893) at 16-18 Colquhoun Square, is by Walter Wood Robertson (1845-1907). The early twentieth century addition of a 5-bay block in the Square is probably by William Thomas Oldrieve (1853-1922). The semi-circular entrance tower of the Post Office is topped with a cupola and louvred lantern. There is an oval panel above the door with a frieze inscribed 'Post and Telegraph Office' and a floreate panel above with the monogram VR and 1893 on the date stone. This handsome building has a rusticated ground floor and quoins that continue round. The cornice between the ground and first floor at first floor level has a cartouche decoration. The parapet level is crowned with urns on pedestals.

The United Reformed Church 39 West Princes Street is the original Congregational Church, 1883, John Honeyman, (1831-1914) an asymmetric Gothic church. This was built at right angles to the original Independent Church, sharing the east gable wall of the old church, which had been built in the Old English style and is now used as the church hall. An even earlier Independent Church (or

The Tabernacle) occupied this site. Varied fenestration includes pointed arch and lancet styles and a rose window on the east gable; a gabled porch with pointed arch doorway with foliate moulding are features of this third church to be built on this site. The interior is pleasing with a 4-bay arcade of granite columns; stone corbels support a timber roof and there is a fine organ below the rose window.

Across the street from the United Reformed Church at *46-60 West Princes Street*, later nineteenth century, William Tait (possibly, the Alexander Thomson influence is apparent) is a handsome tenement continuing round to Colquhoun Square. The semi-circular-headed arcade of the Colquhoun Square ground floor echoes the arcades of the west and east quadrants of the square. Number 48 West Princes Street is *The Central Pharmacy*, which has much of the original furniture of counters and shelving as well as huge glass jars.

74-78 West Princes Street (1896), by Robert Wemyss, is in Arts and Crafts style. This grey-harled tenement building curves round to James Street. The facades have ball finials and a tall bleak chimney breast on the James Street side breaks the regularity. The red-bricked feature around the windows adds attractive colour to the building. By the same architect, *Waverley Place*, 62-66 West Princes Street (1896), has Jacobean details. This most attractive red-sand-stoned, asymmetrical tenement

building with corbelled chimney piece and delightful windows arched on the upper storey, was built for a Mr John McFarlane.

Across Colquhoun Street at *14-28 West Princes Street* is a sober, symmetrical tenement 1878, by William Tait. In contrast at *8-12 West Princes Street* 1911, is a tenement by William Hunter McNab, (d 1937). It was originally meant to continue round the corner into Sinclair Street, as the projecting teeth at the gable end proclaim (one cannot help but grieve that the original plan was not carried out), this half design resulted in an asymmetrical tenement building in Jacobean style. The ornamentation on this edifice is delightful, such as the pilastered windows, one especially eye-catching has a decorated pediment and it is set in a tall chimney stack. Colonettes flanking an upper window topped by an elongated ornate finial, balconies and crenellated parapets are only a selection of the decorative delights for the viewer to enjoy. A rather splendid pend entrance with pilasters, round arched doorway with keystone and twin round-arched lights in the panel above is reminiscent of the entrance to the Victoria Infirmary, a William Leiper building of 1895. (McNab was Leiper's pupil and later partner).

COMMERCIAL TOWN CENTRE

The main commercial area developed centrally around Sinclair Street, Princes Street and Clyde Street, after the extension of the railway further into the town in 1863 (the station was originally at George Street in 1858). The present Central Station (1899) at 3 East Princes Street is Victorian in style, but is a ghost of its former splendid self when urns filled with blooms and hanging baskets adorned its platforms, gaining First Prize in 1932 for the best kept station. The recent Centenary upgrading by Railtrack at a cost of £1 million has made a start to restore this once handsome Victorian structure. An excellent view of the end of the splendid wrought-iron glazed canopy can be enjoyed from the steps of the footbridge at Grant Street.

The neighbouring *Municipal Buildings*, 1 East Princes Street (1878) by John Honeymoon, replaced the old theatre that had served also as the Town Hall. On a corner site in Scots Baronial Style with eye-catching turrets and crow steps, it dominates the busy crossing of Sinclair Street and Princes Street. The main entrance is on Princes Street and above an impressive doorway is the sculp-

Neil Macleod

The 1906 extension to the Municipal Buildings housed the Police Station with carved stone handcuffs

tured head of Henry Bell, while directly above is a balcony. The splendid Provost's office has an attractive oriole window overlooking Sinclair Street. In 1906 AN Paterson added the Sinclair Street extension in a much more restrained Scottish style to house the Police Station and the Fire Station. The carved stone handcuffs issue a warning as well as a touch of humour to the façade, as does the cat reclining on a ledge on the second storey. It had become the pet of the builders and the cat-loving architect immortalised it in stone. An unusually tall feature dominates the rear of the building;

it housed the facility for drying fire hoses. A favourite motif of the artist is the thistle-topped watercourses. These can be viewed from the exit of the adjoining lacklustre, fortress-like structure of the *Co-operative Supermarket*.

Proceeding down Sinclair Street at no. 40 is the interesting former *Conservative and Unionist Association Club Rooms* (1894), Honeyman and Keppie, now *Mackays*. The many Glasgow Style features, such as the elegant carving and roof glazing, the flower and tree motifs and the sinuous line of the whole façade suggests that the young architect, Charles Rennie Mackintosh, contributed to the design of this charming building, while he was employed by the firm. A statue of St Andrew, the crest of the club, occupies a niche in a central position on the façade.

The adjoining *Carlton Buildings*, 1898, by Frank Burton & Boston, was built for James A Reid. In red sandstone, this is a very tall and imposing building with seventeenth century style details. The windows on the first floor have detail in shallow relief above the cornice the same as that used by William Leiper at Dalmore Lodge, 1873, Lower Rhu Road.

Old Parish Church Tower, 4 East Clyde Street, is all that remains of the fine old Established Church, 1847, designed by Charles Wilson (1810-1863) built on land gifted by the then Sir James Colquhoun on a site that was reckoned to be the finest in town. It became the Parish Church in 1862. The Italianate

tower has a clock face on four sides and round-arched louvred windows to the belfry. The nave, hall and outer buildings (once the school) were demolished in 1982.[19] The large tolling bell with the inscription 'Let all things be done to the Glory of God' is still in place. Mr Arnold Fleming presented a clarion of Westminster Chimes to be rung on Christmas Day, 1929. The porch, by Robert Wemyss, 1923, was also dedicated that year to the town 'in memory of those who in time past worshipped here'. (There are many local people who, when they see the remnant, remember with affection those days, not least because so much of their social life was bound up in this church!) The tower now houses the *Tourist Information Centre*.

To the east is *Clyde Street School*, 1903, by AN Paterson, Scottish Revival style with seventeenth century Renaissance details. Bell-cast roofs, mullioned and transomed windows, varied fenestration including a Venetian window, base and string courses, cornice, gabled bays and coped skews ensure that this building will not be overlooked. The interior has a fine hammerbeam roof. The Glasgow-style galleried hall is in the centre and is surrounded by arcaded doorways and windows to the classrooms on the ground and first floor. The cast iron railings are of fine quality. The gates have curved panels with 'Boys' and 'Girls' above the west and east gates respectively. A carved cartouche with the inscription

'SCHOOL BOARD OF THE PARISH OF ROW' on the façade proclaims its function. The two lodges are of different design, the *East Lodge*, 46 East Clyde Street, is a one-storey asymmetrical building with few details. The other, the *West Lodge* at 38 East Clyde Street is a two-storey asymmetrical building in Scots Baronial design, including a bell-capped tower with finial. This complex is now the *Clyde Community Education Centre* administered by Argyll and Bute Council and a voluntary committee.

WEST END

At the corner of John Street and West King Street once stood St Bride's Church, built in 1877 by John McLeod (d1888). Paterson later redesigned the chancel and Leiper the hall. The church was demolished in 1993 and the name is commemorated only in the St Bride's Room in part of the building that was the early two-classroom school of the now West Kirk. (See the West Kirk section). Some of the stained glass windows were stored for years until, thankfully, Helensburgh Heritage Trust and Argyll & Bute Council purchased them in 2001 for restoration. The designer of the windows was Viola Paterson (1899-1981), (daughter of AN Paterson architect and artist, and Maggie Hamilton who was also an artist) and executed by Guthrie and Wells of Glasgow. The Hamilton window of 1924 was gifted by the artist's mother to commemorate her parents and sister; the Gow window (see p149) was installed as a thanksgiving for the safe return of two sons from World War I; the 1934 window commemorates the Rev John Baird, the first minister of the church and father of John Logie Baird. The new *Helensburgh Library* (new home for at least two of the windows) and a tenement building now occupy the site.

The charming tenement at *27 John Street,* (Loch Sloy Place) (1896), with the unusual crazy-paving pattern of the ground floor is an example of Robert Wemyss' individual style. Varied fenestration including Venetian windows to either side of a pend are attractive features of the façade.

St Michael and All Angels Episcopal Church, (1868) 18 William Street, Sir Rowand Anderson (1834-1921), the eminent architect who designed the Museum of Antiquities and the Portrait Gallery in Edinburgh. Built on the site of the earlier Tudor style Holy Trinity Church of 1843, (when Helensburgh was described as a village in the Feu Charter) this splendid church is in the French Gothic Style of the 12th-13th century. The exterior is of red sandstone from Corncockle, Dumfriesshire and the interior is of limestone from Caen in Normandy. There is a fine rose window above the west entrance. The plain entrance was embellished in 1915 as a memorial to the wife of Sir William Raeburn. This took the form of a tympanum (see p54) with exquisite carving depicting God in Majesty in a symbolic mandorla flanked by angels; beneath in the centre is the insignia of the Episcopal Church, a mitre and crosiers, and two Evangelists on either side in stylistic form, Matthew the winged figure; Mark the lion; Luke the bull and John the eagle. An additional gift by Sir William Raeburn in 1930 was the Bell Tower; its completion thus fulfilled the plan of 1886 for the church. In December of 1930 a new Peal of Eight Bells, the only full peal in the town, rang out the Christmas Message. The interior of the church has many fine features such as the alabaster pulpit. Behind the high altar is the reredos and a mosaic picture of the Crucifixion. Among the many splendid stained glass windows are those on the south gable depicting Christ walking on water and another, near the font, Christ with the children commemorating two little children who were drowned. The font has a carved oak cover that is operated by a counter-balance mechanism; in nearby recesses are figures of St Andrew and St Mungo; a splendid brass eagle forms the lectern; the mural on the north wall is by one of the most eccentric of artists, Professor of Mural Painting, Ancell Stronach ARSA (1901-1981).[20] He ran away to the circus and married an acrobatic dancer. He also established *Ancell's Painted Pigeons* that performed aerial acrobatics. Three panels painted by Stronach were commissioned by Sir William Raeburn in memory of his family; the angels' faces are portraits of his children. The lovely little side chapel and a splendid collection of banners are among the delights in this fine church. (Among the original contributors to the Building Fund were the Rt Hon WE Gladstone MP and Field Marshall Lord Roberts).

The First Church of Christ, Scientist, 136/140 West Princes Street, (1956) is by Margaret B Brodie BSc ARIBA who was one of the designers of the 'Women of the Empire Pavilion' at the Glasgow Empire Exhibition 1938. She designed the church with the fine old plum tree that grew on the original site in mind as she believed it would enhance the building. When the tree died a Chearl's Weeping Cherry replaced it. This tree is now mature and is beautiful in bloom, but even without the flowers the silhouette of its shape adds interest to this rectangular building. The attractive entrance front is of freestone of varied shades. The vestibule and west wing have decorative grilles of wrought iron. The interior is pleasing.

Rosebank, (c 1830) 150 West Princes Street, is a charming Georgian villa fronted by a porch with columns and entablature. The approach to the house is by a short, sweeping drive flanked on either side by mature trees. The house sits serenely in the privacy of a large garden behind an attractive red-brick wall even although the house is divided into three and modern buildings have encroached around it. This house was the subject of a disagreement between Thomas Samuel, an early owner, and Sir James Colquhoun. He maintained that Sir James had given him permission to encroach on the site of Campbell Street, hence the narrow street today. In a report of 1849 Sir James denies any such agreement and insisted that the public had to have access across the site on pain of a £100 fine. In 1891 William Leiper designed a large extension to the north of the house with red tiles and a domed bay for William Kidston.

Brandon Grove, 119 West Princes St, is an early farmhouse, pre-1760, and still a charming building.

Carisbrooke, 108 West King Street, (1857) was built for Mr Potter of Glasgow. Additions for a Mr Morrison in 1901 were by William Fraser. Attractive stained glass windows are a feature of this building. (Nora Neilson Gray, the artist and later Major James Gibb DSO lived here.) It is interesting to compare the design and date, 1857, of this house with that of the Rectory of the Episcopal Church at 16 William Street, built to serve the Holy Trinity Church of 1843.

Rosemount, 10 West Argyle Street (1836). Arts and Crafts addition by William Leiper to the east wing for Dr Sewal, raising it a storey, and a single-storey wing to the west side. In 1907 Robert Wemyss added a storey to the west wing in another example of the seamless join in the work of these architects. There is an interesting Art Nouveau gate to the Colquhoun Street entrance.

Bourtrie, 25 Glasgow Street, (1898) Robert Wemyss. In coloured stone at ground level and harling above, this splendid Free Style villa has two pedimented Venetian windows overlooking the south. The variety of the fenestration on the east gable is eye-catching, especially the Wemyss' touch of individuality in the lovely tripartate, stepped stone-traceried window.

40A Glasgow Street, John McIntyre, is an example of a modern house, all white tiles and a wall of windows, its neat compactness is in dramatic contrast with its sprawling commercial neighbour.

Cairndhu Rhu Road Lower, (1871) William Leiper. The architect received the commission to build a grand house from John Ure, Provost of Glasgow. Ure's son became Lord Strathclyde and later lived in the house. Built on an elevated site with magnificent, uninterrupted views over the River Clyde, this splendid miniature French château in Francois I style shows Leiper at his eclectic best with an early French style exterior and a Modern Aesthetic interior. The southwest corner has a circular tower with a French pavilion roof, cheek by jowl with a circular stair tower, the whole topped with towering chimney-stacks. The interior has splendid features such as the dramatic black and gold Anglo-Japanese ceiling with sunflowers, bamboo and birds to delight the eye. Leiper was in the 'vanguard of the Anglo-Japanese manner' [21] with the decorative artist Daniel Cottier (1838-1891). The magnificent stained glass windows are by him; the full-length neo-classical pairs of figures from left to right depict

Kenneth Crawford

Cairndhu was built for the merchant John Ure in the style of a grand château. Its design was a collaboration between the architect William Leiper and the stained glass artist Daniel Cottier.

The Anglo-Japanese ceiling in Cairndhu House

Truth and Beauty; Love and Audacity; Knowledge and Prudence. The panels are surrounded by squares containing sunflowers in multifarious designs. (A vase of sunflowers was the symbol of the Aesthetic Movement; Leiper and Cottier were exponents of this style). Cairndhu is now a Nursing Home.

Cairndhu Lodge (1871), William Leiper, is in Scots Renaissance lodge style. An attractive house built to service the main house it has its own distinctive features such as an entrance with crenellated

parapet and ball finial and a pedimented window with cartouche in tympanum.

Dalmore Rhu Road Lower, (1873) William Leiper. A red sandstone mansion in Scots Baronial style with crow-steps and conical-roofed turrets, et al, it stands fortress-like and impregnable. The Renaissance style entrance to the north has pilasters and a frieze with armorial shield. Built for Robert Little, whose initials R L and the date 1873 are on the ogeed pediment of the window above the entrance. On the south façade the attic dormers proclaim their presence with decorated pediments almost as big as the windows themselves.

Dalmore Lodge, Rhu Road Lower, (1873) William Leiper. He added a circular tower in 1904 to accommodate a bathroom and storage area. Like Dalmore itself this building is in the Scottish Baronial style and has its own particular detail to admire including a triple horseshoe motif over a window.

Dalmore West Lodge Rhu Road Higher, (1893) William Leiper, was commissioned by TO Bishop, a later owner of the house, as a coachman's house. In Scots Baronial including a turret with conical roof and finial. In contrast to the severity of the main house, decoration of this attractive lodge includes a pilastered cartouche, cherubs, and a thistle finial topping the gabled bay, all crowned with a green roof with red ridge tiles and beak skewputts.

Ardencaple Castle, possibly 1566

Kenneth Crawford

when the McAulay stronghold, later sold to the 4th Duke of Argyll. A Duke was born here and the Dowager Duchess lived for a time in the castle. Sold to Sir James Colquhoun in 1862, it changed hands and deteriorated until finally demolished in 1957-59. Part of the retaining wall can still be seen, its vast breadth almost hidden but still impressive in its bulk, while the estate is now absorbed by modern housing. The only easily seen evidence of this historic pile is the tower that is still useful as a navigation aid to submarines and other vessels negotiating the Rhu Narrows.

Ardencaple Hotel (early nineteenth century) (originally named the Ardencaple Inn,[22] it replaced the Cairndhu Inn that once stood in Cairndhu Park, renamed Kidston Park). It was an important posting inn for travellers from Inveraray to Glasgow including the Duke of Argyll from his castle at Inveraray. A handsome building with balustraded parapet crowned with ornamental urns, it has two winged pedimented pavilions with arched panels to south-east and south-west. The exterior is painted in startling white and black, a worthy building to mark the Rhu-Helensburgh boundary.

UPPER WEST END

In 1858 the railway was extended to Helensburgh. Sir James Colquhoun commissioned a feuing plan from William Spence in 1857 in anticipation of the growth of the town. He incorporated sweeping curves and gracious crescents rather than the grid plan on the upper part of the town. The plan was not carried out in the east but fortunately it is at least partially built in the west with Sutherland Crescent.

Terpersie, 2 Upper Sutherland Street, (1871) William Leiper, was the delightful home of the architect, which he built for himself, described as in his English Cottage style. The impressive entrance has a unicorn's head above the doorway. There is also a carved boar's head above the window to the left, supposedly from Terpersie Castle, which he claimed was the ancestral home of his forebears. On the north elevation the stained glass stair window has Aesthetic Movement figurative panels of Lord Darnley and Mary, Queen of Scots, and above monograms of WL and MJ (The house was at one time named Thurloe).

Rhu-Arden, 1 Upper Sutherland Crescent, (1871) William Leiper, is on the adjacent plot to his home. (originally called Bonnytoun and built for John McGregor jp). In this example of a Greek villa Leiper shows his eclectic style by incorporating a Roman porch with Scamozzi-Ionic columns.

Westermilligs, 18 Millig Street, (c1870) William Leiper, (originally

The Long Croft, at the end of Rossdhu Drive West, was designed by AN Paterson for his own use

Redholm), Early French vernacular style. Additions by AN Paterson and Douglas Campbell 1903, of a library and billiard room wing for R Dunlop. The attractive interior includes a stair window with decorated stained glass depicting animal and floral motifs, probably by Daniel Cottier, who worked with Leiper on many commissions. The converted stables, 1898-9 in Arts and Crafts style with the usual Baronial touch, now has an address at *25 Queen Street*.

Moraig 1 Rowallan Street, *West Gables* number 3, and *East Gables* at number 5 (a mirror image of number 3) and *Ard Rhu*, 22 Millig Street, 1895, are by AN Paterson. When he married in 1897, his father made over to him *Ard Rhu* (then known as The Turret), as he had financed this group of houses as a way of introducing his son professionally to the town. These houses, in Arts and Crafts design, are collectively known as 'Canary Islands' the name derived from their original colour, although now all are dazzlingly white. While each

one is individually designed they all have the basic motifs of the architect, such as red sandstone dressings, low dormers, crowsteps and skewputts *et al* used in a variety of ways.

Clarendon, 89 James Street, (mid-nineteenth century) is all but lost in the extensive additions by William Leiper in 1888 and 1891 for John Anderson. This building now houses the primary department of *Lomond School*. The ornamentation of the house includes crow-stepped gables and crenellated parapets; decorated bargeboards; a hoodmould course with animal gargoyles; a corbel course with gargoyles; a date stone '1888'; crocketted ball finials and a crenellated tower, to mention a few of the fascinating details in the decoration of this imposing structure. It is a building impossible to ignore.

The Long Croft, at the end of West Rossdhu Drive, (1901) AN Paterson. He designed this house for himself and included every-thing an architect needed in a home and an office. In a secluded position at the end of a long street, the house sits on an elevated site overlooking the Glenan Burn at the foot of the garden in the west. There are five different forms of turrets that ensure an interesting skyline. The arched main entrance to the north is in the form of a turret topped by a balustrade with carving around the entrance, including sculpted heads of his children, Viola and Alistair; the tower adjacent to the main entrance has a bell-cast roof; a large southwest turret with an unusual octagonal base has a conical cap; a smaller candle-snuffer-like turret with a stairway beneath leads to the garden; and in the south there is a two storey turret roofed with blue-grey Ballachulish and dark green Aberfoyle slates. A splendid tall and decorative west gable completes the picturesque outline. The architect (and artist) had his study with windows to the north and west that contained a fireplace probably designed by his friend and fellow artist 'Glasgow Boy' George Walton (1868-1933) in the Glasgow Style. The interior is handsome with ceilings by G Bankart that add great charm to the rooms. The drawing-room also reflects the interest in the Arts and Crafts and the Glasgow Style of decorative art exemplified in the beautiful embroidered panel in the overmantle of the fire by Maggie Hamilton, the architect's wife. Another embroidered panel in an abstract design is at the other end of the room. The coloured upper panes of the windows are painted with motifs of architecture, painting, music and embroidery reflecting the interests of the family.

Neil Macleod

UPPER HELENSBURGH

The Hill House 8 Upper Colquhoun Street, (1902) Charles Rennie Mackintosh (1868-1928). Built for Mr Walter Blackie, a Glasgow publisher, this is the jewel in the crown of the town's architectural heritage, one of the great houses of the twentieth century. In The Early Modern Movement style it still remains essentially Scottish with conical tower and harling finish. Varied fenestration includes entrancing small-paned windows in French, dormer, attic, small, square and elongated design. The architect, who was a master of space, designed virtually every detail of the house. Contrast continues in the interior with the dark-oak fittings of the library alleviated with details of coloured glass squares, a style echoed in the dark-wooded hall with its splendidly designed and coloured ceiling lamp. A startling change of mood is obtained by the effect of the large south-facing window in the drawing room and the interior decoration in the delicate Glasgow Style. Many of the original features

The Hill House, designed by Charles Rennie Mackintosh, is so well-known that it attracts more than 32000 visitors during its annual seven-month opening

and fittings designed by Mackintosh have been retained. The striking fireplace with a mosaic of coloured enamel and glass and the stylized fire tongs are intact. The beautiful gesso panel 'The Sleeping Princess' above the fireplace is the work of the architect's wife, Margaret Macdonald (1865-1933). Delicately wrought in the subtle colour scheme and mood of the room the green echoes the leaves in the delightful lampshades and the garden. Mary Newbury, a young friend of the Blackie family, has a childhood memory of the artist's technique as icing a cake! The owners were interested in the decorative Glasgow Style for the interior design for their home and the Mackintoshes were leading exponents of this style; both were also talented artists who co-operated in the venture. For example, he designed the standard lamp in the drawing room, and she sewed the lampshade that incorporates clear glass beads. It is said that Margaret pricked her finger while sewing the shade and a tear fell and her husband replicated it in a tiny mother-of-pearl fallen tear at the base of the lamp. The curtains in the drawing room designed by Margaret Macdonald are not originals but one of them can be seen in a showcase with a drawing of her first idea for the curtains. The striking panels by Margaret designed for the master bedroom have recently been replicated, (known to the Blackie children as the 'Skinny Ladies'), adding the finishing touches of colour to this exquisite room of cream-coloured paint, pink roses and silver-plated washbasin and ewer. (The last two items were originally designed for Miss Kate Cranston's home, Hous'hill, in Glasgow). Mrs Blackie took a great interest in the decoration and Margaret Macdonald and she became friends.

The house is now owned by *The National Trust for Scotland* and is open to the public daily from April to October and is visited by thousands of visitors from all over the world every year. An exciting annual exhibition of young designers' work and a well-stocked gift shop are also in the house.

It is fascinating to compare the above with the house opposite, *Morar House* 17 Upper Colquhoun Street by William Leiper (1903). A splendid red-tiled house, (for a while known as *Drumadoon*) built for the McAlpine family who owned a shipping firm. It was built the year after The Hill House, commanding the same splendid view of the Clyde. It is in the style that has given Helensburgh a unique homogeneity, an Arts and Crafts and Shavian style with Scottish elements, such as the corbelled turret. The north entrance is arched with a crocketted ogeed arch above and the columns supporting the roll-moulded architrave have capitals decorated with animals, an example of Leiper's eclectic best and the antithesis to The Hill House's entrance with its stark simplicity of a sandstone surround.

Red Towers 4 Douglas Drive West, (1898) William Leiper, a red sandstone château-like mansion house built for James Allan, grocer. In a exuberant combination of Baronial and Arts and Crafts details including towers with conical hats, protruding bays with a delicate balcony between, mock half-timbering, tall chimneys and a Scottish Renaissance style entrance to the south. This imposing building with a roof of green slate and its picturesque skyline compels attention. *Red Towers* is now a drug rehabilitation centre.

The White House 15 Upper Colquhoun Street (1899) is by MH Baillie Scott (1865 – 1945), commissioned by HS Paul. A Modern Movement building, one of only two houses by Scott in Scotland. To take full advantage of the sunshine there are few details, such as hoodmoulding, for example, to protect the southern aspect of this elegant house from the rain. At first glance only the red-tiled roof and white exterior have anything in common with the neighbouring Arts and Crafts, Voyseyesque villas. However, like many of the other designs no entrance door or stairwell interrupts the southern elevation, all the rooms with their free-form layout will benefit from maximum sunlight. Hardly a shadow will be cast on this pristine white façade with its simplicity of design. Varied fenestration gives character to the building, an attic window breaks the monotony of red tile. On the east elevation stained glass

windows and hopperheads have Art Nouveau decoration. Much of the original interior, including woodwork, chimney pieces and stained glass in windows and internal partitions remain, many designed by Baillie Scott. This house was built a few years before The Hill House and the two buildings herald modernism in the area. Both artists entered an international exhibition for the design for an Art Lover's House. No first prize was awarded but Baillie Scott won second prize for his design. Charles Rennie Mackintosh submitted an unfinished entry and was asked to submit more drawings subsequently winning a special prize. ('The House for an Art Lover' built in 1989 in Bellahouston Park, Glasgow is based on Mackintosh's winning drawings).

Brantewoode 4 Munro Drive West, (1895) William Leiper. Built for J Alexander of Jamieson and Co. Glasgow, oil refiners. The house was named after John Ruskin's but spelt with an extra 'e'. In Arts and

The White House is another excellent example of the housing on and around Upper Colquhoun Street

Crafts style with a strong Norman Shaw influence this is an enchanting house in red sandstone with many delightful features including mock half-timber and architectural details in multifarious patterns. An eye-catching Romeo and Juliet balcony embellished with rosemary fishscale tiles enhances the façade. A splendid entrance on the north elevation has a vestibule door with textured panels and an Art Nouveau door handle. The interior is equally attractive with many original details and also a conversion from a bedroom to a 1930s style bathroom complete with Vitrolite tiles and an open fireplace.

Strathmoyne 6 Munro Drive West, (1899) Robert Wemyss, a large villa for W Snell Anderson with the red-tiling and mock half-timbering details seen in Leiper's work in the area. Wemyss' delicate handling of the Art Nouveau details reflect his individual interpretation of the Norman Shaw influence. His nearby *Rokney* (was Redcliffe) at 118 Sinclair Street, is similar but has also a delightful variety of windows.

Galloway Cottage 41 Colquhoun Street, (c 1865). With Greek Revival details it is probably by Alexander Thomson. The site was given by Mrs Mary Meldrum or Galloway to the Industrial School for a house to be built for the teacher. In 1877 the house was nearly doubled in size by a sympathetic addition by William Spence who followed the original design.

Pynhannot 49 Colquhoun Street, (1875) has a bell-cast roof and a weathervane with ship finial, a Regency-style porch and a corner tower in Glasgow Style. An addition by Robert Wemyss in 1902 doubled the size of the house for the Sloan shipping family.

Space restricts details of all Leiper's houses in the town, but the following houses not already mentioned will enable lovers of his work to view them.

Tordarroch Douglas Drive (c1883) in Arts and Craft style, Leiper's first in this style, built for Mrs R Smith.

Albion Lodge 134 Sinclair Street, (1883) (known as Dorlecote, Dovelcote and later St Bernard's) for Quentin Galbraith is a 'smaller version of Tordarroch'.[23] It was almost doubled in size by an extension.

Glen Kin 76 John Street, (mid-nineteenth century) (originally Cornwall House). Addition in 1889 by William Leiper for William Anderson includes a distinctive tower topped with a large chinaman's hat and a wing influenced by Norman Shaw. The interior has handsome Jacobean features.

Dhuhill Lodge, 125 Sinclair Street, (1898) in Scottish Baronial style. This small house with charming detail was built as a lodge to the sober Dhuhill House, 127 Sinclair Street commissioned by AR Brown.

Ardluss 135 Sinclair Street, (1900) is an Arts and Crafts villa built for William Russell JP, factor for the Luss Estates. The English Villas of 41,43 and 45 Charlotte Street, 1905-9, were built for a local builder, John Jack. Built of red sandstone with half-timbering and attractive fenestration these are delightful houses. Number 45 has a billiard room added by J Hunter McNab, 1913.

Lynton 6 Upper Colquhoun Street, (1908) (formerly Polkemmet built for JF Duncan). An Arts and Crafts style house influenced by Voysey.

Woodend 20 Millig Street, (1872) built for Mr Robertson. This is an example of one of the extensive additions carried out by Leiper and Paterson for a subsequent owner, Sir William Raeburn, a ship-owner. In 1901 Leiper designed a conservatory and in 1910 Paterson designed the splendid Elizabethan window and stair-hall timber screen and added a billiard room to the west on the service wing.

William Leiper RSA FRIBA was an eminent Glasgow architect. The internationally known Templeton Carpet Factory (1889) that he designed is an imitation Doges' Palace in glazed-tiled Venetian Gothic that brings a touch of Venice to Glasgow Green. It also featured on an architectural postage stamp in 1990. The Sun Fire and Life Insurance building in West George Street, Glasgow, his only major commercial building, gives rein to his artistic bent with copies of three of Michaelangelo's statues by William Birnie Rhind, on the façade. Leiper received a silver medal at the Paris Exhibition for this design. He had his office in this building. He left his profession in 1875 to study art in Paris but a prestigious commission in 1880 from the Czar of Russia, Alexander II, to design the interior decoration of the Imperial State Rooms[24] of the royal yacht *Livadia*[25] tempted him home. Another important opportunity in 1888 of overseeing the interior design of the Glasgow City Chambers was offered to him. One of the artists involved in the interior decoration, in painting murals, was the Glasgow Boy, John Lavery. He later asked Leiper to design an architectural frame for his monumental oil painting 'The State Visit of Her Majesty Queen Victoria, to the Glasgow International Exhibition, 1888'.[26] (The picture was damaged and the frame destroyed in an air raid in World War II. Portraits of William Leiper, Sir James Guthrie and EA Walton were included in the picture). Helensburgh residents were happy to enjoy vicariously the success of such artists and commissioned Leiper to design their homes, consequently the town has the most concentration of his domestic architecture. Around 1871 Leiper came to live in Helensburgh with his mother. He subsequently became a JP, an office-bearer and Superintendent of St Columba Church Sunday School and a member of many of the Arts organisations.

Alexander Nisbet Paterson (1862-1947) ARSA RSW FRIBA was also a Glasgow architect. His parents lived in Helensburgh at *Hapland*, 48 Charlotte Street; when he married he settled in Helensburgh. From a talented artistic family himself he married Maggie Hamilton from a similar artistic background and lived at The Long Croft, taking part in all aspects of the life of the town. Like Leiper his artistic talent is apparent in the buildings he designed, leaving the town with this wonderful architectural legacy. Other examples are *Whincroft*, 2 Colquhoun Street Upper (1915). It has the expected detailing of this architect's repertoire. *Greycourt*, Dhuhill Drive West (1911) (was *Courtallan*). An Arts and Crafts villa with seventeenth century details built for J R Caldwell. *Drum-Millig*, 146 Sinclair Street, 1909, is an Arts and Crafts villa in this architect's recognisable style.

Robert Wemyss (d 1955) FRIBA, lived in the town from about 1896. He was also a Glasgow architect. His delicate touch has left the town with many beautiful buildings. His regard for the work of Leiper ensured that the many extensions and additions that he was involved in did not detract from the original. He lived at *Dunvegan*, 35 Campbell Street, at one time. A member of St Andrew's Church, he wrote a short history of the church.[27] He designed *Braeriach*, 4 Colquhoun Street Upper (1909), an Arts and Crafts villa with the usual details such as red sandstone and tiles, harling and timber of the surrounding Leiper houses without losing his individual touch. There are handsome wrought Art Nouveau gates to the front. *The Hollies* 61 John Street (1910), is one of four delightful villas, 63, 65, 67, all with his usual tasteful variety of detail.

William Spence (1806-1883) was a pioneer of the use of cast-iron in the façade of the new department stores being built in Glasgow. He came to Helensburgh to live and built *Ardlui*, 23 Charlotte Street, for himself where he lived for twenty-five years. He had already designed Ardlui House, 5 East Montrose Street, home of Provost Steven, (both now demolished). His commission for large buildings included the impressive *Hermitage Secondary School*, 11 East Argyle Street (1880). (Now sadly demolished and an insignificant building on part of the site houses *Hermitage Primary School*). In Scots Baronial style in bull-faced cream sandstone with turrets, crowsteps, varied fenestration and fine detail it was a splendid building. However, the former *Janitor's Lodge*, 9 East Argyle Street (1879) remains to remind us of what we have lost. *Hermitage Cottage*, 104 Sinclair Street, is by Spence and possibly *Dalfruin*, 1 West Montrose Street, the entrances are similar. *Chapelacre Lodge*, 106c Sinclair Street, (c1850) in cream sandstone with an attractive gabled doorway, bargeboarded gables, quoin strips and hoodmoulds is all that is left of the Chapelacre estate.

There are many traditionally well-designed, well-built Victorian villas, many with central doorways flanked by windows on either side and on the second storey, but also with their individual detailing and charm and gardens with beautiful flora, such as rhododendrons, azaleas and magnolia bushes. *The Grange* 23 Suffolk Street, (1858) has additions by Campbell Douglas and Paterson to the rear. A single storey wing to the west was built as a studio for the artist-owner J Whitelaw Hamilton by AN Paterson in 1910. *The Lodge,* 121 West Argyle Street is late nineteenth century, and added to in 1900. Two cast-iron columns support the porch. On the wall to the left is a commemorative plaque inscribed 'John Logie Baird. Inventor of television. Born in this house 13 August 1888'. *Garthland,* 38 West Argyle Street, (1857) has Tudor details. When the house was called *Westwood* it was the home of JL Baird's great friend, Jack Buchanan, the international entertainer. *Westburn,* 50 Campbell Street, was built possibly in 1855. In pink and cream sandstone, this was the home of James Ballantyne Hannay, inventor of the first artificial diamonds in 1880. •

References (see Bibliography)
1 MacLeod *A Nonogenarian's Reminicences* p204
2 Maughan *Annals of Garelochside*
3 *Ibid*
4 Survey and Street Report Helensburgh 25th June 1845
5 Dumbarton Sasines 1800
6 Maughan *ibid* page 127
7 MacLeod *ibid* page 164
8 Murray *Glasgow and Helensburgh as recalled by Sir Joseph Hooker*
9 McFadzean *The Life and Work of Alexander Thomson* p42
10 MacLeod *ibid* page 167
11 Historic Scotland *Combined Statutory and Descriptive List – Helensburgh Burgh*
12 Handout on visit to house on 'Doors Open Day'
13 *Ibid*
14 Website http://uncommonjourneys.com/pages/qmart.htm
15 Handout on visit to house on 'Doors Open Day'
16 *Ibid*
17 *Helensburgh & Gareloch Times* 4th December 1895
18 Gordon Webster *The Stained Glass Windows, Old and St Andrew's Parish Church, Helensburgh* 1968 (Free booklet provided by West Kirk, available in porch)
19 *Helensburgh & Gareloch Times* 28th November 1980, article by John Thomson.
20 Halsby & Harris *The Dictionary of Scottish Painters* p216
21 Gomme & Walker *Architecture in Glasgow*
22 *Road Book of Scotland* pub London 1826

23 Gow & Rowan (eds) *Scottish Country Houses* (appendix: John R Hume *Chronological List of Houses in Scotland Designed by William Leiper*)
24 Picture, Mitchell Library, Glasgow
25 Model, Glasgow Museum of Transport
26 Glasgow Art Gallery and Museum
27 Wemyss *The Church in the Square*

Glossary

Architrave – the lowest division of the entablature (in classical architecture)

Bargeboard – verge or gable board

Cartouche – decorative tablet often with an inscription

Corbel – projection acting as a supporting bracket

Cornice – projecting upper part of the entablature (in classical architecture)

Crowsteps –stepped gable

Dormer – window in roof

Entablature – contains architrave, frieze and cornice (in classical architecture)

Finial – crowning ornament

Gable – end wall of a building

Gablet – small gable

Gibbs doorway or window – projecting stonework surround

Harling – exterior finish

Hoodmoulding – overhead projection to divert rainwater

Hopperheads – receptacle at top of rainwater pipe

Oriel – window projecting from the face of a wall

Pavilion – wings attached to main building

Pediment – triangular feature above entablature (in classical architecture)

Quoins – corner stones usually long and short

Reredos – screen behind and above altar

Skew – gable coping

Skewputt – bottom of skew sometimes scrolled

String course – horizontal projecting course

Tympanum – triangular area between cornices of pediment

CHAPTER 16

Men of Vision

Henry Bell
Brian D Osborne

Henry Bell (1767-1830), Helensburgh's first provost, is much better and more widely known as the pioneer of steam navigation. His *Comet*, which went into service in 1812, was the first commercially successful steamship in Europe.

Argyll & Bute Council

Henry Bell

Bell's background is significant in understanding his success and his problems. He was born in 1767 at Torphichen Mill, West Lothian, and was apprenticed as a millwright – the family trade. He later worked in the Grangemouth shipyard of Shaw and Hart, learning ship-modelling or ship design. Later he went to widen his experience in engineering in the Lanarkshire coalfield and went to London to work under the great Scottish engineer John Rennie. He returned to Glasgow about 1790 and set up in business on his own account, as a wright (a builder or house-carpenter) in the Gorbals.

Bell's training and experience was essentially practical rather than theoretical. Of course this was the norm for technical training at this time and scientific education was the preserve of the universities – and a man of Bell's background was unlikely ever to attend a university. Bell claimed that it was when he was working at Grangemouth that he became interested in the problem of steam power at sea. His move away from the family business of millwright work and his search for a wide range of experience in shipbuilding and engineering fitted him to work on this problem even if he lacked the theoretical skills to fully cope with it

Bell moved from the suburb of the Gorbals to the City of Glasgow, entering the Incorporation of Wrights in 1797 and becoming a burgess the same year. From 1799 to 1807 he can be traced living at various addresses in Glasgow and his movements suggest a successful business career. Little is recorded but we know he designed a church in Carluke (St Andrew's Parish Church, which is still in use) and there are suggestions of involvement with steam machinery in Glasgow mills. In 1806 he prepared a scheme for a Glasgow water supply drawn from

Stonebyres Linn at New Lanark – a far-sighted proposal similar to the much later Loch Katrine scheme. However the responsible committee adopted a simpler plan put forward by Thomas Telford.

Bell married Margaret Young in 1794. She was apparently something of a beauty and was described as 'a woman of strong practical good sense' – a quality she certainly needed in her life with Bell, whose character was marked by great enthusiasms, doubtful judgement and a cavalier disregard for money. Margaret Young seems to have been from a prosperous family, certainly her stepfather, Thomas Dykes, was a landowner in Eaglesham and the Dykes family were later to invest in Bell's shipowning projects.

By 1806 Bell was in Helensburgh supervising the construction of the Baths Inn (later the Queen's Hotel and now Queen's Court at 114 East Clyde Street). Bell had feued land on the south side of the road 'from Dumbarton to the Kirk of Row' in May 1806 and it was on this land that he was to build his inn, which became the premier bathing establishment on the Clyde. Bell, as we have seen, had practised as an architect as well as house-builder and millwright and there is no reason to doubt that the concept of the Baths Inn as well as the design and supervision of it was his.

The infant town of Helensburgh had only grown slowly since its foundation in 1776 but by 1802 it was well enough established to be granted a burgh charter. Under this Helensburgh was entitled to elect a Provost, Bailies and Councillors, hold markets and take such other measures as were the common practice of the day.

No steps were taken to implement these rights until 12th September 1807 when, at a general meeting of the feuars – the property-owning electors – Hendrey (*sic*) Bell was elected Provost. The new councillors soon were involved in civic business. On 16th October 1807 the Council agreed to 'make a road and side path through the city of Helensburgh' and the minutes of 14th November 1807 saw them resolving that annual markets should be advertised and later that month they discussed forming streets in the township. Ambitious plans were laid, and one can probably detect in them the enthusiastic and scheming spirit of the first citizen. In November ground was purchased to build a town's house and in February 1808 the electorate approved, by a majority of four votes, a plan for the town's house, that is to say a municipal buildings or town hall, and markets.

However the progressive spirit had over-reached itself and by May 1808 the Council had decided to abandon the project and authorised Provost Bell to make the best deal he could with the landowner, Sir James Colquhoun, on the surrender of the feu. The minutes go on to record the sad end of the Council's ambitions:

I Hendrey Bell, Provost this day on behalf of the town of

Helensburgh have hereby agreed with Sir James Colquhoun
for the sum of eighty pounds and to give him up the feu
purchased for the Town from James Smith.

The Town Council Minute Book has no further entries until 12th
September 1808 when the second annual election meeting was held,
with the re-election of Bell as Provost. September 1809 saw Bell elected
again, the only fixed point in an entirely new council.

From what we know from other sources about Bell's involvement
and interest in water supply schemes it is reasonable to detect the
influence of the Provost in the decision of 16th May 1810 to provide
the growing town with a supply of spring water.

This scheme was to be Bell's last major project as Provost. At the
annual election in 1811 he was not elected and he was to take no further
part in civic affairs. Indeed he is not even listed as being present at
election meetings of feuars. The Council apparently had a policy of
not re-electing a Provost or Bailie on more than two occasions without
a break in office and the implementation of this policy would of course
be sufficient to explain his demission from office. However even the
existence of such a policy does not explain why Bell ceased to take any
part in civic affairs. The explanation probably lies in the fact that in
1810 Bell had raised £2000 by mortgaging the Baths Inn to the Glasgow
merchant Archibald Newbigging. This action was presumably
undertaken to raise funds for his steamship plans. Bell continued, with
his wife, in the management of the Baths Inn, but he was no longer
qualified, as a feuar, to stand for the Council or to be an elector. It was
not until 1828 that he again became a property owner in the town and
regained a qualification as an elector.

Even if Bell had remained qualified one may speculate that he would
not have been anxious to continue in office. His mind was now turning
increasingly to his steamboat project, and he would surely have found
difficulty finding the time for burgh administration. It is also probable
that his characteristically ambitious plans – the town's house, the water
supply scheme, etc – were so far in advance of what the cautious and
economical citizens of Helensburgh were prepared to support and pay
for, that he might well have found himself being voted out of office
even if he had been able to stand again.

While the steamboat activities would in themselves have provided
one good reason why Henry Bell might not have had time for civic
affairs in Helensburgh it must also be remembered that he and his wife
Margaret had the Baths Inn to run. Both participated in this, although
it would seem that Margaret carried the main burden of the
management of the Inn – not, perhaps, an easy task when married to a
man like Bell, a man who always seemed better at finding ways of
spending money than ways of earning or keeping it. The nineteenth

century local historian Donald MacLeod wrote, 'He was a child in the matter of money. Nothing delighted him more than to have his pockets full, not for its own sake, but solely that he might pay it away right and left.'

The Baths Inn, as shown in nineteenth century prints, was an impressive square whitewashed property. From sale advertisements we learn that it was a complex building of some substance and character – a large greenhouse or conservatory and a coffee room were features of the ground floor. The baths department was supplied with numerous hot and cold baths. The whole property was completed with stabling for twenty two horses, a coach house for nine carriages, a shed for carts and gigs and the usual outbuildings.

In 1822 the novelist John Galt published *The Steam-Boat*. This concerned the adventures and travels of Thomas Duffle by the new steamboats around the Clyde and in one of his journeys, the intrepid Glaswegian shopkeeper reaches Helensburgh and we get an account of the Baths Inn and its health-seeking clientele. Galt's description is brief but valuable as contemporary evidence:

> When I had ate my dinner and drunk my toddy at the
> pleasant hotel of Helensburgh, in which there are both hot
> and cold baths for invalid persons, and others afflicted with
> the rheumatics, and suchlike incomes, I went out again to
> take another walk.

Such enthusiasm for the health-giving effects of sea-bathing and the fresh air of the Clyde Coast was the making of the Baths Inn and ensured the growth and prosperity of Helensburgh during Bell's lifetime.

The problem of the water supply, both fresh and salt, for the curative baths so much sought after by nineteenth century visitors was solved readily enough, and, despite some statements to the contrary, without the use of a steam engine. The 1810 transfer of the property by Bell to Archibald Newbigging included the liberty to take '. . . a six inch bore of water from the Burn of Milligs below the termination of the mill race of the Milligs Mill and of conveying the water by a Ditch or Cast . . . down to the Baths for the use of the same or of driving a wheel to raise the Sea Water into the said Baths'.

In 1823 Henry Bell placed an advertisement in the *Glasgow Courier* which suggests that the damage done by a fire in 1821 had been made good and that the Bells were perhaps now looking more towards long term residents than to short-term holiday makers.

THE HELENSBURGH BATHS, INN AND HOTEL have
undergone a complete repair, and a good many

improvements made to the Buildings, and are just now ready for the accommodation of the Public. MR BELL can accommodate a few LADIES and GENTLEMEN as BOARDERS on reasonable terms. Also, TWO PRIVATE FURNISHED LODGINGS, TO LET by the Month – the West Wing of the Baths, and the Cottage; each of them consists of a Kitchen and five Fire Rooms and Closets.

For most of its time under the Bells' control the Baths Inn ran smoothly and successfully, an achievement which owed more to Margaret's talents than to Henry's. It swiftly established a position as the town's, and the Clyde's, leading hotel with a distinguished clientele. By the end of Henry Bell's life, and to no small extent due to his work, Helensburgh had grown to have a permanent population of around 1000 but boasted a summer population of three times that number. After Bell's death Margaret continued in management of the Inn until her own death at the age of 85 in 1856.

Helensburgh's growth as a holiday and health resort was of course dependent on the transport revolution brought about by the coming of the steamship to the Clyde, a process that owed almost everything to Henry Bell.

Bell's interest in the problem of steam navigation was shared by many scientists, engineers and inventors all round the world. In Scotland Patrick Millar had successfully experimented with a steamboat on Dalswinton Loch at his home near Dumfries in 1788 and William Symington had constructed the *Charlotte Dundas* and seen her successfully ply on the Forth and Clyde Canal in 1803, until concerns about the damage her paddle-wheels might do to the canal embankment caused her to be taken out of service. In the United States, Robert Fulton, who had visited Scotland and spoken with Symington and probably Bell, put a steamship into service on the Hudson River in 1805. In Europe, however, no successful steamship had yet gone into commercial service.

Bell had a model constructed and tested, and in 1811 placed an order with the Port Glasgow yard of John Wood for the construction of the hull of his steamship. An engine was ordered from John Robertson and David Napier was contracted to supply the boiler. Money problems delayed construction and it was not until August 1812 that the *Comet* was put into service, sailing, as Bell's first advertisement said 'by the Power of Wind, Air & Steam' on the service between Glasgow's Broomielaw and Greenock. Initially the connection to Helensburgh was provided by a traditional passage boat but soon the *Comet's* route was extended to include Helensburgh, landing passengers at a makeshift pier near the Baths Inn – remains of its large boulders can just be made out at low tide at the foot of Hanover Street.

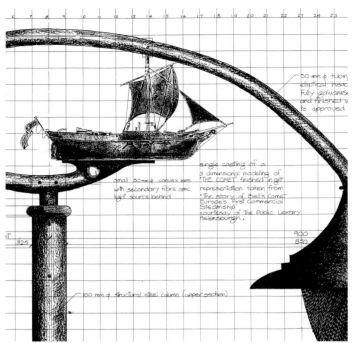

The *Comet* is shown on this architect's drawing by Alex Macgregor of proposed streetlights for Colquhoun Square (1999). Assistance from the wind could be obtained on these first steamships by hoisting a sail up the funnel. The vessel was named after the Great Comet of 1811

Bell's general interest in steam power and steam navigation had been given particular force by his ownership of the Baths Inn and his awareness of the problems of getting his customers down to Helensburgh from Glasgow. The roads of the period were poor and although Bell ran a stagecoach from Glasgow, with his brother Thomas as driver, the journey was a far from pleasant one. The service only operated in the summer months and the journey took six hours. To sail downriver was probably a more comfortable option but the passenger risked long delays if adverse winds were experienced. The Clyde in 1812 was not the deep and carefully dredged river of the high Victorian period and in addition to contrary winds the state of the tide had to be taken into account and many vessels ran aground on one or other of the many sandbanks.

The impact that the coming of the steamship made to traffic on the Clyde was immense. As early as 1816 one writer noted that before the steamers came it was doubtful if more than fifty people sailed between Glasgow and Greenock in a day – after the *Comet* and her successors appeared this rose to over five hundred a day.

Bell was the father of the Clyde shipbuilding and marine engineering industry and started the growth of tourism, and indeed of much of the residential development in the Clyde area. Others swiftly followed where he had pioneered – within months the second steamer had appeared on the Clyde and the numbers continued to grow. The time was undoubtedly right for a successful commercial steamer to emerge but Bell does deserve every credit for being first.

In many ways Bell was an unlikely man to have succeeded. Improvident and rash, he was given to boasting about his accomplishments and indeed to embroidering them beyond the limits of strict truth. He was more of a jack-of-all-trades than a highly trained engineer or scientist. The fact that an artisan rather than a gentleman scientist had been successful caused some of his rivals considerable pain.

There was no single great invention involved in Bell's *Comet*, simply the patient assembly of existing technology. What Bell did have was a passionate belief in his great project and it was this quality and a high degree of determination that undoubtedly carried him through to success, even if, sadly, that success never found appropriate financial reward.

Bell's contemporaries and successors recognised his qualities and achievements. Even those to whom he owed money were willing to support him and endorse his achievements. One of the greatest engineers of the age, Isambard Kingdom Brunel, said that 'Bell did what we engineers all failed in – he gave us the sea steamer; his scheming was Britain's steaming.' Robert Napier of West Shandon, the greatest figure in Clyde ship-building and marine engineering in the middle of the nineteenth century, also recognised Bell's true worth. He arranged for the erection, in 1853, of a statue of Bell above his previously unmarked grave in Rhu kirkyard and was the main contributor to the cost of raising the Bell monument on West Clyde Street, Helensburgh.

Henry Bell died, at the Baths Inn, on 14th November 1830, after a long illness. His mind was however active and occupied to the end. In August 1830 he published a letter to the 'Gentlemen, Freeholders and Merchants of Argyleshire' proposing the construction of a ship canal between East Loch Tarbert and West Loch Tarbert. He had surveyed this route two years earlier and now proposed this as a rival to the Crinan Canal. Like many of Bell's schemes this was a project on the grand scale, perhaps the work of a visionary rather than of a practical man of affairs.

Ann Stewart

Henry Bell's grave in Rhu Parish Churchyard was unmarked for 16 years while the intention of erecting a worthy memorial went unrealised

However it was just this visionary quality which had brought Bell success in the building of the practical steamship, it was this visionary quality which had made him see that steamships were not just a convenient way of navigating rivers and sheltered coastal waters but that they would soon venture into the oceans of the world. Bell put this belief into action when in 1819 he had the *Comet* lengthened and set her off on a service from the Clyde to Fort William – the first steamboat service to the West Highland seaboard.

An obituary of Bell described him as '. . . the ingenious Mr Bell, the practical introducer of steam navigation into Europe. . .' and this, although it omits many of his other activities, certainly warrants Bell's inclusion in this bicentenary volume about the town of which he was the first Provost.

●

Photos provided by Malcolm Baird

John Logie Baird aged about 20, well clad against the Helensburgh weather, standing by his motor tricycle, the 'reaper and binder'. The female passenger is believed to be his cousin Jeanie Coates

John Logie Baird at age 12, while he was attending Larchfield School, in the garden of 'The Lodge'

There are, curiously, very few photos (writes Malcolm Baird) of my father with the family! The best known one of the two of us together was taken in 1938 (when I was 3) in front of a Baird TV

John Logie Baird

by his son, Malcolm Baird

In the late nineteenth century, life in Helensburgh revolved to a great extent around its churches. Among the prominent ministers in the town was the Rev John Baird BD of the West Parish Church. Mr Baird, a dignified figure with a large beard and side whiskers, had been called to his ministry in 1868 and was to serve until his retirement in 1912. His house, The Lodge at 121 West Argyle Street (on the corner with Suffolk Street), had been purchased with financial help from his wife's family, soon after his marriage in 1878. He had what was by Victorian standards a moderate-sized family of four children the youngest of whom, John Logie Baird, was born on 14th August 1888.

JLB in 1944 with his colour television tube, the Telechrome.

His middle name was the maiden name of his great grandmother, and my mother always called him 'Logie' as she disliked the name John. He was always plain John L Baird until his name began to appear in the press and then he always styled himself John Logie Baird. This may have been at first to avoid confusion with his father who was well-known in Helensburgh as the Rev John Baird and who had no middle name.

John Logie Baird was a healthy baby until at the age of two he had an almost fatal illness, sketchily diagnosed as a blockage of the bowels. Always thereafter he was 'delicate' with a proneness to winter chills and colds. This set him back when he entered Larchfield School and he did not do well. His interests lay in science and technology, which were not in the Larchfield curriculum. His imagination was fired by HG Wells' newly published stories. Mr Baird soon realised that his youngest son would not be following him into the ministry.

With some financial help from his mother, JLB (as I will call him) purchased a top-of-the-line camera with rack-and-pinion focussing. Surviving prints show that he was an accomplished photographer. Another early project was the construction of a system of electric light for The Lodge, powered by a small oil engine. This earned JLB a brief mention in the local paper, but one evening the lights failed as his father was descending the staircase and he had a nasty fall. It was time for a new project and this took the form of a telephone system connecting to some of his friends in the neighbourhood. Wires were slung across the street from trees. One stormy night a wire dipped lower than usual and caught the local cabdriver under the chin, yanking him down on to the street. Awkward explanations followed. His parents seem to have shown remarkable tolerance during these goings-on.

As a teenager, JLB detested the conformist football-playing 'hearties' at Larchfield but he had a small circle of friends who, like himself, were looking for something different in life. One of these was a lanky fellow who was fond of pranks and clowning and was nicknamed Chump. Later he became famous on the musical stage as the polished matinee idol, Jack Buchanan. Another friend was Guy Fullarton Robertson, known as Mephy, a philosopher and dilettante who was to cross paths with JLB in future years.

By the time he left Larchfield in 1906, his mind was made up about further education. With the agreement and support of his father, he entered the Glasgow and West of Scotland Technical College as a student of electrical engineering. Years later he recalled that the things he had learnt in his first year at 'The Tech' had stayed with him throughout his life. As part of his training he served as an industrial apprentice. The long hours and miserable working conditions in the factories and the lack of job security for the ordinary workers made a deep impression on him and he acquired left-wing views. These were reinforced when he looked at the glossy magazines like the *Tatler* and the *Sphere*, showing the aristocracy and the idle rich disporting themselves in luxury.

In the midst of his courses at the college and the drudgery of the apprenticeships, JLB still found time for outside hobbies. He owned a succession of noisy and dilapidated motor vehicles, one of which was known in Helensburgh as 'Baird's reaper and binder'. He contributed short pieces of a humorous or satirical nature to the Technical College Magazine. Last but not least, he thought about the possibility of television, using a rotating perforated disc (known as the Nipkow disc) to break up an image into strips of light which could then be picked up by a selenium cell and converted into an electrical signal. He even experimented with a piece of selenium but found that the electrical current change due to light effects was so small as to be barely detectable on an ammeter.

Eventually, in October 1914, he graduated as an Associate of the Royal Technical College. (The College had received its royal designation in 1912). He then enrolled at the University of Glasgow with the intention of taking a further degree, but this was cut short by the outbreak of war. JLB was rejected for active service on medical grounds and he joined the Clyde Valley Electric Power Company, based at Rutherglen, as Assistant Mains Engineer. He had to be on overnight call in case of breaks in the underground power cables. More often than not, a break would occur in a period of heavy rain and then JLB would go out in charge of a work gang, to find the break and repair it. The labourers were rough characters and sometimes the worse of drink. Fights occasionally broke out while they worked with their picks and shovels. JLB stood patiently in the cold rain, trying his best to direct the operations.

After two years at the Clyde Valley Company, he was being worn down. As he put it in his memoirs, 'I saw myself as the years went by, working through one wet winter after another until at last one of my winter chills brought the sorry story to an end.' He decided to resign and set up in business on his own, but what business? Eventually he hit on the idea of a treated sock, which would reduce dampness of the feet. With his small capital he bought a few dozen pairs of plain socks which he sprinkled with borax and packaged as the Baird Undersock. Publicity was needed and he hired a jobbing carpenter to build a large plywood replica of a tank, plastered with signs 'The Baird Undersock for the Soldier's Foot'. This contraption was trundled through the Glasgow streets with a push bar inside it, so it seemed to be moving under its own power. The advertising campaign was successful and he was inundated with orders from the big department stores. He hired extra staff but when he came down with his usual winter chill, the business suffered.

An old college friend wrote from the United States about an exciting business opportunity in Trinidad, where fruit grew abundantly but much of it rotted because of the lack of any processing facilities. Sugar was abundant and cheap. The prospects for a jam factory seemed excellent and the warm climate would surely put paid to JLB's winter chills. In the autumn of 1919, he wound up the undersock business and sailed out to Trinidad.

Robert Burns wrote that 'the best laid schemes o' mice an' men gang aft agley', and JLB's sojourn in Trinidad was a case in point. The jam factory was duly set up but conditions were primitive and the jam was of dubious quality. The tropical climate was no benefit to his health as he contracted malarial fever. After a year he returned to Britain physically frail and with most of his savings gone.

Fighting his ill health, he set up a small business in London, trying to sell his jam and dealing in other products such as soap, on the wholesale and retail markets. The business had its ups and downs and it kept him going for a couple of years. For a while he stayed with his older sister Annie who was working in London as a nursing sister and she recalled that he felt the cold intensely. On one winter night he took the rug off the floor and used it as an additional blanket on his bed. Eventually, he went to a doctor who urged him to leave London for a cleaner and warmer area, or the doctor could not vouch that he (JLB) would last another year.

The town of Hastings, on the Sussex coast, has a dry, mild climate. It was here that JLB arrived in the spring of 1923, in his own words, 'coughing, choking and spluttering and so thin as to be almost transparent'. His old friend Mephy Robertson was there and had arranged for JLB to share his lodgings. In a few months, JLB's health began to rally.

One day he went for a long walk over the hills above Hastings and his thoughts went back to television. He already knew about photoelectric cells and the splitting up (scanning) of an image by the rotating Nipkow disc. An important recent development was the valve amplifier, which could overcome the problem of the very weak signals from the photocell. He came back to his lodgings fired with the possibilities of television and over the dinner table he put his ideas to Mephy, who was at first sceptical. 'I hope that doesn't mean you are going to become one of those wireless nitwits. Far better keep to soap. You can't afford to play about you know.'

But JLB went ahead, slowly gathering a collection of electrical and mechanical items, bought cheaply or in some cases salvaged from scrap. His first Nipkow discs were cut out from the sides of tea-chests, but the later ones were of sheet metal. He attracted a coterie of interested and unpaid helpers including a local teacher, Victor Mills, who was knowledgeable in the new science of electronics. In July 1923 he filed his first patent and in January 1924 a demonstration was held for the press. Although the moving images were only silhouettes, the public interest was raised and some badly needed funds came in for the project. The Rev John Baird donated £50, and the cinema owner Wilfred Day invested £200. The latter proved to be a mixed blessing because Day became impatient for a financial return and as time went on he hounded JLB to show more results. It is strange to note that in 1999 the letters between JLB and Day were sold at auction for £70,000!

Throughout 1924, steady progress was made towards television. JLB moved his laboratory from his lodgings to a rented room in the Queen's Arcade. The signals from the photocells were faint even after amplification, and in his words the need was for 'light, light and more light'. One day he received a near-fatal electric shock from his 2000-volt battery pack but fortunately the explosion threw him away from the terminals. His landlord put pressure on him to leave and later in the year he moved to London, to a small top floor room at 22 Frith Street in Soho. Money continued to be a problem and Baird again sought publicity and possible financial backers.

His old Helensburgh friend Jack Buchanan, by now a star in the West End, was happy to be of help. Although most of his capital was tied up in shows, Jack put on a luncheon at the fashionable Romano's restaurant to introduce JLB to the London press. In June 1925, the world's first television company, known simply as Television Limited, was incorporated with John Logie Baird and Wilfred Day as the co-directors.

Work continued in the Frith Street attic and at last, on a dark evening in October 1925, the breakthrough came. For the first time, a lifelike television image with half-tones was obtained by reflected light from a stuffed tailor's dummy, known as 'Stooky Bill'. JLB rushed down to the solicitors' office on the floor below, in search of a human subject. A teenage office boy named William Taynton was singled out. The bright lights and spinning wheels frightened William and he had to be bribed with half a crown ($12\frac{1}{2}$p) for the privilege of being the first living person to be televised. The picture was small, about 4 by 6 cm, and it contained only 32 lines of definition, but it was television for the first time ever.

The full story of the development of British television has been written up in some excellent books and only a brief summary can be fitted into these pages. Television was formally demonstrated to leading scientists at Frith Street in January 1926 and soon afterwards a successful share flotation of Television Limited was carried out, allowing JLB to move to larger premises. For the first time in his life he had no financial worries and he took on a small but enthusiastic staff including a gifted radio amateur, Ben Clapp. The late 1920s were truly the glory years for JLB and a series of television 'firsts' was achieved: long distance transmission from London to Glasgow (which is commemorated by a plaque in the Quality Central Hotel in Glasgow); primitive colour and stereoscopic television; and the newly named noctovision in which infra red radiation was used as a source of illumination instead of visible light. In another form of television, ultra-short radio waves replaced light as the illumination and this has been compared with some modern radar systems. In February 1928, television was sent across the Atlantic from London to New York, using Ben Clapp's transmitter on a wavelength of 45 metres.

These achievements aroused great public interest and JLB became

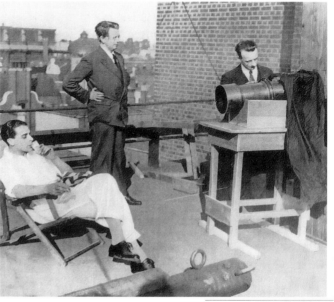

There are very few photos of my father with Jack Buchanan. This is another press photo, from 1928 showing colour television tests on the roof of the Baird Television Ltd headquarters at Long Acre, London. Typically, Jack is the elegant figure reclining with his glass of a cooling beverage, while my father looks anxiously on.

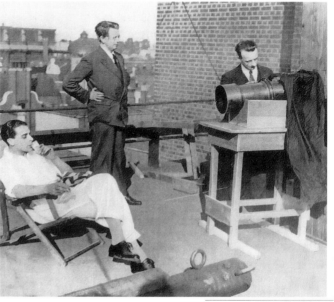

from the files of the Royal Television Society

a celebrity. He was an invited speaker at the meeting of the British Association in Glasgow in 1928 and he found time to visit Helensburgh for a reunion with his father and his sister Annie. Mr Baird was now 86 years of age and Mrs Baird had predeceased him in 1924.

In September 1929 the BBC was persuaded (with reluctance) to open the first public television service. The corporation was at pains to point out that the service was only experimental, but the 30-line signal had a long range and could be picked up in most parts of Britain by anyone with a radio and a 'televisor' which converted the radio signal to a picture. There is a televisor on display in the Helensburgh Library and a working model in the Glasgow Science Centre.

Programmes were broadcast at first from the Baird studios in 133 Long Acre, London. Among the artistes who came to the studios was a young classical pianist, Margaret Albu. Born and raised in South Africa, she had moved to London with her mother a few years earlier and had studied at the Royal College of Music. She caught JLB's eye and what followed can only be described a whirlwind courtship. In October 1931 JLB was on a business trip to New York and with typical impulsiveness he telephoned Margaret and asked her to join him. Margaret sailed over and the two were married before a judge on 13th November 1931.

Soon after the Bairds returned to London the news came that the Baird company, which had been in some financial trouble, had been taken over by Gaumont British Pictures. JLB was increasingly isolated from the day-to-day management of the company and to some extent he welcomed this as he found his laboratory work on cinema television much more interesting than boardroom politics. He was still the main 'asset' of the company and he received an after-tax salary of over £3000 per annum, an extremely good income for those days. The Bairds moved first to a house in Hampstead and soon afterwards to a large Georgian style house at 3 Crescent Wood Road, near the Crystal Palace in Sydenham, South London. My sister Diana was born in 1932 and I was born in 1935.

By the mid 1930s the Baird company faced a serious rival in the development of broadcast television. The Marconi-EMI company, with the help of American patents and a well-funded research team, developed a workable electronic television camera capable of a 405-line picture. Although the Baird system was also upgraded, the electronic system had the advantage, particularly under studio conditions, and in early 1937 it was adopted by the BBC. JLB was downcast but the Baird company was still viable as a manufacturer of receivers, and he continued to receive his salary and support for his research on large screen television.

The outbreak of war in 1939 changed everything. The BBC shut down its television broadcasts and the market for receivers dried up overnight. JLB found himself without an income although fortunately he had accumulated substantial savings. His first action was to move his family to the safety of Bude in North Cornwall. He himself decided to work on at his small private laboratory adjoining the house in Sydenham and use his savings to develop new ideas for high-definition colour and stereoscopic television. He achieved great technical success but his demonstrations to the press were under-reported because the limited space in the papers was dominated by news of the war.

Wartime conditions and the heavy workload took a steady toll of JLB's health. In 1941 he had a mild heart attack and he spent three months recovering at a health farm where he found time to write a draft of his memoirs. Later in 1941 he took on a new project sponsored by Cable and Wireless, on the use of television to send messages at very high speed. He continued to drive himself and by late 1945 he was so weak that it took him several minutes to climb a flight of stairs. The family moved to Bexhill, a few miles along the coast from Hastings, and it was here that John Logie Baird died on 14th June 1946 at the tragically early age of 57. He was buried in the family grave in Helensburgh.

The Burgh Council commemorated him by attaching a plaque to the Municipal Buildings, another was attached to his birthplace, and then in 1961 J Arnold Fleming presented a bust of JLB to the town which can now be seen on the West Esplanade.

The surviving members of the Baird family continued to be part of the Helensburgh scene for many years. At the kind insistence of my aunt Annie, my mother and Diana and I moved into The Lodge in April 1947. Diana and I both went to school in Helensburgh, she to St Bride's and I to Larchfield. Later I studied at my father's *alma mater*, the Royal Technical College, which has since become the University of Strathclyde. By 1960 Diana had married and I was starting work as a chemical engineer. My mother returned to the sunshine of South Africa where for the next twenty five years she resumed her musical career as a teacher and occasional performer. Annie Baird passed away peacefully in June 1971.

In August 1988, the birth centennial of John Logie Baird, my mother and Diana and I returned to Helensburgh to attend the service of dedication of stained glass windows in the West Kirk, commemorating his life and work. Margaret Baird died on 14 July 1996, fifty years and one month after the death of her famous husband.

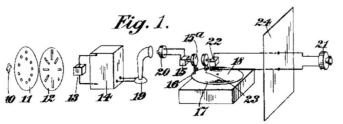

Fig. 1.

John Logie Baird also invented the world's first video recorder as this 1927 patent for his Phonovision shows. It used 78 rpm gramophone records

CHAPTER 17

The Benefactors

In the past it was not uncommon for individuals or families to make substantial donations of one form or another to a town. In Helensburgh the Colquhouns as founders of the town obviously played such a role, but they were not alone. Donations could be big or small, but naturally because they make a bigger impact, bigger donations tend to be best remembered. Thus for example the donors' board in the entrance hall of the Victoria Infirmary records only the larger donations that were made in the days before the establishment of the National Health Service in 1948 – many individuals also gave regularly out of their wages, but they are not recorded.

We look here at four of the more prominent benefactors to the town, because it is important to remember just how much we owe to them. And in these days when local government is no longer expected to provide everything, perhaps it is worth considering that they may constitute an example that we should try to emulate.

The Kidstons

John Johnston

The Kidston family have lived in and been involved with Helensburgh since the 1830s. In one of their obituaries in the local paper it was said: 'The name of Kidston is writ large in all the recreative and philanthropic institutions of our beautiful town.'

The background of the family is of some interest as it explains the source of their business interests and fortunes in the first half of the nineteenth century and is a fascinating illustration of the entrepreneurial developments of the West of Scotland at that time.

There had been Kidstons living at Logie, close to Stirling, since the middle of the sixteenth century and for generations they had been farmers – not always successful. In 1765 a Richard Kidston, born in 1736, emigrated to Virginia and later the same year his wife and family joined him. In 1773 Britain attempted to start taxing her American colonies, which then joined together to form the United States of America. Richard joined the United Loyalists being a Royalist like his forebears in Scotland. In 1776, when the American War of Independence started, he fled to Maine. It would appear that he with many other United Loyalists fought with the British army and he was captured by the colonists at New York on 25th November 1783. Managing to escape from the prison in New York he fled in a small boat with only what he was wearing. He was lucky to be picked up in the Atlantic by a ship proceeding to Halifax, Nova Scotia.

Richard Kidston established himself as a merchant at Halifax and eventually as a ship owner. He exported timber to Glasgow and imported goods from that city. He died in 1810 at the age of 79. His many ships passed to his son, William Kidston, who had by this time moved to Glasgow and formed his own business, William Kidston and Sons, with offices and warehouses in Queen Street.

William Kidston had been born in 1757 at Logie and in 1784 married Catherine Glen at Halifax and they had a family of seven; he died in 1831. Business prospered and by 1820 the firm was involved in wholesale china manufacturing, shipping (they acted for Cunard, another Halifax family) and general merchanting. The potteries in Glasgow at Anderston and Finnieston, Verrivale and Lancefield were extensive with a large export trade to South America and the East Indies – the Scottish Pottery Society has identified several pieces found in Indonesia.

By 1839 the firm had become too large with too many Kidstons trying to run it and it was decided to divide the business as follows:

i) Richard Kidston – the home market (William Kidston & Sons);

ii) Archibald Glen Kidston – the export and shipping fleet (AG Kidston & Co). This business prospered under his son, George Jardine Kidston (1835-1909) who lived at Finlaystone near Langbank in Renfrewshire. His grand-daughter married General Macmillan whose descendants live there today. At the top of the stairs is a large portrait of George Jardine Kidston in hunting pink. The shipping business prospered and developed into The Clyde Shipping Company;

iii) Robert Alexander Kidston – the potteries (Kidston & Co). There are a number of articles on the history of the potteries in the journals of the Scottish Pottery Society. Although or possibly because the products were of a high quality the firms were not financially successful and eventually Robert Kidston moved to Stirling. His son, Adrian, worked for the family firm, William Kidston & Sons, and then went into banking, becoming Manager of the Helensburgh branch of the Clydesdale Bank in 1885.

Richard Kidston

Richard Kidston (1784-1865) It is said that Bailie Richard Kidston came to Helensburgh in 1845 but he was provost of the town in 1836! He had been Bailie in Glasgow from 1835 to 1845 and a partner in William Kidston & Sons. He was also involved in the early days of the Clydesdale Bank and became a director of the Bank in 1843 and Chairman in 1851 and 1862. Until 1856 a director had to live within ten miles of Glasgow, the coming of the railways rendering this qualification unnecessary. Perhaps Richard Kidston had more than one house as he lived, together with his two unmarried sons William and Richard and daughter Catherine at Seabank, a villa said to have been built about 1820 in classic palladian style, on the river side of East Clyde Street, opposite the foot of Grant Street. He was Provost of Helensburgh in 1836 and again from 1840 to 1849.

His latter years as Provost were taken up with the vexed question of a new pier. An Act of Parliament had been obtained in 1846 authorising the local authority to erect a pier and levy rates on it. But an unfortunate agreement had been made with the promotors of the Caledonian and Dumbartonshire Railway by which they, in consideration of certain privileges to be granted, undertook to advance money to build the pier. The line was not at that time completed; but an ill-advised litigation was raised by the council against the company to compel their implementation of the bargain which after years of delay was decided against the council. Various attempts at arrangement and compromise were made by Mr Kidston and a minority of the council, and would have been successful but for the litigious inclinations of his colleagues who wrangled constantly over every subject. The action ended with the House of Lords and the Town Council obtained nothing more than a large place in the Law Reports. Fame is dearly bought.

The foundation stone of the West United Free Church (now known as the West Kirk) was laid in 1853 and the cost of £4,500 was to a very considerable extent contributed by Mr Richard Kidston.

The East End Park for the town was walled and laid out by him and the gift of the land by Sir James Colquhoun secured through him. He liberally aided the building of Park Free Church and Manse and he fostered many religious and philanthropic schemes. He died in 1865.

William Kidston (1813-1889) On his father's death William Kidston continued to live with his brother and sister but in 1869 moved to the newly built mansion of Ferniegair, West Clyde Street, in what was then the Parish of Row. Similar in scale to Cairndhu, its next door neighbour, Ferniegair (architect, John Honeyman) had very large grounds stretching back to West Argyle Street, which over the years were whittled away. In the 1960s the house was demolished and A Trail and Son built a modern housing estate on the site, but one of the roads was named after the house. The coachman's lodge was retained, enlarged and

Ferniegair around 1900; the house stood immediately to the east of Cairndhu on Rhu Road Lower

modernised and sold as a private house – it stands today at 196-198 West Princes Street.

William Kidston was closely involved with the Free Church Sunday School and in the early days of the Free Church came to the front as a leader of the Highland Host. In this context he was known all over Scotland. He supported Park Church and as the senior Elder was involved in the dispute in 1874 when there was an attempt to change the long established custom of 'standing during prayer and sitting during the exercise of prayer'.

In 1874 he became involved with saving as an open space the piece of land then known as Neddy's Point and now as Kidston Park. It has been written that a 'well-known local artist of worldwide fame' has decided he wished to acquire the point and build himself a villa. On the point was a cottage occupied by the Duke of Argyll's fisherman, by name of Neddy – hence the name. William Kidston organised a subscription, supported by himself, Sir James Colquhoun and Provost Breingan to acquire the land from the Duke of Argyll and lay it out as a park. The cost was £552 (£320 per acre, or £790 per hectare) and included the rights to the foreshore and the mussel beds, but the Duke retained the right to land from and embark to the Castle of Rosneath. A local writer, though full of praise for the new park, thought it rather small. William Kidston offered a subscription of a further £500 to add to the land but nothing further was done. How it now comes to be known as Kidston Park is not clear as there is correspondence showing that Sir James Colquhoun wrote that, in his view, the park should not bear the name of any of the contributors, but an inscription still in existence states that the park was chiefly the gift of William Kidston and that he left funds for maintenance. Since then road widening, a car-park and the building of houses on the land not acquired have reduced the attraction of the park but there are photographs showing the bandstand and there was a jetty at the water's edge.

In 1877 Mr Kidston was honoured by a dinner in the Queen's Hotel for his spirited action in the Helensburgh Railway Station dispute. There were diverse opinions on his and others' efforts which prevented the railway company from forming their 'station in the sea' at Helensburgh pier, and thereby laid them under the necessity of making the station and pier at Craigendoran. But there were hundreds who agreed it would have been ruinous, reducing Helensburgh from being a flourishing and favourite watering place into 'a dirty coaling place'. The Bill before Parliament by the North British Railway Company was opposed by what was known as the Kidston Bill and the House of Commons declared that the 'preamble had not been proved'. William Kidston was presented with a portrait painted by Sir Daniel McNee.

In 1863 a number of magistrates and other gentlemen connected with the West of Scotland interested in the cause of Sabbath Observance and Sobriety, in testimony of their appreciation of his zealous and efficient services involving the Scottish licensing system and the Public Houses Acts, presented to William Kidston a solid silver table piece three feet high in the form of three nubile girls holding aloft the dishes for fruit. This can be seen in a formal New Year photograph of an assemblage at Ferniegair about 1900.

There were never any doubts about the political party that their cousin and future Prime Minister, Bonar Law, would join if he entered politics. The Kidstons, unlike the great majority of the Scottish middle class to which they belonged, were ardent Conservatives. There is a tradition that Disraeli once visited Ferniegair. Middle class Scotland was in general at that time a stronghold of Liberalism.

William Kidston had sponsored his cousin Andrew Bonar Law into the family firm of William Kidston & Sons. When in 1885 William and his brothers wished to wind up the affairs of the firm and retire, the Clydesdale Bank offered lucrative merger terms. However they realised that such a deal would have left Bonar Law in a difficult situation. His recent biographer describes how Bonar Law found a position in William Jacks, a metal trading company in Glasgow, and how William Kidston and his brothers advanced him the money to buy a partnership in that firm. Incidently William Jacks was a Helensburgh neighbour.

Richard Kidston (1816 – 1894) was a partner in the family firm who inherited Ferniegair on William's death and who died unmarried. Like his siblings he was involved with the church and in 1860 a new manse for the West Parish Church was acquired and new bedrooms added principally through his generosity. In 1893 he gave £1,000 to the Victoria Infirmary as shown on its Donor Board.

Charles Kidston (1820-1894), a brother of William lived at Glenoran, Glenoran Road, Rhu, another large house now demolished. He was married but had no children and was a director of the family firm. Both he and his wife left substantial fortunes which together with the house went to Bonar Law's family. Donations by Charles and his wife to the Victoria Infirmary are shown on the Donor Boards in the entrance to the Infirmary – £525 in 1895 and £1,000 in 1898. The year after his death his trustees donated £2,600 to the Commissioners of Helensburgh Pier, thus enabling the abolition of pier dues (ie charges to passengers). This was the cause of much festivity within the town.

Catherine Kidston (1824-1906) spent nearly all her adult life in Helensburgh moving at the age of eighteen, following the sudden death of her mother, with her father Richard and brothers to Seabank and later to Ferniegair.

Her father was closely involved with the St Enoch Free Church in Glasgow and after the Disruption the family continued to be closely involved with the Free Church as well as her work with Sunday Schools and as a District Visitor. In addition she was a partner in the family business, unusually for a lady in these days. Her obituary refers to band performances at Kidston Park by the boys from the *Empress* being due to her thoughtful kindness (presumably financial). The boys disembarked at the jetty at Kidston Park and marched through the town to their appointments. It continued that she was esteemed for her religious, temperance and philanthropic work and many acts of unostentatious benificence and it was said her motto was 'to live as we would wish to have done when we come to die'.

Shortly after the death of the Rev Alexander Anderson in 1891, who had retired from the West Kirk in 1882, she gifted the spectacular porch, designed by William Leiper. This much-crocketed extension is alive with fantastic birds and beasts munching their way around the stepped cornice. When he retired he had been presented with a silver fruit set which consisted of a central raised basket, embossed with a view of the church, and four silver dishes. This set was apparently left to Catherine by the Rev Anderson.

Adrian MMG Kidston (1848-1912), son of the pottery director Robert Alexander Kidston, became a banker and came from being agent at Crieff to Helensburgh in 1885 as manager of the Clydesdale Bank in James Street and lived in the house attached to and over the bank until he moved to Ferniegair. He served on the parish council for eighteen years, became a town councillor in 1902 and Provost in 1911, dying in office in October 1912, a month after he had welcomed the dignatories who came to the celebrations of the *Comet* centenary. His obituary refers to his involvment with the Girls' Schools Company (of which St Bride's was part) and also with Larchfield. It also says that the town owes in a large measure the building and equipping of the Victoria Infirmary to

Adrian Kidston

family photo

his wonderful gift of raising money. Like other members of the family he was a keen sportsman being Captain of the Golf Club 1901-5 and President of the Curling Club and Vice President of the Royal Caledonian Curling Club in 1907-08. There is also mention of cricket, tennis, quoits, bowling, swimming and rowing. He was also President of the West of Scotland Rosarian Society and the Helensburgh and Gareloch Horticultural Society.

In the late nineteenth century the property on the west side of James Street between Princes and King Streets was somewhat notorious. Originally the 'Barracks' had been built as dwellings for railway or construction workers and had become a very poor class of house. They were in the area covered by Miss Catherine Kidston as District Visitor for the Sunday School. Her obituary said that she had handed it to the town but the deed of gift was signed in 1907, after her death, by Adrian Kidston with the condition, accepted by the Provost, Magistrates and Councillors that it be preserved and used at all time coming hereafter 'as a place of recreation for the inhabitants of Helensburgh' but he carefully added that 'being used otherwise would revert to him or his heirs'. It now serves as a children's playground.

In 1988 a plan was put forward by private developers to build a medical centre together with flats on the site and a small play area under cover on an adjacent site – the plan also involved converting the adjoining but disused St Bride's Church into a new library. Admittedly the playground had been allowed to run down and there was a need for a new medical centre but a number of local residents and others were unhappy at the loss of the open space of which there was little in or near the centre of the town. Descendants of the donor raised objections to the proposals on the grounds of the loss to the community and after lengthy legal correspondence and a site meeting the plan to use the playground was dropped. In due course a new and larger site was found for the doctors and a new library was built on the site of the demolished church.

In 1999 the playground was refurbished, with splendid new railings, with financial help from local businesses and also by members of the Kidston family.

RAPR (Dick) Kidston (1894-1972) inherited Ferniegair from his father, Adrian Kidston. Educated at Larchfield, Fettes and Cambridge University he served throughout World War I in the Royal Field Artillery in Egypt and Palestine where he was mentioned in General Allenby's despatches. In 1922 he married Penelope Paul the daughter of Henry Paul, a Director of Matthew Paul & Co, engineers in Dumbarton, who in 1897 built the White House in Upper Colquhoun Street. The architect there was Baillie Scott who was awarded the second prize in the competition to design a House for an Art Lover. This competition made the reputation of Charles Rennie Mackintosh even though he failed to complete his entry – no first prize was awarded. Regrettably after the house was sold in the 1920s some of the major features were changed.

Also in the 1920s Ferniegair was sold and Mr and Mrs Kidston moved to Edinburgh returning to Helensburgh in 1939. Dick Kidston served throughout World War II in which his only son Adrian, a Lieutenant in the Royal Artillery, was killed in action. Adrian was in the 52nd Lowland Division which was designated as a Mountain Division – there was no other such unit in the British Army. They added 'Mountain' to their Divisional shoulder flash but in the end went into action below sea level where he was killed in the amphibious landing on Walcheren, Holland. After the war Dick Kidston was a Town and County Councillor in the 1950s and 60s.

WH Kidston (1852-1929), a nephew of George Jardine Kidston, lived at Rosebank, 150 West Princes Street. He was Chairman of AG Kidston & Co Ltd whose business in the twentieth century was iron and steel merchants but he concentrated on the insurance broking side of the business and became a senior executive and later a Director of the Royal Insurance Company. He was a keen sportsman playing rugby for Scotland against England in February 1874. He was also an enthusiastic bowler, being Club President in 1921; as a devotee of golf, he was one of the original founders of the Helensburgh Club – Captain in 1894-96 and President in 1927-28; he was also a member of Helensburgh Curling Club. His obituary in the local paper said that for a long number of years he was closely identified with the public life of the burgh and in many ways contributed to the advancement of the town and the welfare of its people. It was said his philanthropy was well-directed in particular to the Town Mission and practical interest in the religious teaching of the young. The Plotholders Association had, in him, a sympathetic friend and it was typical that he should grant the use of a large field in front of his house for the culture of vegetables. It was his custom to visit the field and watch the progress being made on the various plots. There are now houses on this field. His only son William, who was unmarried, a Captain in the Argyll and Sutherland Highlanders, died of wounds suffered at Ypres in 1917 and is buried in the Commonwealth War Cemetery at Etaples.

A printed letter to the congregation of the West Kirk dated 11 December 1914 details sixty members of the congregation who were serving King and Country – nos 20-23 were members of the Kidston family – Dick Kidston, William Kidston, James Kidston Law and Charles Law – the last three were all killed.

Annabel Kidston (1896-1981) was another member of the family who lived in Helensburgh, a wood engraver, etcher and painter who studied at the Glasgow School of Art, under Greiffenhagen and Forrester Wilson and at the Slade School of Fine Art under Henry Tonks and Wilson Steer. She moved to St Andrews and became first President of the Art Committee of that town.

The present members of the family living in Helensburgh are: **Mrs Marion Watson**, a granddaughter of Dr Robert Kidston FRS, and a cousin of William Kidston, a noted paleobotanist who lived in Stirling. Mrs Watson has lived all her life in the town and has been and is on many local committees and synods; and **Mrs Penny Johnston** daughter of Dick Kidston.

The Cramb Family
Jenny Sanders

John Stuart Ltd

John Cramb

The Cramb family whose origins were in Crieff came to live in Larch Villa, 67 Colquhoun Street by way of Dundee, Glasgow and Gourock. The head of the family of seven was David Cramb, a retired leather merchant who had run a large shoemaker's business and had been closely identified with the Chartist movement.

Of the six sons and one daughter, Helensburgh owes much to John Cramb, the fourth son and to his sister Susannah, youngest of the family.

The first professional studies in daguerrotype photography were produced in the 1840s at the same time as John was developing his aptitude for photography in Dundee. By 1859 'Cramb Brothers' were 'photographers to Her Majesty' at 67 West Nile Street, Glasgow where John Cramb described himself as 'Professor of Penmanship'. William Collins & Sons, publishers, commissioned John to visit Syria and the Holy Land to photograph places of interest for Collins' illustrated Bibles and other publications. It was on his return that John's interest in public affairs manifested itself in service on Glasgow City Parochial Board and other institutions.

After coming to Helensburgh in 1868 John played an active part in municipal affairs for almost twenty years as a member of the Parochial Board and of the Police Commission. He was an advocate of the station at the pier; under his supervision the Ballevoulin water scheme was introduced to the Burgh; a local hospital was erected and equipped while he was 'convener of Local Authority'. When the Roads and Bridges Bill was before Parliament he was mainly instrumental in obtaining amendments which prevented burghs such as Helensburgh being taxed along with the county and secured for them the control of the highways within their bounds. As a member of the first School Board of the Parish of Row John Cramb took a deep interest in education.

The family had moved to Hermitage House, later The Hermitage, by 1879 when John was describing himself as a 'Property Agent', significant in terms of the sale of ground at The Hermitage to allow for the building of Hermitage School, formally opened in 1880. The building of Prince Albert Terrace in Victoria Road capitalized on another portion of the ground. However the story goes that Susannah Cramb was being courted by the young man from 'across the road' in Lansdowne House. He is supposed to have jilted her and consequently Prince Albert Terrace was built facing north as an act of revenge; Lansdowne House would have been overlooked, its occupants would have lost their privacy, and their view towards the Clyde would have been blocked!

Donald Fullarton

Instead of facing south for the sun Prince Albert Terrace looks north across Victoria Road – does this add credence to the tale of the Crambs' revenge?

John was no stranger to controversy, successfully leading the group against building a public hall next to the Municipal Buildings. The account of his part in this reveals the affection in which he was held, while telling us of the tenacity contained in a body 'housed in such a frail tabernacle that you might expect that it would burst its bonds at any moment so as to roam o'er the trackless fields of air "uncribbed, uncabined, and unconfined".' He had risen from his sick bed on that occasion, his constitution had never been strong and he died on 31st May 1894 at the age of 69.

Duncan, the last of the brothers, died in 1900 leaving Susannah as sole survivor of the family. She had cared for John throughout his final illness and was obviously devoted to him. Now she was in a position to pay tribute in a practical way and this she did when she gave to Hermitage School ground for a playing field, bounded by Grant Street and East Argyle Street and fronted by ornate wrought iron gates under the name Cramb Park. Owing to ill health Miss Cramb was unable to open the park in person. The plaque commemorating the gift can still be seen to the right of its original position and bearing the inscription:

> This Park was presented by Miss Susannah Cramb
> to the School Board of the Parish of Row
> 15 May AD 1909 in memory of her brother
> John Cramb Esq. of the Hermitage
> a member of the Board from 1873 to 1879

Susannah died on 13th May 1911. She endowed a music scholarship at the University of Glasgow and left money to St Bride's and Hermitage Schools, at the latter 'to provide bursaries, medals and prizes' for 'the scholar who had proved most efficient each year'. This continues in the form of the Cramb Medal which has been awarded since 1912.

The owners of Hermitage House and the grounds remaining were 'representatives of the late Miss Cramb' and in 1911 gave the town the option of purchasing the house and grounds. Dr Ewing Hunter, a councillor, was largely responsible for the layout of the grounds as a park and for the choice of flowering shrubs and trees, the Wishing Well and the bandstand. Between the wars the house was used as a day nursery and as an Annexe to the School until the opening in 1926 of the new Primary School building (which still stands behind the modern Hermitage Primary School).

Andrew Buchanan
Alistair McIntyre

Helensburgh & Gareloch Times

Andrew Buchanan

Known affectionately as 'Sweetie' Buchanan, Andrew Buchanan was a great benefactor and good friend to the people of Helensburgh. Born in Glasgow in 1869, the 'Sweetie' association stemmed from the fact that the family ran the business of John Buchanan and Brothers, manufacturing confectioners, and he was to be associated with the firm for most of his working life, rising to become company chairman in 1941. After various changes, the business continues today in Greenock as Buchanan's of Scotland Ltd, but without any family connection.

In 1922 he was the sole survivor of the Loch Maree Tragedy, where all the others in a fishing party died from botulism poisoning caused by contaminated potted cold meat in their picnic.

The move to Helensburgh took place before World War I, with Dean House, 5 East Abercromby Street, becoming home for the rest of Buchanan's life. Elected to the town council in 1925, he donated a gold chain and other regalia to the Provost and Bailies the following year, along with finely carved oak chairs. In 1929 there came the gift of the outdoor swimming pool at the pierhead to the town – probably the main act of generosity for which he is still remembered today. It was to continue in use until 1977, one year after the opening of the indoor swimming pool, and many in the town have fond memories of it – despite the often chilly temperature of the salt water! The paddling pool was built the year after that on the seashore immediately in front of the Henry Bell Monument at the foot of James Street, once again at his expense.

Buchanan became Provost of Helensburgh in 1930, in which capacity he remained until 1936. During this time he continued to benefit the town, for example through the refurbishment of the Victoria Halls in 1935, to celebrate the silver jubilee of King George V. He also paid for repair work to the footpath section of the Old Luss Road.

Apart from his work on behalf of the town council and his

commitments to the family business, Buchanan was involved with a host of other activities. Some of his time was spent on various trade and industry bodies at regional and national level, but quite apart from that, his range of interests was truly astonishing. A staunch supporter of the temperance cause, he was connected to the Glasgow Abstainers' Union for most of his life, becoming Chairman in 1928. He was Vice-President of the Helensburgh and Gareloch Horticultural Society, President of Helensburgh Swimming Club, Chairman of Helensburgh and District Nursing Association and was involved with the Buchanan Society, the Glasgow-Dunbartonshire Benevolent Society and the Glasgow-Kilmun Convalescent Society. He represented the burgh for six years on Dumbarton County Council.

A liberal in politics, he was President of Dunbartonshire Liberal Association. He was a follower of the Congregational Church. As if all that were not enough, Buchanan also found time for angling, and indeed represented Scotland internationally at competitions on Loch Leven, Loch Lomond, Loch Maree and other places.

Andrew Buchanan died at Dean House in April 1952 at the age of eighty-three. He was survived by his wife, a son and a daughter, and was interred at Faslane Cemetery.

The Anderson and Templeton Families
William FT Anderson

James Templeton, originally from Kintyre, was an East India merchant and sugar planter in Georgetown, Demerara, British Guiana (now Guyana). His wife, Susan Trimingham, came from St John's, Newfoundland, Canada. They came back to Scotland and to Helensburgh in 1869 chartering a boat to transport their young family and household. They soon became established at Drumgarve, 51 John Street. Drumgarve had been the name of the Templeton farm in Kintyre. More children were born in Helensburgh and the roll-call of the family was Annie, Susie, Agnes, James, Lizzie, John, Archie, Frances, Rosa and Ralph. Only Annie married. After the parents died the rest of the brothers and sisters continued to live at Drumgarve until the last survivor, Frances, died in the late 1940s.

William Anderson about 1898

John Stuart Ltd

They were a cultured, lively and liberally minded family. Rosa Templeton was a noted watercolourist. Frances was an embroiderer who trained at the Glasgow School of Art. She was a member of the Leek Embroidery Society in Staffordshire which was associated with William Morris. Examples of her works have been exhibited at and belong to the Victoria and Albert Museum in London.

Annie Templeton (1858-1928) married William Anderson (1854-1928). He was a silk throwster in Glasgow and involved in other businesses. He was one of the first directors of the Girls School Company of which St Bride's School was part and was also on the Larchfield School board. He was Colonel of the Renfrew and Dunbartonshire Artillery Volunteers and Provost of Helensburgh (1898-1902).

William and Annie had three daughters, Mary, Frank and Annie (otherwise known as Nance) and two sons, John and Kenneth. Their house, Inistore at 76 John Street, was redesigned by William Leiper and is now known as Glen Kin. Mary died young. Frank married a Newfoundlander and lived in St John's. John and Nance moved to a house at 58 James Street which they renamed Inistore. John and Kenneth were both involved in the Anderson family silk business. John was chairman of the Larchfield School board of governors.

Nance lived in Helensburgh all her life and was an influential and public-spirited person. She was educated at St Bride's and after reading geography at Oxford (before the days when they allowed women to take a degree!) and after Froebel Teacher Training at Bedford she returned to teach at St Bride's for a time. She was a Brownie leader establishing one of the first packs, if not the first pack, in Helensburgh in 1920. She produced regularly during the 1930s for the Helensburgh Amateur Dramatic Society (her casts including the future Poets Laureate, WH Auden and C Day Lewis). She served on the Burgh Council from 1939 to 1967. She was chairman of the Library Committee and a member of the Vale of Leven Hospital Board and was the first woman Bailie in the town. She received the MBE in 1941 in recognition of her work with the Women's Voluntary Service. Her sister, Frank, had received the MBE for war work in Helensburgh during World War I.

When the last of the Templetons died, the Anderson family gave Drumgarve to Helensburgh as its first public library. The Templeton Library in John Street continued in use until 1998 when its modern replacement was eventually built. The retirement houses built in the garden remain today.

Nance was closely connected with the Helensburgh Art Club, latterly as Honorary President, and had a fine collection of pictures of Helensburgh and District including among them some by the Glasgow Boys and their associates and other well-known Scottish artists. In accordance with her wishes this collection has been kept together for Helensburgh. The Trust which owns them also has a small purchase fund, the income from which is used to add to this collection from time to time. Selections from the collection are regularly exhibited in the new Library. The trustees include Kenneth Anderson's sons, Dr John Anderson (a retired GP who lives near Cambridge), William Francis Templeton Anderson (a solicitor in Falkirk), and one of Kenneth Anderson's grandsons, Jim Anderson, who is a professional artist.

The interest of the Templeton and Anderson family in Helensburgh dating from 1869 thus continues. •

230

CHAPTER 18
The Famous and the Infamous

In 1997 Leslie Maxwell's 'Eye on Millig' column in the *Helensburgh Advertiser* started to produce a 'Hall of Fame' of Helensburgh residents past and present. Needless to say it was a long list!

The problem for the editors of this book has been to decide who to include and who to omit. We decided that to be included, firstly, an individual had to be dead. Secondly, he or she must either have been born in Helensburgh or have lived here for at least five years. Lastly, the individual should be reasonably well-known – a nice subjective criterion! And if all this were not enough, we added the rider that 'the editor's decision is final'!

Consequently, of course, many who did appear in the 'Hall of Fame' are omitted. Notable examples are the two future Poets Laureate who briefly taught at Larchfield School (and are mentioned in Chapters 6 and 17), and the large numbers of players from Rangers Football Club who chose to stay in the town from the late 1980s onwards.

The Murder of John Arrol
Stewart Noble

In the late eighteenth century the schoolteacher was one of the very few educated people in an area. It was therefore common to find that the schoolteacher often took on other work which required higher levels of literacy and numeracy. John Arrol, the school master of Row, was just such a man.

In the year of 1759, and already into his fifties, he was not only session clerk of Row Church (and probably also its precentor) but he also occupied the very honourable position of banker to the neighbourhood. There only were three banks in Scotland in those days and they confined their activities to the larger towns. Not only did he look after the savings of the people, but he also lent money out at interest when he saw a safe opportunity to do so. Unfortunately not all borrowers could be relied on to repay their debts promptly and in full.

John Arrol had lent money to a resident of Dumbarton called

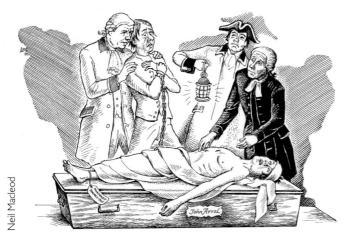

Neil Macleod

The touching of
John Arrol's corpse

Cunningham and was owed £30 by him – a considerable sum in those days. Having previously given notice that he wished the money to be repaid, and having heard unfavourable reports of Cunningham, John Arrol started off one day in January 1760 to Dumbarton to collect the debt. He got there safely, was seen by many people in the company of Cunningham during the day, but failed to return home that night. Within a few days the alarm was raised and the inhabitants of Row en masse scoured the countryside for him, all to no avail. Three weeks later the body of the murdered schoolmaster was found floating in the River Leven near Dumbarton Castle. A knife wound, probably straight into the heart, was the cause of death; no money nor valuables were to be found on the body, which had obviously been fairly recently placed in the river as the inside of his pockets were dry. He was buried in Dumbarton Parish Kirkyard, and legend had it that no grass would grow on his grave.

From the very first Cunningham was suspected of the murder, but there was no evidence against him. However in these days it was believed that if the murderer merely touched the body of his victim, the wound would bleed. Cunningham was given the opportunity of proving his innocence, but on the advice of his friends he declined to undertake the test, not because they feared for his innocence, but because it was also believed that the body would bleed if touched by a man who had shaved on a Sunday! To try to overcome this objection, the Rev Mr Freebairn, the Minister of Dumbarton Parish, offered to touch the body, having previously admitted that he had shaved on a Sunday. At Mr Freebairn's touch the body did not bleed. Consequently it was suggested once more to Cunningham that he could prove himself innocent by touching the body, but he resolutely declined.

There the matter lay for many years until Cunningham on his deathbed confessed that he was the murderer. He had repaid the £30 to John Arrol and got a receipt for it, but then stabbed him. He rifled the body and then he hid it up a disused chimney in his house where, shortly after, it was discovered by his servant girl. She received such a shock that she went raving mad. He had later carried the corpse off to the river one pitch black night. 'Having made that revelation, he breathed his last, and went to where he had to give an account of the deeds done in the body.'

'Yesterday's heroes of mine'
Personal Memories of Jack Buchanan
Jimmy Logan

Jack Buchanan with Anna Neagle in *Street Singer's Serenade* around 1935

1890 was a momentous year. In France an unknown Dutch painter called van Gogh died after shooting himself in the chest. The critics said he had only sold one painting and an article in the *Mercure de France* suggested that one day his mystical and original art might become fashionable, although it seemed unlikely then. The Forth Bridge was completed, described by the poet and artist William Morris as 'the supremest specimen of all ugliness'. New York introduced a new form of capital punishment: the electric chair.

In 1890 Queen Victoria agreed to the East African border being redrawn to give Germany Mount Kilimanjaro. Victoria was anxious for this, as her grandson, Wilhelm the Kaiser, had no mountain in Africa!

And in Helensburgh a baby was born on 2nd April; he was to become an international star of stage, screen and records, and a giant of the entertainment world on both sides of the Atlantic. He was called Jack Buchanan.

Jack Buchanan's early years at Larchfield School in Helensburgh were shared with the son of the minister, John Logie Baird, and they remained friends all their lives. Later Jack became a director of the Baird Television Company and introduced Logie Baird to the press in 1926 when Logie Baird gave the first public demonstration of this new medium, television. Buchanan was on the roof of the building in Soho with his school friend and took part in the first Logie Baird television transmission across the Atlantic, and after the War when Logie Baird died he made all the legal arrangements for Mrs Baird to receive a pension from the company.

When Jack's father died Jack's mother moved to Glasgow and opened a boarding house to make a living but she made sure Jack had a good education and it was at Glasgow Academy he acquired the polish that stayed with him through life.

In search of a career he went to London in 1912 and made various appearances in revue as he seemed to have a flair for comedy. A leading man, who was over six feet tall, could dance and sing, and could understand laughter was a rare commodity and by 1917 he was appearing in films and on stage in the leading revues in the top London theatres. He starred in various plays and musicals but by 1922 he made his first appearance in a play where he was also part of the management and in 1924 after a successful season in London he starred with Gertrude Lawrence at the Times Square Theatre on Broadway in New York in the 'André Charlot Revue'.

He was now the toast of London and New York and in time owned three British theatres and built what was to become the Leicester Square Theatre. In the 1930s he decided to make his own films and established his own studio making over forty films starring artists like Maurice Chevalier and a very young Anna Neagle and at the same time presenting and appearing on stage in many revues and plays and in his lifetime making at least 120 recordings with many hit songs.

For years the back page of the London telephone directory carried only two words: Jack Buchanan. He spent a great deal of time travelling and was a regular at least three times a year on the Cunard liners.

After World War II, in 1949 he returned to America and when the press met the great British star and his new bride Suzzie they were invited to his suite on board the *Caronia*. What they did not know was in the hold of the ship was Jack Buchanan's Rolls Royce and by the time he left the ship with the American press there was the Rolls with his driver waiting for him on the dockside.

Jack Buchanan always wore a pearl grey trilby hat and was regarded by those who did not know as the perfect Englishman! He had a great warmth and personality that could 'charm the birds off the trees'. He was very proud of his Scottish birth returning to Arran for holidays and when he died a book of poems by Robert Burns was at the side of his bed.

I was brought up to believe that if I could look like Jack Buchanan and sing like Harry Lauder I might make a name for myself and the day came when I met my two heroes. The opening night of Scottish Television in 1956 was a nerve-wracking occasion for all who took part. I was appearing with Stanley Baxter and singers and dancers of the 'Five Past Eight' revue and in one of the sketches we were Teddy Boys, far removed from the immaculate appearance in top hat and tails of Jack Buchanan. I met Jack's wife Suzzie and she was needing help. Jack's valet had only packed three buttons for his evening dress waistcoat instead of four and the wardrobe was not yet organised. 'What are the buttons like?' I asked and she said, 'About the size of a gent's fly button.' So I tore off a button from my Teddy Boy's flies and so Jack Buchanan appeared with the assistance of a Teddy Boy's fly button! In 1953 Jack had starred with Fred Astaire and Cyd Charisse in the Hollywood film *The Band Waggon* singing such hits as 'By Myself', 'I Guess I'll Have To Change My Plan', and 'That's Entertainment'.

When he came off stage at the STV opening show I did not realise he was ill and in pain. He stopped at the foot of the stairs and asked me, 'When are you coming to London, Jimmy?' I said, 'not for another three months as I am in 'Five Past Eight' till then.' He said, 'Come to my theatre, the Garrick, and ask for me and we will go out for dinner.' I could not believe that I would be seen in London with one of the greatest stars of the theatre.

It was not to be because Jack Buchanan died on 21st October 1957. Later on when I went to London his wife said, 'Let's have that dinner Jack promised you.' I met her at their apartment and she showed me all the personal momentoes from his life and we went to dinner.

Donald Fullarton

38 West Argyle Street was known as *Westwood* when Jack Buchanan was born there. Today it is called *Garthland*

Two years later I received a parcel from her with Jack's kilt in the Buchanan tartan and a note saying, 'I am sure Jack would like this to return to the theatre and to Scotland.' Jack Buchanan's kilt is now part of the Logan Theatre Collection at Glasgow University along with many other items that I collected through the years that are a part of Scotland's theatre history.

I still think that there are two school pals, 'ghosts of the past', going round Helensburgh, one always remembered by family and friends as neat and tidy and the other with his head in the clouds and the appearance of one who had been drawn through a hedge backwards. Each man makes his mark in the book of life and these school pals are part of our great history that is Helensburgh and Scotland.

Postscript by Stewart Noble.

Jimmy Logan was a very busy man and I was therefore delighted when he decided to accept my request to write a piece on Jack Buchanan. The subject obviously appealed to him, because he sent his script to me within a matter of weeks. The above piece was all Jimmy Logan's own work, and it is certainly not for me to amend it, particularly now that Jimmy is dead. However there were one or two small gaps that I wanted to see filled, so hence this postscript.

Jack Buchanan was born and brought up in 38 West Argyle Street in Helensburgh, close to the birthplace and home of John Logie Baird. When Jack was twelve his father died and for financial reasons his mother was forced to move to Glasgow. Jack Buchanan became one of the most highly paid entertainers of his time, and Jimmy Logan recounted how Jack normally gave his leading lady a diamond bracelet on the opening night of a new performance.

Jimmy Logan writes of Jack Buchanan's friendship with John Logie Baird, and he tells how Jack Buchanan arranged a pension for Baird's widow. However that was not the whole story as he also personally helped Baird by investing heavily in his last company, John Logie Baird Ltd. The company produced high quality television sets between 1946 and 1948 and at Jack's suggestion the models were named after London theatres: the Adelphi, the Lyric and the Garrick. After 1948 the company came under new ownership, but the new owners continued to pay Margaret Baird's pension. The Baird family today acknowledge that without Jack Buchanan's help, they would have faced a life of severe financial hardship.

AJ Cronin – The Man behind Dr Finlay
Stewart Noble

AJ Cronin
from a painting by
Stephen Conroy

One of the most successful BBC Television and Radio series produced in the 1960s was Doctor Finlay's Casebook, and its popularity was so great that Scottish Television revived the series thirty years later. The programmes were based upon stories written by a man who was born in Cardross and who spent part of his childhood in Helensburgh: Dr AJ Cronin.

Archibald Joseph Cronin was born at 'Rosebank', a cottage to the west of Cardross on 19 July 1896. His father was an Irish Catholic whose parents owned a public house in Bridge Street, Alexandria. His mother, Jessie, was the daughter of a staunch Presbyterian, Archibald Montgomerie, who owned a hat shop at 145 High Street, Dumbarton. A 'mixed marriage' such as this across the religious divide was highly unusual in those days and children born of such a marriage often had a difficult childhood. Archibald, the only child of the marriage, was no exception. His parents moved to Helensburgh and set up home at 7 Prince Albert Terrace. He attended Grant Street School, known as the Ragged School because many of its pupils were the children of poor Irish immigrants who had come to Scotland to escape the dire economic situation in their homeland. He hated his Helensburgh school days and desperately longed to mix with the children of the better-off Presbyterian community, but because of his background he was not accepted. He became a lonely and unhappy child.

Unfortunately his father died young, and so he and his mother left Helensburgh and she went to live with her parents in Dumbarton. However initially his grandparents refused to allow young Archibald to live under their roof, and he was sent to live with relations of his father. After a change of heart his grandparents eventually allowed him to live in their home with his mother, but no love was shown to the boy and he had to cope with being transferred from the strong Catholic influence of his father's relations into the staunch Presbyterianism of his mother's family.

Jessie Cronin herself was a remarkable woman. Firstly, it had been courageous of her to embark on a marriage across the religious divide. Secondly, she later became the first female public health visitor employed by Glasgow Corporation, an achievement at a time when women were expected to remain in the home.

Rosebank, Cardross, Cronin's birthplace

Archibald's grandparents made it possible for him to attend Dumbarton Academy, despite continuing to show little affection. At his new school he quickly became a star pupil, as well as being a good athlete and footballer. However his fellow pupils gave him the nickname 'The Wee Pope' and he thoroughly disliked this. After leaving school he became a medical student at the University of Glasgow, but before he could complete his studies he had a period of war service as a Surgeon Sub-Lieutenant in the Royal Navy. He finally graduated with honours in 1919, thus repaying his mother for her years of sacrifice. He then worked in South Wales, at least one medical practice in Scotland, Bellahouston and Lightburn Hospitals in Glasgow, and as a medical inspector of mines. He eventually became a doctor in 1925. He married a fellow medical graduate, Agnes Mary Gibson and they had three sons.

Between 1926 and 1930 he had a practice in London's famous Harley Street, but when he needed complete rest after an illness he went to Dalchenna Farm near Inveraray. There he wrote his most famous novel, *Hatter's Castle*, published in 1931. The Hatter of the title, James Brodie, was obviously based on Cronin's grandfather. It was a powerful tale of life in a Presbyterian family and became an instant bestseller. However the success of the book had one negative effect – it completely finished the relationship between grandfather and grandson.

Following the success of *Hatter's Castle* Cronin decided that a career in writing was to his liking, and so he gave up medicine. His books sold well and he produced several in rapid succession. *The Citadel* was based on his own experiences as a young doctor in a mining village in Wales, and *The Stars Look Down* was also set against the same background. In an autobiographical novel, *The Song of Sixpence* (1964) a fictitious family called the Carrolls even moved into 7 Prince Albert Terrace in Helensburgh! He wrote that 'there existed an air of *tone* which mother immediately liked, father ignored and which at first intimidated me'. He was also one of the first writers to cash in on the lucrative world of films.

The character of Dr Finlay of Tannochbrae was made into a popular TV series by the BBC. It ran from 1961 until 1967 and the episodes were based on characters from his *Adventures in Two Worlds*. However Cronin was upset when other writers were brought in to work on new plots for his characters. He demanded that the series be brought to an end and it was only when he was made to realise how greatly loved his characters had become that he relented and allowed the production to go ahead. In 1993 Scottish Television made a further series of *Doctor Finlay*.

His successes as a writer made Cronin into one of the world's millionaires and, to avoid the high taxation payable in Britain at that time, he emigrated to Switzerland. Once there he became increasingly reclusive and so little of his later life is public knowledge. He died there on 6 January 1981 at the age of 84. Thus ended the colourful life of a man who had been a pupil at Helensburgh's 'Ragged School', then an eminent Harley Street physician, and finally one of the best-loved writers in the world.

Sir James George Frazer OM
David Arthur

Sir James Frazer (1854-1941) may be counted as the father of modern anthropology. He was born in Glasgow at the corner of Blythswood Square, but left when young, perhaps because the trial of Madeleine Smith brought notoriety to Blythswood Square! His parents moved to Helensburgh, where he was brought up at Glenlea, 16 East Argyle Street. He was educated first at Larchfield and then Glasgow University, and then went on to read classics at Cambridge and became a Fellow of Trinity College where he read, but never practised, law.

He became interested in comparative religions from which stemmed his massive work – twelve volumes in all – entitled *The Golden Bough*, published between 1911 and 1915. He brought together a wide range of cultures and practices in which he saw a progression from magical, through religious to scientific thoughts and beliefs. He strongly influenced major writers and thinkers such as DH Lawrence, TS Eliot and Ezra Pound. While much of his thinking is nowadays discarded, he remains a major milestone figure in anthropology. He became Professor of Anthropology at Liverpool University in 1907, was knighted in 1914 and was awarded the high honour of the Order of Merit in 1925.

Andrew Bonar Law
Prime Minister of Great Britain, October 1922 – May 1923
Joe Craig

Andrew Bonar Law was born in New Brunswick, Canada in 1858. His father was the Rev James Law, a Presbyterian Minister from an Ulster farming background. Andrew was the youngest of four sons. His mother, Eliza Ann Kidston, died when he was two years old. Her sister, Miss Janet Kidston, came to New Brunswick to keep house for the Laws. They were daughters of William Kidston of Halifax, Nova Scotia who had left his father's firm in Glasgow in 1810 and returned to Canada where he had joined his grandfather's firm of merchants and shipowners. When Bonar Law's father remarried in 1870, Janet returned to Scotland and brought Bonar, aged twelve, with her for upbringing and education by his relatives who lived in Helensburgh.

Bonar Law first attended Gilbertfield House School in Hamilton where he was 1st in Greek (1873) in the junior class, then to Glasgow High School, where he was again 1st in his class in French (1874). One of the houses in the High School is still named after him. He left school at sixteen and after an undistinguished period at Glasgow University, joined the Kidston family business, a firm of merchant bankers specialising in the financing of trade in iron and steel. In 1885 the firm merged with the Clydesdale Bank in which Bonar Law became a Director. With financial help from his Kidston cousins he bought a partnership in William Jacks, Glasgow Iron Merchants and Traders, who acted as factors between the manufacturers of the raw metal and the users. In the next fifteen years Bonar Law made the firm extremely profitable and he himself became a man of property.

Andrew Bonar Law

Neil Macleod

He joined the Glasgow Parliamentary Debating Association and so impressed the Conservative and Liberal Unionist Association that they made him their Parliamentary candidate for the Glasgow Blackfriars ward. In 1900 he won the election and became an MP at the age of 42. Winston Churchill was also elected at that time.

Bonar Law began to make his mark and was appointed Secretary to the Board of Trade. At the next election (1906) he lost his seat in Glasgow but was within months re-elected at a by-election in Dulwich.

The early days of the twentieth century were a time of internal divisions within the Conservative party. Under Balfour, the party had lost three general elections. In late 1911, Balfour resigned as leader and Bonar Law was elected as the new leader. He was a compromise candidate after the leading contenders, Austin Chamberlain and Walter Long, withdrew to allow him to be elected unanimously on 13th November.

Because of the early setbacks in World War I, including the need for military conscription and the futility of the Dardanelles campaign, a coalition government was formed in 1915 and Herbert Asquith appointed Bonar Law Secretary of State for the Colonies and a member of the War Committee. When, after some political intrigues, Asquith resigned on 5th December 1916, King George V asked Bonar Law to form a government but he declined because he felt that David Lloyd George was the right man for the job, and so Lloyd George became Prime Minister forthwith. In the new coalition, Bonar Law was leader of the House of Commons and Chancellor of the Exchequer.

Kintillo, home of Prime Minister Andrew Bonar Law

Donald Fullarton

In January 1919, by which time he was the MP for Glasgow Central, he resigned the Chancellorship in exchange for the office of Lord Privy Seal. He also remained leader of the Commons until March 1921, when he was forced to resign due to ill health.

In October 1922, David Lloyd George was forced to resign as Prime Minister by the Conservative party, and the coalition government was dead. The King, on the recommendation of Lloyd George, asked Bonar Law to come out of retirement and form a new Government, which he only agreed to do if he had again been elected Conservative party leader. This the party – peers, MPs and candidates – did on 23rd October.

On 16th November 1922, the Tories ruled Britain again after winning an election with an overall majority of 75. The Liberals were badly beaten but Labour more than doubled their MPs to 147 and became the main opposition. A new Labour group called 'The Red Clydesiders' emerged. Churchill lost his seat. Bonar Law became Prime Minister.

On 21st May 1923, Bonar Law resigned on being told that he had incurable throat cancer. Although a lifelong abstainer from alcohol, he was a heavy smoker of cigars and a pipe, which may have contributed to his condition. Stanley Baldwin succeeded him. Five months later Andrew Bonar Law died on 30th October 1923. In his will he expressed the wish to be buried beside his wife in Helensburgh. However, the family were persuaded to allow his ashes to be buried in Westminster Abbey.

After the ceremony, Asquith is reported to have said, 'It is fitting that we should have the Unknown Prime Minister by the side of the Unknown Soldier.' It is endemic in the game of party politics to demean or discredit the opposition. The players accept this as part of the game but sometimes the mud sticks into history and distorts the true facts. Bonar Law was a man without vanity and such a comment from Asquith would not have bothered him. His consuming passion was the unity of his party. He is reported to have stated in 1922, that keeping the party united was more important than winning the next election. It is due to him that the Conservatives came through the crises of World War I and its subsequent aftermath as a united party. The Liberals were not so fortunate.

Bonar Law had a phenomenal memory, a very quick grasp of the factors involved in debate and the ability to articulate the issues in a clear and unambiguous way. He was a trusted leader who could be relied upon to listen to his peers and unite the party behind the agreed policies. He would compromise his own convictions if necessary for the sake of the Party and the country.

Andrew Bonar Law spent nearly forty years in Helensburgh. His first home was Seabank with his aunt Janet Kidston at 40 East Clyde Street (opposite the foot of Grant Street). This house has been demolished and there is a small football pitch and a scout hall on the site now. At thirty he established his own bachelor household. His aunt gave him Seabank and she retired to Partick, his sister Mary coming to keep house for him. It was shortly after he acquired Seabank that at the age of 32 he married Annie Pitcairn Robley in 1891. They had four sons and two daughters. James (1893) and Annie (1895) were born there. The other four children were born after the family moved to Kintillo, West Stafford Street, (now entered at and addressed as 34 and 36 Suffolk Street): Charles (1897), Harrington (1899), Richard (1901) and Catherine (1905). Only a few years later, Bonar Law's wife Annie died in 1909 shortly after he had sold Kintillo and gone to London, and his sister Mary again took charge of his household.

Charles became a 2nd Lieutenant in the 2nd battalion of the Kings Own Scottish Borderers and was killed in action at the second battle of Gaza in April 1917. James died in September 1917 when he was reported missing after an air action whilst serving in France with the 60th Squadron of the Royal Flying Corps. Their youngest son followed his father into politics as MP for South-West Hull and later became Lord Coleraine.

Bonar Law was a member of the first committee of the Helensburgh Golf Club in 1893. The club has in its archives a membership list from 1922 which includes Bonar Law with his address as 10 Downing Street, London. His membership is well recognised in the Golf Club's Centenary book (published in 1993), and he was also one of the founders of Helensburgh Lawn Tennis Club. He also enjoyed billiards and had William Leiper add a billiard room to Kintillo but his greatest love was perhaps chess.

There is a magnificent headstone in the Helensburgh Cemetery in memory of the Bonar Law family; it stands against the North Wall. There is a Bonar Law Avenue named after him off West Clyde Street in the Ferniegair estate, which stands on the site of the demolished house of that name owned by his Kidston cousins and where he had lived with them when he first came to Helensburgh.

From boyhood, he became a member of the West United Free Church – now the West Kirk of Helensburgh. He was a Sunday school teacher and it was there that he had his first experience of public speaking. Perhaps the finest local memorial to Bonar and Annie Law is in the back gallery of the West Kirk. It is a five-light stained glass window with a carved stone inscription at the base and a long carved wooden bench below. The window is the work of Oscar Paterson. It was installed and dedicated when the church was restored after being destroyed by fire in 1924. Stanley Baldwin unveiled the memorial window. As a matter of course every Prime Minister has his portrait painted and hung in 10 Downing Street; this stained glass window is believed to be the only other memorial to him in Britain. However the National Portrait Gallery of London commissioned Sir James Guthrie, then living in Rhu, to paint a life-size group of Statesmen from the Great War in which appear, among others, Winston Churchill, Lloyd George and Bonar Law.

Jimmy Logan OBE
Stewart Noble

Jimmy Logan

Jimmy Logan's connections with Helensburgh go back even to the time before he was born, as it was in Helensburgh that his parents, Jack Short and May Dalziel, met each other. They formed a successful show business partnership and it was natural that Jimmy would follow in their footsteps. Jimmy was born as James Allan Short but after entering show business he took on the name of Jim Logan – it became Jimmy later – because, in his own words, 'my father soon decided it wasn't a good idea to have the same name as him because the audience wouldn't think they were getting their money's worth' and it was later under the name of Jimmy Logan that he was subsequently known to everyone. Over the years he became, in the words of his obituary writers, 'a consummate performer and inspiration to many entertainers' (*The Herald*) and 'a gentleman, a very generous man, and one of Helensburgh's best loved residents' (*Helensburgh Advertiser*).

Jimmy was born in Glasgow on 4 April 1928 – the same year as Mickey Mouse, as he pointed out – and he first appeared on stage at the age of twelve, although his career in the theatre actually started at the age of seven – during holidays he would sell programmes, chocolates and cigarettes at his father's summer show in Northern Ireland. He left school at fourteen with no qualifications, but already certain that his future lay in the world of entertainment. His belief in himself was justified as his natural flair for comedy was so great that by the age of nineteen he was principal comedian at the Metropole Theatre in Stockwell Street, Glasgow. His career instantly blossomed and he shortly started a ten year run in the famous 'Five Past Eight' show at the Alhambra Theatre in Glasgow. He also appeared on the first night of Scottish Television in 1956. Although he was principally known as a comedian and entertainer in his earlier days, he nevertheless showed his abilities as a dramatic actor in his first film *Floodtide* at the age of twenty-one.

The trappings of success followed rapidly and while in his twenties he was living in a wing of Culzean Castle, had his own Rolls-Royce with personalised number plate, and flew his own plane. It seemed that nothing could go wrong. But it did.

He wanted to be not just an actor, but an actor-manager, in the best old traditions of the theatre. Consequently in 1964 he bought the old

Empress Theatre at St George's Cross in Glasgow, refurbished it and renamed it the Metropole, having paid £80,000 for it. He knew that the theatre itself would probably lose money, but he believed that by building a complex of bars and restaurants with entertainment on the plot next door, he could subsidise the losses of the theatre. However planning permission was refused for this and over the years the Metropole ran at a loss. Finally in 1973 the bank pegged his overdraft at £170,000 and so he had to close the theatre. In his own words 'my responsibilities to the building and my debts were destined to crush me for another decade.' His first marriage of twenty-one years standing had already failed in 1969, and he believed that his financial problems played a large part in the failure of his second marriage. Consequently at the age of forty-nine he now also lost his home and all that he owned. As a result, for the next two years he slept on the settee in his father's one-bedroom flat in Ibrox, and hung his clothes on the back of the upright piano.

Tigh na Mara, Jimmy Logan's East Clyde Street home

Donald Fullarton

However, typically, Jimmy Logan bounced back. He was making more and more of a name for himself as a serious actor, and he even wrote and performed in a one-man play on Sir Harry Lauder, one of his great heroes. But even then, life was not always kind to him.

At the age of twenty he had married a dancer, Grace Pagan. When that marriage was dissolved in 1969 he then married a world famous fashion designer, Gina Fratini; this marriage lasted eight years. In 1985 he married Pamela Donald and the following year twins were born. Jimmy was delighted as he believed them to be his first children and three years later the family moved to part of 152 East Clyde Street in Helensburgh. However this marriage too broke up when Pamela walked out taking the twins who Jimmy adored. Worse was to follow. During the subsequent divorce Pamela insisted on DNA tests which eventually revealed that Jimmy was not the biological father of the twins. Jimmy was distraught, but with typical courage bounced back, helped by his sister the famous jazz singer, Annie Ross, who flew over from the USA to be with him for several months. He was also helped by sympathetic neighbours, especially Angela Mackenzie who lived in the east wing of the house; she later became his driver and dresser during his continuing career. The separation meant selling his house, a move to East Princes Street in 1990 and disposing of his wonderful collection of Harry Lauder memorabilia. This loss was a gain for the University of Glasgow and the people of Scotland as these items now form part of the Logan Theatre Collection in the University Library, thanks to the MacFarlane Trust. In 1993 his divorce was completed, he survived a quadruple heart bypass, and then to the delight of his friends married Angela and enjoyed eight years of happy life together. Typically of Jimmy he continued to cherish 'his' now distant twins.

Jimmy continued to raise money for charity; Erskine Hospital was a favourite because he had been so impressed with the treatment which his father had received there when he had had to have a leg amputated. Jimmy's career had taken him to the Albert Hall in London and to the Carnegie Hall in New York; but he still continued to take part in his real love, pantomime. Latterly he performed regularly at the Pitlochry Festival Theatre, one summer revelling in performing three very different plays on successive nights. In 1988 the Royal Scottish Academy of Music and Drama made him a Fellow and, as a consequence, in his own words 'in a way I became respectable'! In 1994 he was granted the honorary degree of Doctor of Letters by the Glasgow Caledonian University and then in 1996 he was awarded the OBE. When Helensburgh Heritage Trust was set up the same year, he became its first Honorary President, and as such contributed a piece on Jack Buchanan, another of his great heroes, for this book.

It was while performing at the Pitlochry Festival Theatre in the summer of 2000 that he learnt that he had incurable cancer. Typically he carried on acting until the end of the season before making the news public. In March 2001 Scotland's show business stars led a stage spectacular, 'A Celebration for Jimmy Logan', in his honour at Glasgow's Pavilion Theatre; it was sold out even before the box office opened! During this event he made his last appearance on stage. Jimmy set up the Jimmy Logan for Cancer Trust to deal with the £30,000 raised by the occasion. He began the arrangements to produce video tapes to be made available to newly diagnosed cancer sufferers to console them, but he died on Good Friday, 13 April 2001 in the HCI Hospital in Clydebank. The following Thursday a memorial service was held for him in Glasgow Cathedral - once again he had a packed house. And during the service he was given a round of applause because Billy Connolly (who was inspired to take up entertainment by watching Jimmy) believed it was more appropriate than a minute's silence!

In 1998 he produced his bestselling autobiography aptly entitled *It's A Funny Life*.

Dr Fordyce Messer and the Rhu Coach Tragedy
Alistair McIntyre

Dr Messer is best remembered today for his connection with the tragic and mysterious disappearance of his coachman, coach and horse on a dark winter's evening at Rhu. But as we shall see, he was a memorable figure in his own right.

Born in Portobello in 1841 the young Messer studied at Edinburgh University before launching out as a general practitioner in Penicuik.

The Rhu Coach Tragedy

Neil Macleod

The move to Helensburgh took place around 1874, when he was appointed to take over from Dr Skene, who had been struck down by a fatal illness. Dr Messer rapidly established himself as a highly popular and proficient family doctor. An account by another doctor refers to him as 'having a magnetic personality. . . being kind and persuasive rather than overbearing, with the power to instil into the minds of his patients an essentially hopeful outlook.' Such a style had enabled him to build up a large following 'who indeed were mostly content to accept him at his own valuation.'

The fateful event for which Messer is remembered took place on the evening of Monday 22nd November 1886. Called out to a case at Rosneath, the doctor had been deposited by his coachman, Andrew Carson, at Rhu Point, where he was to be ferried to the Rosneath side. This was about 8pm, and Carson was instructed to wait at Rhu Inn, and return to the Point for 10.30pm. According to a contemporary newspaper report, Carson in fact went instead to Clifton Villa, where he collected his brother and his brother's wife, and they all proceeded to the Rhu Inn. After a refreshment there Carson returned to drop the others off before he returned to Rhu. There he spoke to several people, who revealed that he seemed sober, before returning to Rhu Point for the 10.30pm rendezvous.

Around that time, the ferryman and the Rosneath constable noticed that the carriage lights had suddenly gone out, while a plunging sound was also audible. However, on landing at the Point and finding no trace of coach or coachman, they assumed that Carson had for whatever reason decided to drive off. The two then returned to the other side of the Loch to collect the doctor.

On his return to Rhu Point, Messer also concluded that Carson had gone away, but inquiries soon revealed that he was nowhere to be

The 'Mesopotamian Devils' leer down across William Street at the rectory of St Michael and All Angels Church

Neil Macleod

found. Subsequent examination of the scene of the disappearance showed by the tracks of the coach that it had apparently turned round several times well out on the Spit, where the bank shelved away quickly into very deep water. Next day no fewer than twenty boats were engaged in dragging and searching the area, but without result.

On different days of the following week the driving box of the coach and the coachman's hat were picked up from the shore at Kilcreggan while on 22nd December, a carriage seat was retrieved from the shore at the Cloch Lighthouse near Gourock. Other than that, no trace was ever found, except that fifteen years after the tragedy, the skeleton of a horse with bits of harness attached was washed up on the foreshore at Blairvadach.

Dr Messer was held in such high esteem that the community subsequently presented him with a new horse and brougham (coach), although the whole episode must have affected him deeply. Throughout the period of his employment as a doctor in Helensburgh, Messer resided at Craigellachie, 9 William Street. The house in question is notable for two red, grotesque, animal-like figures, which surmount the roof-line and which appear to be leering across the street at St Michael's Church on the other side. These 'Mesopotamian Devils' (to give them their official name) were almost certainly erected by Dr Messer although this cannot be substantiated by the title deeds of the house. The popular account is that Messer, a Roman Catholic, fell out with the Episcopalian rector, Rev John Stuart Sime, and set up the two figures both as a provocative gesture and to match the Church's gargoyles.

Whether or not the explanation is true it should not obscure the many positive qualities possessed by Messer. Apart from his work as a doctor, he was also an active member of the Artillery Volunteers, in which he rose to the rank of Major, being recalled as a very popular commander, greatly liked by his men. Again he served for a number of years as a member of the school board of the parish of Rhu, and was a strong advocate for the promotion of higher education. He also lectured to various organisations on a variety of topics such as geology and travel.

Owing to ill-health, Dr Messer was forced to retire from his practice in 1905, when he moved to Woodlands, Garelochhead. Such was the high regard in which he was held that a testimonial was organised at which the doctor was presented with two hundred sovereigns (£1 gold coins) along with a gold bracelet. Unfortunately Messer's health deteriorated such that after a few years he returned to Craigellachie which had evidently been retained in the family. After a long and painful illness he passed away in January 1911, being survived by his widow and a grown-up family. In conclusion, one thought. If Dr Messer did indeed erect the 'Devils' on his house opposite St Michael's Church, and if there is such a thing as Divine Retribution, then it would appear that the Almighty got the wrong man!

Neil Munro – novelist, poet and journalist

Catriona Malan

Neil Munro's sixty-seven years of life began on 3rd June 1863 in Inveraray and ended in Helensburgh, in whose east end he spent the last years of his life, until he died on 22nd December 1930. While a resident of the town, he lived in Cromalt, East Clyde Street, a fine house which was built in the eighteenth century. The fact of his illegitimate birth was hardly a rarity among the servant classes in Victorian times – rumour gives his father as a family member of the Duke of Argyll, while his mother, Ann Munro, was a kitchen maid in Inveraray and Neil himself was brought up a barefoot boy, speaking both Gaelic and English. However his inauspicious beginnings did not stop him from becoming an author of note and one of Helensburgh's most famous inhabitants. Nor did the fact that his education lasted only until he was aged thirteen.

Neil Munro

Neil Munro Society

He began his writing career as a journalist and he became assistant editor of the *Glasgow Evening News*. After four years he left journalism to dedicate himself for a dozen years or so to writing poetry, short stories and novels – it was about this time that he moved firstly to Gourock and then in 1918 to Helensburgh. In his historical novels such as *John Splendid* (1898) and *The New Road* (1914) he voiced, through the themes and characters, his own regrets that the influence of the South was altering the ways of life of the Gaelic-speaking North.

During this period he continued writing humorous stories for the *Evening News*, as author of 'The Looker-On' column, giving a light-hearted weekly social comment on the times. The sketches included the antics of Master Mariner Para Handy sailing his puffer, the *Vital Spark*, up and down the west coast of Scotland, along with his mate Dougie, Hurricane Jack and the rest of the crew. These characters first appeared in 1905. Munro had very little interest in the popularity of these humorous tales, and it was only after considerable persuasion from his newspaper colleagues and friends that he permitted them to appear in book form. Even so, they were published cheaply and under the pseudonym of Hugh Foulis, for fear of compromising his reputation as a serious author. Although the book became an instant bestseller in Glasgow and the West of Scotland, and although more humorous tales were to follow, Munro made it clear that he had no desire to encourage any wider circulation.

Cromalt, Neil Munro's Helensburgh home which he renamed after a burn in his beloved Inveraray

Donald Fullarton

It was only later when the stories were retold on radio, film and television that they reached a wider audience. His characters in these, possibly his most accessible and best-loved stories, were to be immortalised by such actors as Roddy McMillan, John Grieve, Duncan Macrae, Rikki Fulton, Gregor Fisher and Angus Rennie. There never was a *Vital Spark* and its part was played in the 1990s by the puffer *Auld Reekie*.

The best-known of his other short stories introduced Erchie and Jimmy Swan. However he always played down his humorous writings, hoping that he would be recognised as a major writer of historical novels – indeed in his lifetime he was regarded as the successor to Sir Walter Scott. Sadly, for many years since his death the opposite has been true, although recently his historical novels have been enjoying a revival.

Perhaps it was the loss of his son, Hugh, during World War I, that curtailed his enthusiasm for writing, for he returned to journalism again now as editor of the *Evening News* and wrote little else. Although there is nothing to commemorate him in Helensburgh – he was buried in Inveraray – a monument to Neil Munro can be seen in Glen Aray, between Inveraray and Loch Awe and a plaque is on the wall of his birthplace at Crombies Land in Inveraray.

This is how he wrote of Helensburgh in his book *The Clyde*:

> There is a certain air – not strictly speaking hauteur, let us call it dignity or self-respect – about Helensburgh which makes it stand aloof from the vulgar competition of the other coast towns for popular recognition. And although the burgh is, in a generous sense, a suburb of Glasgow, it is in secret communicable relation with the wild.

That is how he viewed us – we should remember him with respect and affection, and perhaps a little awe.

Rev AE Robertson

Neil Macleod

Archibald Eneas Robertson MA, BD (1870-1958)
– the first 'Munro-Bagger'
Pat Mitchell

Archie Robertson was born in Helensburgh on 3rd July 1870 and brought up at Parkhill, 7 Kings Crescent (which is now Barbreck, 1 Granville Street). Details of his childhood are difficult to follow, but he and his two brothers did attend Miss L Nichol's Ladies School, a boarding school at Kintyre Villa, Charlotte Street. However by the 1881 Census only he remained – his father had died shortly beforehand and his two brothers were no longer recorded as living in Scotland, while his mother was in Glasgow. He was educated at Glasgow Academy and Glasgow University where he obtained his MA degree in Natural Philosophy (Mathematics and Physics) under Professor Sir William Thompson (later to become Lord Kelvin).

Although Robertson had climbed Ben Cruachan 'with some other lads' in 1889, it was to be nearly a year before he became a devoted mountaineer after his ascent of Glencoe's Bidean nam Bian in company with experts: 'This day showed me the delights of scientific mountaineering – the use of maps, aneroid, compass, etc – and ever since that day I have steadily pursued the Quest.' Four years later he commenced his first walking and climbing tour, well-equipped even to his aneroid barometer-cum-altimeter obtained for him by his former professor, Lord Kelvin. The instrument was 'especially suited for checking the heights of the Scottish bens' if used intelligently. Now an heirloom, it is handed down to each new President of the Scottish Mountaineering Club.

At the end of that year he became a member of the Scottish Mountaineering Club. From its inception in 1889 there had been debate as to how many mountains there actually were in Scotland. Hugh T Munro, an Alpinist, was entrusted with the task of compiling a list of Scottish mountains of 3,000 feet (914.4 metres) or higher but went a step further, that of identifying those he judged to be separate mountains and those which he regarded as being subsidiary tops, using arcane criteria of dip, distance and difficulty. He used one inch and six inch to the mile Ordnance Maps of 1870 vintage, much inferior to those available nowadays, so it was an immense task, completed in 1891 with the publication of Munro's Tables. These listed 538 tops of 3,000 feet or higher, of which there stood out 283 he had classified as being separate mountains. Archie Robertson coined the name 'Munro' for these, but although he climbed extensively, sometimes during SMC meets, it was to be several years before he developed an ambition to do them all, but not necessarily climb the subsidiary tops as well. Munro, on the other hand, eager to check the validity of his tables, steadily visited all but three of his 538 'tops' until first illness, then death, sadly intervened, but not before he became Sir Hugh T Munro, a hereditary baronet.

In 1892 Robertson began to study Divinity at New College in Edinburgh and graduated in 1896. By 1898, having climbed a large proportion of the Munros, he realised that by sustaining his efforts it might be possible to complete (or 'bag') the lot, within two or three years.

Despite the absence of tarmacadam roads there were some advantages in those days: shepherds' and keepers' cottages on tracks leading into the hills; hirings of pony and trap; lifts on mail carts; passengers on goods trains; rowing boats saving long detours; but most importantly the readiness of the cottagers to put him up, where there was great mutual respect. At a later stage he used a bicycle when it was advantageous. He mostly climbed solo, but sometimes had companions, including his cousin Kate McFarlan whom he married in 1900.

In 1901, accompanied by Kate and an old friend, Sandy Moncrieff, he completed his last Munro, Meall Dearg on the Aonach Eagach ridge on the north flank of Glencoe. On attaining the summit they broached a bottle of champagne, then 'Sandy made me first kiss the cairn and then my wife!' Some may find it difficult to imagine today that by 1939 only eight had completed the Munros, whereas now some two thousand have managed this feat.

Robertson continued to climb for many years after this. Kate died in the mid 1930s, but after her death he married Winifred Dorothy Hutchison who accompanied him on many a climbing trip until he became enfeebled with old age. He became Vice-President and Honorary Fellow of the Royal Scottish Geographical Society, Chairman of the Scottish Rights of Way Society, President of the Scottish Mountaineering Club, and was elected a Fellow of the Royal Society of Edinburgh.

He died at his home in Edinburgh on 22nd June 1958. Winifred presented his aneroid to the President of the Scottish Mountaineering Club. It had survived his only mountain accident when, in a blizzard and thunderstorm on Ben Nevis, he had gone over the edge and was battered unconscious, bleeding profusely. Not seeking help, he walked six miles to Fort William where a doctor put twenty stitches into his scalp wounds. Not one to make a fuss, his diary recorded: 'April 5th, 1905. Left Imperial Hotel Fort William at 9.05 for Ben Nevis via path. Struck by lightning about 1 on ridge of corrie overlooking Glen Nevis. Got home at 4.15. Dr MacArthur dressed my head for 2 hours. 20 stitches! Temperature about 1 degree above normal at 10pm.'

Madeleine Smith

Pierre Emile L'Angelier

Neil Macleod

Madeleine Smith – Murderess?

Joe Craig

Madeleine Smith was tried for the murder of her lover, Pierre Emile L'Angelier. The trial began on 30th June 1857 at the High Court in Edinburgh and finished on 9th July. The jury returned a verdict of 'Not Proven' – a uniquely Scots Law verdict, which some say is a finding of innocence with a caution not to do it again!

Madeleine was born in Glasgow in 1835. Her father, James Smith, became an architect of distinction and Madeleine was the eldest of five children. James Smith designed and built the country house at Rhu (then known as Row) called Rowaleyn in which the family, like many wealthy Glaswegians, lived during the summer months. The house stands at the top of Glenarn Road and is known today as Invergare.

Pierre Emile L'Angelier was born in Jersey, also the eldest of a family of five. The family owned a seed shop, and Emile came to work in a nursery in Edinburgh. He became restless however, and after sojourns back home and to Paris and Dundee, he eventually settled in Glasgow. Although born and brought up a Roman Catholic, he joined St Jude's Episcopal Church at 278 West George Street (now transformed into the Malmaison Hotel) and was found lodgings by the Rev Charles Miles at the home of the Curator of the Royal Botanic Gardens.

When Emile first saw Madeleine, he was immediately smitten. He was well aware that he was attractive to women and resolved to somehow make the acquaintance of Madeleine in spite of the social chasm that divided them. When they eventually met, Emile's French flair and flamboyant style obviously captivated Madeleine, and from that brief encounter began a series of clandestine meetings. Madeleine was only nineteen when she wrote the first letter to Emile. It was written from Rowaleyn and expresses the charming walks which would be better enjoyed in his company although she stipulated that he must not turn up at Rowaleyn.

THE FAMOUS & THE INFAMOUS

251

Her next letter reveals that someone had reported to her father that they had seen them together and that he was very angry. A Scottish Victorian father was akin to God in the family and his word was law. Despite this, an increasingly passionate exchange of letters took place and they became secretly engaged. Eventually 'Mimi' (her pet name in their correspondence) confronted her father and family at Rowaleyn, and declared her love for Emile and her desire to marry him. Madeleine was left in no doubt that such a match was totally out of the question. She was forced to give her word of honour that she would have no more communication with Emile.

However the letters began again and meetings took place in the Smith home at India Street in Glasgow and at Rowaleyn, and it was at Rowaleyn that they first had sex together in the early summer. Her subsequent letter relating to the encounter was graphic enough for the Judge at the trial to forbid its being read aloud. To the modern reader, this may be hard to understand.

Meanwhile James Smith's business prospered and the family moved to 7 Blythswood Square, Glasgow. A business friend of Madeleine's father was William Minnoch and he came to be regarded as a possible suitor for the wayward daughter. Emile was jealous of the Minnoch presence but was robustly reassured by 'Mimi' that he was her only love, until at the end of January some sign of strain appeared in Madeleine's letters.

On 28th January 1857, Minnoch proposed and Madeleine accepted. A few days later she wrote to Emile breaking off the engagement with him (not mentioning Minnoch) and begging that he, as an honourable gentleman, return her letters. Emile, enraged at such a sudden change of attitude, sent her a note that has not survived. In a very frightened reply, Madeleine begs him not to send her letters to 'Papa'. Emile replies to her letter – there is no record again of this, but from her reply, it could be interpreted that Emile either intended to blackmail her or, in his hurt, to disgrace and humiliate her. Her reply is a lengthy grovelling appeal for pity and forgiveness and an attempt to justify her change of heart. She begged for a meeting and that seems to have taken place and some normality in their discussions was restored.

Exchanges of letters and meetings continued. On 22nd February prior to one meeting, as the records of Murdoch Brothers in Sauchiehall Street showed, Madeleine bought some arsenic. Emile had an attack of illness afterwards. His health was not all that good, with periodic attacks of stomach disorders. However, at the trial later, conclusions would be drawn from circumstantial evidence.

On 6th March, Madeleine with a friend, visited a druggist, John Currie in Sauchiehall Street, purchasing an ounce (27 grams) of arsenic 'to kill rats'. If the intention was to poison her lover it is perhaps surprising that these purchases were made so openly. On the other

Rowaleyn, Rhu

Donald Fullarton

hand, she still wrote affectionately to Emile, even a day after confirming her engagement to William Minnoch and setting the month of June for the wedding. Emile meanwhile when entertaining various friends on a short leave from work was making oblique remarks about being poisoned.

On Monday 23rd March Emile arrived home at 2.30am, obviously sick, and his landlady sought immediate medical help. When the doctor arrived for the second time at 10.30am he found that Emile L'Angelier was dead. There were immediate suspicions as to the cause of his death, but despite these he was buried three days later, on Thursday 26th March, in an unmarked grave in the Ramshorn Church at 98 Ingram Street, Glasgow. On the morning of his funeral Madeleine fled on an early steamer from Glasgow, heading for Rhu. William Minnoch arrived that morning at the Smith household to find it in a state of uproar at Madeleine's disappearance. He learnt then for the first time of Emile's death and believed that the reason for Madeleine's flight had been shock at hearing the news.

Along with Madeleine's brother, Jack, he therefore took the train from Glasgow to Greenock and then the steamer to Helensburgh. Madeleine turned out to be on board it already and they disembarked at Helensburgh where they hired a coach. They paid a brief visit to Rowaleyn and then returned in the coach to Glasgow. Some have suspected that the purpose of her journey was to destroy evidence at Rowaleyn.

After the post-mortem, Madeleine was interviewed and signed a long statement which included a denial of having administered arsenic to Emile. The arsenic she purchased, she said, was mainly used by her for a cosmetic. Meantime the medical investigations had been continuing, and finally Emile's body was exhumed on 31st March, and on the same day Madeleine was arrested by the Procurator-Fiscal in Glasgow and taken to prison.

Rumours began to spread in the streets, and in the class culture of the day the 'have nots' were making sure through the strongly expressed public voice that the 'haves' would not be allowed to cover up this crime. Throughout it all, Madeleine remained cool, calm and composed and her family staunchly supported her

The trial was conducted under the spotlight of intense national and international interest. After the jury returned a verdict of 'not proven', loud applause rang out within the Court, and outside the uproar was also loud with people shouting and dancing. Betting had been heavy on the outcome of the trial and that no doubt contributed to the ecstatic behaviour of some. The press had a field day for a long time after.

As for Madeleine, after an unsuccessful marriage and two children to George Wardle, a drawing teacher, in London, there was an amicable separation, and at the age of seventy she went to join her son in the United States. George Wardle having died by this time, she met and married a gentleman called Sheehy who predeceased her. The following year she was given legal notice to leave the United States as she was in danger of becoming a charge on public funds, but was eventually allowed to stay. Throughout her life she never commented on her trial, and she refused an offer from a Hollywood company to make a film of her life. She died in New York on 12th April 1928 at the age of ninety two, and her gravestone carries the name Lena Wardle Sheehy.

Modern researchers have revisited the evidence and cast some more doubt on the generally assumed guilt of Madeleine Smith. They point to the fact that Emile had sometimes spoken of suicide to his friends. He was blackmailing Madeleine and telling friends that she was poisoning him. On the day that Madeleine begged for her letters back, he started a diary with daily references that she was poisoning him.

The truth of the matter will never be known for certain.   •

CHAPTER 19

Out of the Past and into the Future
STEWART NOBLE

You can only predict things after they have happened.
Eugene Ionesco

*What all the wise men promised has not happened,
and what all the damn fools predicted has come to pass.*
Lord Melbourne

Never make predictions, particularly about the future.
(unknown)

Although this Valentine's postcard photo was taken in 1959 or 1960, it could easily have been from fifty or more years ago because little had changed over many years. However it can be precisely dated because the teenager on the left with his back to the camera is the author!

I came to live in Helensburgh for the first time in 1951 and apart from six years when I 'emigrated' to Edinburgh I have not left Helensburgh. In this chapter what I propose to do is give a snapshot of the town as I found it on my arrival and contrast this with the town as it is today, almost exactly fifty years later. As slightly more than a babe in arms fifty years ago I could certainly not have predicted the changes that would come to the town over this period, and I have no great faith that my predictions now will be of any great accuracy. Nevertheless, I do hope that readers in the future will find some interest in trends that are taking place at the beginning of the twenty first century and in seeing if these trends ever work out in the way predicted.

So, dear reader, I would ask you always to have one question in the back of your mind while you read this chapter: 'who would ever have expected things to work out this way?'

Size of The Burgh

The 1951 Census gives the population of the Burgh of Helensburgh as 8,760; no exactly comparable figure exists yet for 2001, but the 1991 Census gave a figure of 15,852 and there is unlikely to have been a substantial increase since then. Of course the boundaries today are not the same as they were fifty years ago – after all the Old Luss Road and Craigendoran Avenue marked the eastern extremities of the burgh – but the traveller would certainly notice differences coming to the town.

Arriving from Cardross only the estate of 1930s bungalows at Colgrain existed – there were green fields between the main road (not a dual carriageway in those days) and the West Highland Railway. Although building of the Kirkmichael estate by the town council had started in 1935, a wartime pause meant that much was not built until the late 1940s, with the flats at Nursery Street and Drumfork Court coming later. Within the town the big houses still had their big gardens – they had not yet been split up to accommodate one or more smaller modern houses, but some of the houses were already flatted.

Arriving from Loch Lomond, not long after passing the Walker's Rest Park one would find green fields on the left-hand side, where the estate accessed today through Sinclair Drive was built in the late 1950s. Millig Farm, still using horses as well as tractors for ploughing, occupied the land where the houses of the Glade Estate now stand, and the Clyde Arran Estate and the Churchill Estate were still many years in the future.

Leaving the town along West Clyde Street, Ferniegair House still stood immediately to the east of Cairndhu. Only the first half of the houses along Kidston Drive and the streets behind it had been built, and Ardencaple Castle was very visible on top of its cliff. The burgh boundary was reached after Dalmore House, but in those days only the big house itself was to be seen. No building had taken place behind the western half of Queen Street or at the west end of Queen Street – Woodend Farmhouse survives today, but all the surrounding fields have vanished.

It is interesting to note that almost all those developments took place prior to 1980. To a large extent the activities of the Green Belt Group (founded in 1990) have stopped geographical expansion of the town in recent years, and the limited growth in population latterly has therefore been due to more intensive use of the land within the town boundaries.

The Structure Plan produced by Argyll and Bute Council in 2001 predicts a 20 per cent growth in population over the next twenty years. This would be a major reversal of trends and will, I suspect, be firmly resisted as it must imply an encroachment on the jealously guarded Green Belt.

Even the view out into the Firth of Clyde is different! The wreck of the *Captayannis* lies in the middle of the estuary, and is visible at all states of the tide and from much of Helensburgh. She was Greek-owned and was bringing a cargo of sugar cane from Africa to the refinery in Greenock in January 1974. She dragged her anchor in a severe gale, but before she could get under way she collided with the anchor chain of a tanker which ripped a gaping hole in her side. She began to fill with water very quickly and settled on her port side, grounding on a sandbank. The cost of salvaging her was much greater than her insured value, and consequently no attempt has been made to raise her.

Transport

An incident in the 1950s provides a graphic example of how different transport in the past was from today. At that time there was a regular bus service from Helensburgh to Luss and one Saturday lunchtime in the early 1950s the bus's brakes failed on the way down Sinclair Street. In those days the only set of traffic lights in the town was outside the Municipal Buildings, and most shops closed over lunchtime on a Saturday – nowadays we have three sets of traffic lights on Sinclair Street and very few shops (if any) close over lunchtime on a Saturday. Furthermore, the pier car park at the foot of Sinclair Street had not yet been infilled.

The driver of the bus held his hand on the horn and, to avoid ending up on the beach, when he reached the foot of Sinclair Street he drove into the front of the Granary Restaurant (where the Clockworxs pub stands today, immediately opposite the Tourist Information Centre). He and his passengers escaped with slight injuries, no pedestrian was injured, and no other vehicle was damaged on his way out of control through the town centre. Given current levels of congestion, that could certainly not happen at lunchtime on a Saturday in 2002!

Car numbers round the town were beginning to increase from the 1950s, but for those who had to rely on public transport within the town Garelochhead Coach Services had a fleet of double-deckers, which also provided services up the Garelochside and round the Rosneath Peninsula on a road which was very much narrower and more twisting than it is now. Similarly there was also a regular coach service provided by Central SMT from Glasgow Street to Glasgow, but this time on a road which has scarcely changed between here and Dumbarton over the last fifty years! Today the bus service to Glasgow has just restarted after a gap of about twenty years. Garelochhead Minibuses and Wilson's of Rhu jointly provide the services up Garelochside and round the Rosneath Peninsula, but there are also many more taxis in the town.

On the railways there was only steam power, and a sound which I always associate with my childhood is that of steam trains on the West Highland Line skidding as they tried to make their way up the hill when rails were wet and slippery – indeed sometimes they had to split the train on the hill and take half of it to the Upper Station. For a young boy the West Highland Line also held the attraction of engines with names! The 'Glens' and the 'Lochs' were all running, as well as the

K4s with such names as *Lord of the Isles, Macleod of Macleod*, and *The Great Marquess.*

Beside the Helensburgh Central Station there was a substantial area of sidings and sheds where the Co-op supermarket and the medical centre now stand at the corner of Sinclair Street and East King Street. Furthermore, there was a siding diagonally across East Princes Street into the gasworks, and frequently East Princes Street was blocked by a train shunting coal wagons across there. Although Helensburgh Central Station is now looking much better after its recent refurbishment and the reglazing of its canopies, it misses out on the range of plants and hanging baskets that there used to be – it even won the prize for the Best Kept Station in 1932.

On the West Highland Railway, Helensburgh Upper and Craigendoran (Upper) both had not only passing places but also their attractive chalet-style station buildings. No trains stop at Craigendoran (Upper) any more and there is no sign of any building there either, while at Helensburgh Upper the buildings have disappeared and only one platform is in operation. The Upper Station was staffed by a station master, two signalmen and a boy. The station master's stone-built house still survives at 116 Sinclair Street, while immediately to the east of it at 32 Maclachlan Road stands the brick-built house put up for one of the signalmen, although now considerably extended. One of the duties of the station master was to shout out the station's name whenever a passenger train arrived, and I well remember him shouting 'Elllllllllns-brupper'! The 'Wee Arrochar' push and pull train went up and down several times a day from Craigendoran to Arrochar & Tarbet, providing a local passenger service. There was also a regular local goods train and it would drop off and pick up coal wagons from the sidings at Helensburgh Upper station (where the flats in Maclachlan Road stand today). A further regular goods service ran down the Faslane branch to pick up the steel from the ships which were being broken up there.

Perhaps I am tempting fate, but it seems to me that today we have a reliable and efficient electric train service to Glasgow, even although some of the trains are still the original electric units from 1959, albeit refurbished. The number of people using the train appears to be going up again, but there is no sign of any goods service returning to Helensburgh Central. On the other hand on the West Highland Line goods services also appear to be picking up, and several times a year steam trains pass through Helensburgh Upper on their way to provide locomotive power for the daily summer steam train service between Fort William and Mallaig. Both *Glen Douglas* and *The Great Marquess* have been preserved and the latter ran on the West Highland Line to mark its centenary.

Helensburgh Pier closed shortly after my arrival, largely because of insufficient depth at low tide. Craigendoran continued to provide a service with four steamers in summer and two in winter, and frequently Station Road at Craigendoran was crowded out with coaches meeting the steamers. Regular and special trains also called in at the pier platforms at Craigendoran to connect with the steamers, and continued to do so into the early years of the electric trains. In 1955 an adult could travel on all the Clyde steamers (except the MacBrayne service to Tarbert and Ardrishaig) for a whole week for just 45/- (£2.25p), and so excursions by ship were possible almost every day to such places as Ayr, Campeltown, Inveraray and Glasgow.

Today most of the timbers of Craigendoran Pier have fallen into the sea, and with winter gales can act as battering rams along the seafront in East Clyde Street. Part of the area has been infilled, and it all has a sad and desolate look now, compared to how it used to be. The owners of the pier have had plans to convert the area into a water sports centre, but a huge injection of cash will be required. Helensburgh Pier continues to receive small ferries however, and in 1998 a winter service started, operated on behalf of Strathclyde Transport by Clyde Marine Motoring of Greenock.

However the restoration in 1975 of the *Waverley* by the Waverley Steam Navigation Company as 'the last sea-going paddle steamer in the world' (despite the fact that six others were sailing on the Clyde alone in 1951) coincided with the dredging of Helensburgh Pier and consequently the *Waverley* is now a frequent visitor once more during the summer. As her maiden voyage was in 1947, she is now more than fifty years old, but recent refurbishments have meant that she should continue to sail for many years yet.

In the days before jet aeroplane travel, transatlantic liners used to call at the Tail of the Bank, when I arrived in Helensburgh in 1951, but they disappeared just a few years later. However in the last few years there has been a steady increase in cruise ship business at Greenock, and many Helensburgh residents and businesses look enviously across the water thinking about the business which is not coming their way. A plan was produced in 2000 to build an extremely long extension to Helensburgh Pier so that it would stretch right out into deep water where cruise ships could come alongside. One suspects that such a venture would only be profitable if the number of ships calling at Greenock reached saturation point, and this is probably many, many years in the future, even if global warming does not rule out the whole idea totally.

However probably the most controversial transport issue facing Helensburgh today ironically does not concern the use of transport. Rather it concerns what to do with the transport when it is not in use! The issue in question is parking. In 1951 the infilled area beside the pierhead was still many years away, but the pressure on parking space over the years ensured that this infill started to take place in 1967, although in winter it is far from ideal because a large proportion of it can be under water during storms! However the increase in car ownership has meant that the demand for parking is becoming ever greater. In 1999 Argyll and Bute Council introduced parking charges in the majority of off-street car parks, almost entirely as a revenue-raising exercise. The Council's motivation was the cause of their lack of success – the correct use of parking charges is to ensure the best possible use of on-road and off-road space by vehicles. The Council's failure to realise this meant that the car parks became deserted and on-street parking spread beyond the town centre.

At the time of writing various remedies have been suggested. However many are coming to believe that parking problems cannot be tackled in isolation, but must be considered as part of an overall plan for Helensburgh.

Shopping

Fifty years ago there were many more small privately-owned shops in the town than there are today. In fact in 2001 the only shop in the bottom two blocks of Sinclair Street which was still there was CG Reid Ltd, the ironmonger at No 8, although it had changed out of all recognition. However in 2002 it was sold and became Wright's Home Hardware. The arrival of the supermarkets largely brought about the demise of the small shops.

Probably the first supermarket to arrive in the town was William Low's (now Tesco) at 23 Sinclair Street. It took over the space previously occupied by Spy's coalyard! However this transformation of the main shopping area was not unique to Helensburgh.

Butchers, grocers and other shopkeepers would frequently make home deliveries, although by 1951 the age of the delivery boy on his bicycle was dying out. With the arrival of supermarkets home deliveries died out completely, with the exception of milk and newspapers which still continue to be delivered to some houses. However over the last five years the supermarkets themselves have started home deliveries again.

Across Sinclair Street from the first supermarket another major change took place. Waldie's Garage, the biggest in the town, was accessed through a pend at 32-34 Sinclair Street, with a ramp to the upper section. The business today belongs to Arnold Clark Ltd with a frontage at 15 East Clyde Street where there was previously a row of tenements. However the main garage workshops in behind the showroom are still those of Waldie's, although the petrol pumps through the pend have long since gone. RB Steel & Company's furniture showroom and removals business occupies much of the original Waldie premises.

The vigilance with which the green belt has been protected has ensured no out of town shopping in the Helensburgh area. The principal 'brown field' site in the town was the old railway sidings and sheds at the corner of Sinclair Street and East King Street and a large new supermarket was built there, owned by the Co-op since 2000. However over the years many Helensburgh people have felt that supermarkets as far away as Dumbarton and Clydebank offered a better selection, to a large extent because they were even bigger. And where people do their main supermarket shop, many may also tend to do their other shopping. All of this (it is argued) has been to the detriment of Helensburgh where smaller shops have been closing down and have been replaced by either public houses or charity shops.

The only other major shopping development in the town centre has been the south side of Colquhoun Square, and round the corner into West Princes Street. In 1951 the Tower Cinema occupied the south-east corner of the square, but it was badly damaged by a storm in 1968 and closed a few days later. Munro and Pender's Garage occupied the south-west corner of the square, while the stretch of West Princes Street which was redeveloped was occupied by an old tenement with shops underneath and gardens behind. The development took place in two phases in the 1980s. However although major for Helensburgh, it was a development of small shops and offices, with flats above them.

Thus although almost all the old business names have disappeared from the town centre over the last fifty years, the actual buildings themselves are on the whole much as they were half a century ago.

The absence of space in the town centre has meant that supermarket operators have cast their eyes elsewhere in their bid to stop spending leaking out of the town – and of course to earn profit for themselves! The first to come up with an innovative proposal was the Co-op when in 1994 they proposed a substantial further infill at the foot of Sinclair Street but as a consequence of great public opposition to their ideas their planning application was rejected. In 1999 two new proposals emerged. Luss Estates and Glenmorison jointly proposed a large supermarket between the pierhead and Clockworxs pub, with a new swimming pool and leisure centre being built to the west side of the Clyde Community Education Centre (formerly Clyde Street School) as planning gain – however many regard the whole concept of 'planning gain' as simply a euphemism for a bribe which is on offer so that the unacceptable becomes accepted. Palisade Properties proposed a large supermarket at Colgrain, but with the redevelopment of the Pierhead area as 'planning gain'. Both proposals have major consequences for other businesses within the town and for traffic movements.

Against all this shopping on the internet is only just starting and it may be that in another fifty years the need for people to go shopping every week for their household necessities will have almost entirely disappeared.

As when the North British Railway Company proposed extending its line through Helensburgh Town Centre down on to the pier in 1877, opinion within the town appears almost equally divided. Once again, as with the parking problem, many are claiming that the whole issue of shopping can only be decided within the context of an overall plan for the town centre.

Outside Working Hours

When King George VI died in 1952 my father almost immediately decided that he wished to watch the forthcoming great spectacle of the Coronation on a television set. He got one from Small and MacDonald's, 61 Sinclair Street, and was told there that we were probably about the twelfth household in Helensburgh to own a television set. In those days it was easy to spot who had one, because the the aerials were about the size of an armchair!

All this is a bit ironic because John Logie Baird, the inventor of television, was born in Helensburgh and gave his first public demonstration of television in London in 1926. However, it is a good example of what life in Helensburgh was like in those days. There were of course also no mobile phones – in fact to make a telephone call in Helensburgh prior to 1966 one had to lift the phone and wait until someone at the telephone exchange asked you for the number which you wished to call – and it could be a long wait! There were also no personal computers and in fact during 1951 the world's first commercial computer became functional at Manchester University. And lastly there were no video recordings, despite the fact that like television this was an invention of John Logie Baird.

When Scottish Television was started in 1956, it could not be received in Helensburgh at first, and finally arrived the following year. Likewise, when colour television broadcasts started in 1967 a freak signal meant that those living in the upper half of the town could unexpectedly receive it; those living in the lower half of the town had to wait until the mid 1970s when changes were made to the Rosneath mast. Even the siting of the mast was not simple because the engineers discovered that the strength of their signal varied depending on whether it was high or low tide!

So what did people do in those days?

Some sports were already well-established. There was, of course, only the outdoor swimming pool – which was supposedly heated! So swimming was therefore only a summer pastime. The New Year Day's swim used to take place at the pier until it was moved to Rhu Marina in 1984 when the pier steps finally became too dangerous. And despite the highly polluted waters of the Clyde at that time, there was a swimming race from Craigendoran Pier to Helensburgh Pier every summer until 1972.

Winters were also much colder in those days (and also less wet and windy) and hence skating was a regular occurrence. The Council used to charge for admission to the skating pond at the top of the hill, and they even issued season tickets. If the ice was bearing for more than a fortnight, it was worthwhile taking the gamble of buying a season ticket! In 1947 and 1963 the winters were so cold that Loch Lomond was frozen solid and it was possible to skate on the Loch for several weeks – in 1963 I skated from Duck Bay to Balloch Pier and back again. Because of all this skating there was a roaring trade in second-hand skates largely conducted by Macneur & Bryden's shop immediately opposite the station entrance at 16 East Princes Street. This firm also produced the *Helensburgh & Gareloch Times*. Like many other newspapers in that era it carried only advertisements and public notices on the front page until 1961, when news was permitted. The *Helensburgh Advertiser* started in 1957 and the *Helensburgh & Gareloch Times* was eventually closed at the end of 1980, just a few months short of its centenary.

Although the 1968 hurricane badly damaged the Tower Cinema it continued to show films for about two more weeks, albeit with half the seats closed off! Newly engaged at the time, the author remembers taking his fiancée to see *Bonnie and Clyde* in the usable half of the cinema

The rugby club was not founded until 1963, and likewise the Naval rugby pitches at Duchess Wood were also many years away. Helensburgh Sailing Club was only starting in 1951, initially just racing off the pier.

For those who were of a more sedentary nature there were the two local cinemas. The Tower in Colquhoun Square (the bigger of the two) was closed in 1968. The La Scala at the foot of James Street was split up in the 1970s, but the cinema portion was closed in 1984. The other portion continued to offer snooker and gaming machines for about six more years, but since then it has stood unused.

Church-going was also much more common then than it is today, and many of the churches had an evening service as well as the morning one. Evidence of the decline in church-going can be seen from the closure of churches – the Old Parish Church, of which only the tower remains, was at the foot of Sinclair Street; where St Bride's Church stood at the south-east corner of West King Street and John Street there is now a block of flats and the library. On the other hand, the First Church of Christ, Scientist at 138-144 West Princes Street was built only in 1956. The decline in church-going in Helensburgh is similar to that in other British towns, and the trend for closure of churches seems likely to continue.

The reverse side of this coin is the proliferation of shops opening on Sundays. In 1951 this was unheard of, yet despite the fact that research has shown that Sunday opening does not lead to more spending by consumers, more and more shops are opening on Sundays. To the astonishment of some, there are even people today who regard shopping as a leisure activity rather a necessary evil!

Helensburgh had in those days the wide range of clubs and societies which it still has today, but as with most other towns and villages then more entertainment took place in the home. More people could also play a musical instrument then than now, and people probably also read more. And in the evenings people went to bed earlier – on the basis that all decent folk were in bed by about eleven o'clock, all the street lights in Cardross were switched off at that hour until about 1964! By contrast, in Helensburgh in 2001 permission was given for the opening of a disco until three o'clock in the morning!

It is hard to resist the temptation to say that times were better then!

Despite this large number of clubs and societies, many Helensburgh residents nowadays fear that the Clyde Community Education Centre is proving too expensive to maintain and is hence threatened with closure. Likewise the Victoria Halls have been in need of substantial refurbishment, although some has been done by volunteers – an interesting sign of changing times! On the other hand, many young people in the town believe that there is nothing for them to do, and all ages argue that there is a requirement for better sports and leisure facilities. If one of the supermarket developments does go ahead, then there is hope that one or more of these problems might be addressed by way of planning gain.

Over the last fifty years the leisure options open to people have become wider, and it seems highly probable that this trend will continue, probably with increasing use of technology. On the other hand some smaller towns like Helensburgh have seen a return to the old ways with the reopening of the local cinema. As people become more affluent the demand for leisure is also likely to grow while people work fewer hours or take more holidays or both. It would not be difficult to draw up a wish list of new facilities for the town – for example a youth centre, an arts centre, an indoor sports arena or a heritage centre. However the days are past when one could expect a local authority both to provide and run such facilities. In the past a mix of local authority money and public subscription was used, probably the most recent example being the construction of the indoor swimming pool in 1976. It seems a method of financing facilities whose day is once more coming, particularly when coupled with planning gain.

Of course it will only be possible to provide any of these facilities if the perennial problem can be solved – the lack of available sites in Helensburgh. And once again this brings us round to the growing desire for an overall vision for the town.

Industry, Commerce and Employment

Despite the fact that Helensburgh was never an industrial town and has been home to many commuters, there have been changes over the last fifty years as far as industry and commerce is concerned. In 1951 there were more farms on the periphery of the town than today and they provided some employment. Prior to World War II the big houses had provided employment for many domestic servants and gardeners, but over the years bits of the gardens have been sold off and consequently many fewer now work as gardeners. Likewise the spread of labour-saving devices such as vacuum cleaners and washing machines into almost every home has meant that the demand for domestic servants has all but disappeared.

On the other hand however the increasing longevity of the elderly has led to an increase in the number of carers helping people in their own homes, and to quite a number of residential care and nursing homes in and around the town.

Within the town probably the largest employer in any way approaching manufacturing industry was Garvie's lemonade and fizzy drinks factory which was situated at 67 James Street, premises now occupied by RM Prow (Motors) Ltd. However about 1959 Garvie's decided to close their Helensburgh plant and concentrate all their production in Milngavie. Another significant employer in the area, but not in the town, was the shipbreaking business of Metal Industries at Faslane. The closure of the gasworks, the transfer of the railway depot to Yoker, and the closure of the steam laundry are all examples of areas where jobs have been lost over the years.

The biggest employers today are in the public sector, notably the naval bases at Faslane and Coulport, both of which employ civilians as well as naval personnel. Likewise, the many arms of local government also provide much work, although privatisation of some local government services has meant that some local government work is now actually carried out by private sector businesses.

Probably the largest single employer in Helensburgh today (other than the Co-op with its supermarket at the corner of East King Street and Sinclair Street, and its shops at 8-28 West Princes Street) is Derwent Information Ltd at 13 East King Street which currently has a workforce of about forty-five, largely engineering and science graduates with computer skills – and this of course is a type of business which did not exist fifty years ago! It is also important to note that a business such as this could be sited almost anywhere. Thus Helensburgh has gained from the presence of Derwent Information, but it has also lost when the computerisation of printing meant that the *Helensburgh Advertiser* was no longer printed locally; ironically Derwent Information now occupy the old printworks.

The Seven Ages of Man

When I arrived in the town in 1951 it was still possible to be born here. Braeholm Maternity Hospital at 31 East Montrose Street was the birthplace of many babies until its closure in 1989. At that point maternity facilities were transferred to the Vale of Leven Hospital in Alexandria and Braeholm lay derelict until in 1995 it was restored and today functions as the Aggie Weston Royal Sailors Rest.

Because the percentage of housewives out working was extremely low in those days, very few children had any form of education prior to going to primary school. When the big day came there were the Primary Department of the Hermitage School in East Argyle Street and Clyde Street School on East Clyde Street or, for Roman Catholic pupils, St Joseph's Primary at the north-east corner of West King Street and James Street (where Waverley Court stands today). Thereafter for secondary schooling it was once again the Hermitage School in East Argyle Street, but in the old Scots baronial building not dissimilar to the Victoria Halls which was demolished in 1967 and replaced by the new Hermitage Primary School. For private education boys went to Larchfield School until they reached secondary school age, but girls could have their entire education at St Bride's. The Larchfield School building at 37 Colquhoun Street is now private housing, while the St Bride's School building today forms part of Lomond School at 10 Stafford Street (although the front part of the original building was destroyed by fire in 1997 and rebuilt).

My acquaintance with the medical profession in Helensburgh happened extremely shortly after my arrival. We came to Helensburgh on a Friday in September 1951 and two days later, to get me out from under foot, my parents sent me out bramble-picking. On my way back home an accident occurred which resulted in a broken arm for me. Prior to coming to Helensburgh my parents had learnt that there was a Dr Noble in the town and, as he shared our surname, they reckoned he must be a good doctor!

Dr Jimmy Noble was one of a three-man practice, the other two being Dr John Harper and Dr Harold Scott, the senior partner. Their surgery was situated at 25 Colquhoun Square, and patients just turned up and waited for an appointment, and waited, and waited, and waited! Dr Scott occasionally saw patients in a surgery in his house in Glenan Gardens and, when in 1973 all the medical practices in the town combined and built a new surgery at 45 West Princes Street, the flats above it were named Scott Court in his memory. Since 1997 the surgery has been known as Scotcourt House (misspelt!) and occupied by Argyll and Bute Council as offices.

Then, as now, a trip to the doctor could of course also mean a trip to hospital and Helensburgh's hospital was the Victoria Infirmary in East King Street. Fifty years ago health services had been nationalised only recently. Inside the entrance to the Victoria Infirmary there are boards listing the names of benefactors and as a child I could never understand why the list came to an end in 1948! Operations were still carried out there until 1988, and when my appendix was removed there in 1954 I was somewhat disconcerted to find that the view from the window beside my bed was of a gate through to the graveyard next door – fortunately it did not seem to have been used for a while!

From 1951 there was also a second hospital on the periphery of the town at Camis Eskan House. In those days the scourge of tuberculosis (or 'consumption' as the Victorians called it) had not been cured. Cities were dirty, smoky places and it was felt that pure air could help sufferers of tuberculosis, and so hospitals such as Camis Eskan were provided. The use of BCG, streptomycin and the pasteurisation of milk led to the disappearance of TB, and so in the late 1950s Camis Eskan became an old folk's home, and then in 1979 it was converted back to private housing.

From the outside the Victoria Infirmary looks exactly the same now as it did fifty years ago. The gate through to the graveyard which the author could see so clearly from his bed after the removal of his appendix was immediately to the right of the building

Because of increasing longevity and because of Helensburgh's attractions for retired people there has been, as already pointed out, a steady growth in the number of homes catering for the elderly. The first of these was the Clydeview Eventide Home established by the Church of Scotland in 1953. It was originally entered from King's Crescent where a small number of modern houses now stand. The entrance today is at 12 East Montrose Street.

Improved health care has also led to an extremely active retirement for many people and the adult education courses which are available today were unheard of fifty years ago. Indeed the whole concept of a Community Education Centre was unknown then.

However death comes to us all eventually and, as the Cardross Crematorium was not built until 1960 in common with most crematoria in the West of Scotland, burial was the only option. Thus when John Logie Baird died in 1946 he was buried in the town's cemetery in Old Luss Road alongside his parents. Today Argyll and Bute Council wages an ongoing war against vandalism in the cemetery.

Local Government Administration

Fifty years ago many local services in Helensburgh were still provided by Helensburgh Town Council, although the most expensive service of all, education, was provided by Dunbartonshire County Council.

In 1951 the town was still largely run from the original municipal buildings plus its 1906 extension. Thus the town's one and only fire engine had its own garage in the extension where the Moss Pharmacy now stands at 52a Sinclair Street. Likewise, the police station stood just a few doors southwards of the fire station, and its entrance is still visible, complete with its name and two sets of handcuffs carved in the stone above the door!

The area outside the burgh boundary – for example Colgrain, most of Craigendoran, Glen Fruin, and Rhu and Shandon – was known as the landward area and this was under the care of Helensburgh District Council for whom Dunbartonshire County Council provided the services. To do this they used an office at 25 West King Street which still stands today and has the name 'Rhu Parish Council Chambers' carved in the stone above its entrance.

In the last fifty years we have had two reorganisations of local government. The pundits will tell us that small local authorities such as the old Helensburgh Town Council were inefficient and had other disadvantages. However against this it might be argued that the residents of the town had a better chance of knowing their councillors and their council officials then than they have today – although the town was of course smaller then. Nevertheless one also senses that an indefinable air of civic pride has disappeared.

What price another reform of local government in the next fifty years, perhaps even with a return to the burghs?

A Vision for The Future

So far in this chapter I have looked at what the town was like in 1951 and compared that with what it is like now. And I have asked you, the reader, continually to bear in mind the following question: 'who would have dreamt fifty years ago how things would have developed by 2001?'

In 1999 I attended a meeting where the guest speaker was George Harper, Director of Development and Environment Services for Argyll and Bute Council. He said that he felt when Argyll and Bute took over responsibility for Helensburgh that the town had a neglected appearance, particularly compared to the other large towns within Argyll and Bute such as Dunoon and Rothesay. Few in the town would disagree, and this has led to many calls recently for some form of overall plan, for a vision for the future.

Many feel that Helensburgh stands at something of a crossroads. Furthermore different people feel that it performs different functions – for example to some it is a commuter town, to others a town of retired people, for some a retail town and for others a navy town. Many feel that the town no longer looks as good as it once did, while others more bluntly say it is dying on its feet, at least as a shopping centre.

Yet a major problem in resolving all these feelings is that the town appears very split on the way forward. For example, some believe that the establishment of a supermarket at the pierhead would revitalise the town, while others believe that it would kill off the town's small shops and its aspirations for tourism – and given the establishment of Scotland's first National Park at Loch Lomond currently many feel that there are now even greater opportunities for Helensburgh to attract tourists. Another example concerns pedestrianisation of the town centre. Many feel that this would make the town a pleasant a place in which to shop, but the Helensburgh Independent Retailers Association are worried that it would drive business away .

Attempts to solve one problem can just lead to other problems elsewhere. For example if a supermarket were to be established at the Pierhead, already scarce parking spaces would be lost – so how could that be remedied? Some have suggested a park-and-ride scheme at Craigendoran, while others have suggested that the gasworks site in East Princes Street between Grant Street and Maitland Street could provide the answer.

Writers to the *Helensburgh Advertiser* often suggest that the Council

What elegant small boys wore to the swimming pool in 1953! Note particularly the corner of the rolled up towel just protruding from inside the author's coat (right). A professional street photographer who snapped passers-by at the corner of Colquhoun Street and West Clyde Street took this photo of Jock Troup and Stewart Noble. Despite this, they are still good friends and even became best man for one another

should do this, that or the other. Unfortunately the Council's abilities to follow their advice is often severely restricted in three ways: firstly, the Council does not own the property in question; secondly the Council must follow the correct legal planning procedures; and thirdly, the Council no longer has the money although some argue that Helensburgh is entitled to a larger share of the Council's spending.

Regrettably the crystal ball is probably even cloudier than ever! However let me just stick my neck out and make a few predictions – but I refuse to be tied down as to when, where or how these will come to pass!

Helensburgh will get another supermarket, simply because the town is too tempting a prospect for potential developers. The town centre will be pedestrianised, because it will give a more pleasant shopping environment. Parking charges will apply to both on-street and off-street parking, and consequently people who work in the town will become less inclined to bring their cars in and just leave them unused for the day. Sporting facilities will be improved because at the moment we seem to be slipping further and further behind other towns of a similar size. The green belt will be maintained substantially unaltered, largely because people are coming to value it more and more, and also because commuters nowadays appear to prefer to live in places such as Bearsden rather than Helensburgh if house prices are any guide. On the other hand this differential may force buyers to look more closely at Helensburgh in the future, and there are signs that it has been narrowing in the last few years.

Lastly, I predict that the latest reform of local government will last longer than the previous one did. However in about forty years time the idea will have been accepted that as a matter of civic pride it is better to have smaller towns like Helensburgh which are in control of their own affairs. Consequently there will be a return to the burghs and in 2052 the residents of the town will be able to celebrate 250 years of the burgh charter, when they once more have a burgh of their own.

And perhaps someone will do something about bringing this book up to date at the same time! •

Other Helensburghs

Stewart Noble

Because Scots are scattered around the globe it is not at all uncommon to find that they have taken their Scottish placenames with them – Falkland, Perth, Aberdeen, Calgary and Dallas are just a few examples. So far we have come across two other Helensburghs, one in Australia and the other in New Zealand. But quite how and why the names got to the Southern Hemisphere is a bit of a mystery.

Helensburgh, New South Wales, Australia is a smallish coal mining township south of Sydney and to the north of Wollongong. It is located about four kilometres inland and on top of a coastal escarpment, the rest of the City of Wollongong being approximately thirty kilometres of the coast and squashed into the flat parts up to one kilometre wide between beaches and rising cliffs. The township is surrounded by National Parks, recreational areas and the catchment area for the Woronora Dam. The main occupation used to be coal-mining and railway maintenance but now many inhabitants commute to Sydney, Campbelltown (*sic*) or Wollongong. The first settlement was largely a tent town of railway workers engaged on the construction of the Illawarra Line. While drilling for the railway, coal was discovered and a mineshaft was sunk by the South Cumberland Coal Mining Company. The township was laid out on the tableland above the mine in 1887.

Known as Camp Creek until 1888, it is believed in Australia that the township acquired its name through Charles Harper who, legend has it, was born in Helensburgh, Scotland. Furthermore he called his daughter Helen. He was born in 1835, but unfortunately research at Register House into the official Scottish records has produced no trace of him. He became the first coalmine manager at Helensburgh in 1886 but unfortunately was killed in a mine accident two years later – whilst supervising the haulage of a new steam boiler, a wire rope broke and he was killed in the recoil. When the township celebrated its centenary in 1984 Charles Harper Park was named after him.

There have been one or two official exchanges between Scotland and Australia, but the most puzzling dates back to 1911. An exchange of flags between the schools of the two Helensburghs took place in that year, and a flag has been found in the Hermitage Academy with the inscription 'Lest we forget 1911'. Its twin has been preserved in Australia. Given the difficulties of communication between the two countries in those days, the exchange is most intriguing.

Helensburgh, New Zealand is a suburb of Dunedin, lying four kilometres north-west of the city centre. Its population at the last census was 1,041 and it covers an area with a very rough rectangular shape of about one kilometre by half a kilometre. It has an attractive setting sloping basically to the north (the sunny direction in the Southern Hemisphere) with a lot of trees and native bush.

It is of much more recent origin than Helensburgh, New South Wales. According to the *Otago Daily Times* of 23 November 1951, 'The name Helensburgh has been given to the area fronting Helensburgh, Wakari and Balmacewen roads. . . A decision to this effect has been made by the Works Committee of the Dunedin City Council. The committee reports that . . . it concurred with a suggestion submitted by the subdividers that a name be alloted to the new suburb which will eventually be created, to distinguish it from Wakari and Maori Hill'.

According to one of a series of articles in the *Evening Star* newspaper in 1959 about the origins of Dunedin street names: 'Miss Helen Hood . . . at one time owned the township of Kirkland Hill, along the top of which Helensburgh Road runs. The name was originally Helensburn; how the change to Helensburgh came about we do not know for certain, but the cause could have been the similarity of the old name to that of the port (*sic*) on the north bank of the Clyde'. Unofficial local opinion is that Helensburn turned into Helensburgh because at least some of the local population who were from Scotland thought that was what the name should be.

All thoughts of brave pioneers from Helensburgh, Scotland vanish in smoke!

General – Books

Anon (actually George Maclachlan) *The Story of Helensburgh* Macneur and
 Bryden c1894

Crawford, Kenneth N & Roberts, Alison *Images of Scotland: Around
 Helensburgh* Tempus Publishing Ltd 1999

Drayton, Patricia *Helensburgh In Old Picture Postcards* European Library
 1985 (Vol 1), 1990 (Vol 2)

Drayton, Patricia *Helensburgh Past & Present* Argyll & Bute Libraries 1999

Fleming, JA *Helensburgh and the Three Lochs* Macneur & Bryden Ltd
 c1957

Glen, Norman M *Helensburgh Town Council 1802-1975* Craig M Jeffrey
 Ltd 1975

Groome, Francis H (ed) *Ordnance Gazeteer of Scotland* Thomas C Jack 1885

Helensburgh Directories 1867 – 1940
 Helensburgh Directory 1867 William Battrum, Helensburgh 1867
 *Helensburgh Directory 1875-76, 1882-83, 1885, 1887-90, 1901-04,
 1907-08, 1911-13, 1915-16, 1919-26, 1928-40* Macneur & Bryden
 Ltd, Helensburgh 1875-1940

Helensburgh Guides 1864-1973
 Helensburgh Guide 1864-65 William Battrum, Helensburgh 1864
 *Helensburgh Guide 1878, 1939 (Helensburgh and Environs), 1950,
 1952-54, 1956, 1959, 1963, 1965-67, 1969, 1972-73* Macneur &
 Bryden Ltd, Helensburgh 1878-1973

Hood, John *Old Helensburgh, Rhu and Shandon* Stenlake Pub. 1999

Laing, Ronald M *Helensburgh (Miligs Town) and Rhu - The First Hundred
 Years* Macneur and Bryden 1973

MacLeod, Donald *A Nonogenarian's* (sic) *Reminiscences of Garelochside and
 Helensburgh* Macneur and Bryden 1883 (the nonagenarian was the
 author's uncle, Gabriel MacLeod)

Macphail, IMM *A Short History of Dumbarton* Bennett and Thomson 1962

Maughan,William Charles *Annals of Garelochside* Alex Gardiner 1897

Murray, David *Glasgow and Helensburgh: as recalled by Sir Joseph Hooker*
 Macneur and Bryden 1918

Osborne, Brian *Helensburgh and Garelochside In Old Pictures* Dumbarton
 District Libraries 1980 (Vol 1), 1984 (Vol 2)

Pettit's Guide to Helensburgh and Neighbourhood c1876

Sinclair, Sir John (ed) *The Statistical Account of Scotland 1791-1799, vol IX
 (Dunbartonshire, Stirlingshire & Clackmannanshire)* EP Publishing
 Ltd 1978

General – Newspapers

Helensburgh Advertiser 1957 to date
Helensburgh & Gareloch Times 1880-1980
Lennox Herald 1851 to date

Chapter 1 Before 1802
Blaeu, Joannis *Theatrum Orbis Terrarum sive Atlas Novus* c1654
Dunrobin Castle Pilgrim Press Ltd 1996

Chapter 3 The Lairds
Calhoun, Stephen Lance *The Clan Colquhoun – A History of its Chiefs and
        Their Clan* unpublished 1992 (Dumbarton Library Local History
        Section holds a copy)
Fraser, William *The Chiefs of Colquhoun and Their Country* published
        privately? 1869
Macphail, IMM *Lennox Lore* Dumbarton District Libraries 1987
Moncrieffe, Sir Iain of that Ilk *Rossdhu, Home of the Chiefs of the Clan
        Colquhoun* published privately c1970
Murray, WH *Rob Roy MacGregor - His Life and Times* Richard Drew
        Publishing 1982
Skene, William F *The Highlanders of Scotland* Eneas Mackay 1902
Welles, Edward Randolph *Ardincaple and Its Lairds* Jackson, Wylie & Co 1930

Chapter 4 Public Administration
Glen, Norman *Helensburgh Town Council 1802-1975: A Record of Some of
        The Decisions of The Council* published privately 1975
Scottish Local Government Information Unit *Local Government in
        Scotland: A Short History* Scottish Local Govt. Info. Unit 1990
Glen, Norman *The Progress made by Helensburgh Burgh Council in its last
        years* Helensburgh Advertiser, October 1993

Chapter 5 Religion
Anon *Helensburgh Old Parish Church, Centenary 1847-1947* published
        privately 1947
Anon *Helensburgh United Presbyterian Church Jubilee* published privately
        1894
Anon *St Michael and All Angels Church, Centenary 1968* published privately
        1968
Galbraith, Iain B *A Village Heritage – the Parish of Rhu 1648-1980* Rhu &
        Shandon Kirk Session 1981
Herron, Andrew *The Law Practice of the Kirk* Bell & Bain Ltd 1995
Logan, Rev George R *The First Hundred Years – The Park Church,
        Helensburgh* published privately 1964
Muskett, Keith *Two Hundred Years and still Counting – a History of the
        Helensburgh Congregational Church* (now United Reformed Church)
        published privately 1999
Smout, TC *A History of the Scottish People 1560-1830* Fontana 1985
Wemyss, Robert *The Church in The Square* Macneur & Bryden 1925

Chapter 7 Commerce
Ashworth, John B *The History of Helensburgh and the Surrounding Area*
        Portico Gallery 2001

Chapter 8 The Geology of the Lands of Malig
Lawson, Judith *Building Stones of Glasgow* Geological Society of Glasgow
        1981
Walker, Frank Arneil *The Buildings of Scotland – Argyll and Bute* Penguin
        2000

Chapter 9 Natural History
Mill, Robert R *Flora of Helensburgh* Macneur & Bryden 1967

Chapter 11 Transport
Brown, Alan *Craigendoran Steamers* Aggregate Publications 1979
McCrorie, Ian & Menteith, Joy *Clyde Piers – A Pictorial Record* Inverclyde
    District Libraries 1982
McQueen, Andrew *Echoes of Old Clyde Paddle-Wheels* Gowans & Gray Ltd
    1924
Thomas, John *The North British Railway* David & Charles Vol 1 1969; Vol
    2 1975
Thomas, John *The West Highland Railway* David & Charles 1965

Chapter 12 Sport and Leisure
Browning, Robert HK *Helensburgh Golf Club* The Golf Clubs Association
    1940
Helensburgh Bowling Club *Helensburgh Bowling Club 125 Years: 1861-
    1986* Craig M Jeffrey Ltd 1986
Helensburgh Bowling Club *The History of Helensburgh Bowling Club 1861-
    1971* Macneur & Bryden Ltd 1971
Helensburgh Sailing Club *Helensburgh Sailing Club: The First 21 Years
    1951-1972* Helcar Press Ltd 1972
Lyall, R & MacKenzie, G *The First Hundred Years of Helensburgh Cricket
    Club 1882-1982* Craig M Jeffrey Ltd 1982
Orton, Ian *The Dumbarton Libraries 1881-1981* Dumbarton District
    Libraries 1981
Stark, Jim & Lowe, Douglas *Helensburgh Golf Club: A Celebration of the
    First 100 Years* Helensburgh Golf Club 1993
Taylor, Michael C, Walton, Julia & Liddell, Colin *A Night at the Pictures*
    Dumbarton District Libraries 1992

Chapter 13 War and Peace
Hall, Keith *The Clyde Submarine Base* Tempus Publishing Ltd 1999
Royal, Dennis *United States Navy Base Two – Americans at Rosneath 1941-
    45* The Douglas Press 2000

Chapter 14 Art and Artists
Billcliffe, R *The Scottish Colourists* John Murray 1996
Billcliffe, R *The Glasgow Boys* John Murray1985
Burkhauser, J (ed) *Glasgow Girls* Canongate 1990
Caw, J *Scottish Painting 1620-1908* Kingsmead 1908
Ellis, A *The Hill House* (Catalogue) National Trust for Scotland
Glasgow Art Gallery and Museum Catalogue Collins 1987
Hardie, William *Scottish Painting* Studio Vista 1990
Halsby, J and Harris, P *The Dictionary of Scottish Painters* Canongate 1990
Macmillan, D *Scottish Art* Mainstream 1990
Moon, K *George Walton* White Cockade 1993
(Tanner, Ailsa) *The Anderson Trust Collections* (catalogue) c1991
Tanner, Ailsa *Bessie McNicol* published privately 1998
Tanner, Ailsa *Helensburgh and the Glasgow School* Helensburgh & District
    Art Club exhibition catalogue 1972
Tanner, Ailsa *West of Scotland Women Artists* Helensburgh & District Art
    Club exhibition catalogue 1976

Chapter 15 Some Architectural Gems

Eyre-Todd, George *Who's Who in Glasgow in 1909* Gowans & Gray 1909

Glendinning, Miles; MacInnes, Ranald & MacKechnie, Aonghus *A History of Scottish Architecture* Edinburgh University Press 1996

Gomme, Andor & Walker, David *Architecture in Glasgow* Lund Humphries 1987

Historic Scotland *Combined Statutory and Descriptive List of Buildings of Special Architectural or Historic Interest – Argyll and Bute – Helensburgh Burgh* Historic Scotland 1993

Gow, Ian & Rowan, Alistair (eds) *Scottish Country Houses 1600-1914* Edinburgh University Press 1998 (in particular articles by John R Hume, Anne Ritches, and Simon Green)

McFadzean, Ronald *The Life and Work of Alexander Thomson* Routledge & Kegan Paul 1979

Walker, Frank Arneil with Sinclair, Fiona *North Clyde Estuary – An Illustrated Architectural Guide* Royal Incorporation of Architects in Scotland 1992

Wemyss, Robert *The Church in The Square* Macneur & Bryden 1925

Chapter 16 Men of Vision

Osborne, Brian D *The Ingenious Mr Bell* Argyll Publishing 2001

Baird, John Logie (ed. Singleton, T) *Sermons, Soap and Television* Royal Television Society 1988

Kamm, Antony and Baird, Malcolm *Tea with Mr Snodgrass – A Personal Biography of John Logie Baird* National Museum of Scotland 2002

Chapter 17 The Benefactors

The Kidstons

Tait, John Kidston *The Kidstons of Logie* unpublished

Thorburn, AMC *The Scottish Rugby Union – the official history* Scottish Rugby Union with Collins c1985

Chapter 18 The Famous and the Infamous

Marshall, Michael *Top Hat & Tails – The story of Jack Buchanan* Elm Tree Books 1978

Downie, R Angus *Frazer and The Golden Bough* Gollancz 1970

Frazer, Sir James George *The Gorgon's Head* Macmillan 1927

Adams, RJQ *Bonar Law* John Murray 1999

Blake, Robert *The Unknown Prime Minister – The Life and Times of Andrew Bonar Law 1858-1923* Eyre & Spottiswoode 1955

Logan, Jimmy with Adams, Billy *It's A Funny Life* B&W 1998

Campbell, Robin N *The Munroists's Companion* The Scottish Mountaineering Trust 1999

Morland, Nigel *That Nice Miss Smith* Souvenir Press 1988

Chapter 19 Out of the Past and into the Future

Moir, Peter & Crawford, Ian *Clyde Shipwrecks* Moir Crawford 1988

Stewart Noble (editor) was born in Glasgow and came to live in Helensburgh just shortly before his eighth birthday in 1951; apart from a six year gap when he 'emigrated to the Far East' (Edinburgh), he has lived in the town ever since then. He has led a varied career and, amongst other activities, works part-time as a Scottish tourist guide; this frequently involves sitting at the front of tourist coaches and (so his wife, Judy, claims) boring a captive audience. Stewart is currently chairman of Helensburgh Heritage Trust and is also a member of Helensburgh Community Council, having served for three years as its chairman.

Kenneth N Crawford (assistant editor) had been Honorary Secretary of the James Brindley Mill and Museum and its Preservation Trust in Leek, Staffordshire for 27 years before retiring from his employment as Chief Legal Executive with the Borough Council of Newcastle-under-Lyme in 1993. Since appointment to the board of Helensburgh Heritage Trust he has edited its quarterly newsletter and been joint compiler of *Around Helensburgh*.

David S C Arthur MBE was born in Kenya and educated at Loretto School, Musselburgh. He graduated from Edinburgh University in History and then taught his subject in Helensburgh at Larchfield School (where the editor of this book was one of his pupils!), then at other schools before becoming Rector of Greenfaulds High School, Cumbernauld. He came back to Helensburgh when St Bride's and Larchfield merged to become the first Principal of the new Lomond School. He was founder of Edinburgh Samaritans, Chairman of Scottish Samaritans and then Chairman of Samaritans UK, and he also became a Director of the Cystic Fibrosis Trust (Scotland).

William FT Anderson OBE After Shrewsbury and Oxford and working for some years in the family textile business he qualified as a solicitor and has practised with Russel & Aitken in Falkirk for more than thirty years. Not a native of Helensburgh but a regular visitor throughout his life. He has been Chairman of the Anderson (Local Collection) trust since its inception twenty years ago. Proud to be both a Templeton and an Anderson.

John B Ashworth OBE was born in 1936 and came to live in Helensburgh in 1974. He is married and has three children who were all educated in the town. He retired in 1996 after twenty-three years as managing director of Chivas Regal whisky company and Vice-Chairman of its holding company Seagram Distillers plc. He has a long interest in local history and published his first book *The History of Helensburgh and the Surrounding Area* in 2001.

Malcolm Baird was born in 1935 at the family home in Sydenham, South London – the only son of John Logie Baird, the inventor of television. After his father's death in 1946 the family moved to Helensburgh where they stayed with his father's sister and where Malcolm attended Larchfield School. In 1957 he graduated in Applied Chemistry from Glasgow University and in 1960 he gained a PhD at Cambridge; he then spent a few years working in industry followed by a spell at Edinburgh University. In 1967 he moved on to McMaster University in Hamilton, Ontario, and has stayed there ever since, ultimately obtaining a Professorship. He retired in 2000 and this has allowed him time to write, as co-author with Antony Kamm, a detailed biography of his father.

Joe Craig OBE was born in 1931 and after leaving school served a craft apprenticeship as a mechanical fitter before becoming a draughtsman. In 1957 he joined John Brown and Co (Clydebank) Ltd and worked his way up to become Manufacturing Director of John Brown Engineering Offshore Ltd. In 1977 he was invited to become Managing Director of Marathon Shipbuilding Company at Clydebank and held that post through its change of ownership to UIE Scotland. He finally retired from his own consultancy company in 1993. He is a keen golfer and a former captain of Helensburgh Golf Club and also enjoys gardening.

Norman Glen CBE, TD was born in Glasgow in 1911 and was educated there. After graduating from Glasgow University, he trained as a retail salesman, before joining the family business of Glens. He married Dr Janet Clark in 1936. After active service throughout World War II he entered the field of politics as well as rejuvenating the family business, and he moved to Helensburgh in 1956. In 1966 he transferred his scene of political activity from national to local politics as a Town Councillor, County Councillor and then District Councillor, consequently giving thirty years continuous service to Helensburgh. He was the last Provost of the town from 1970 to 1975 and for many years leader of the Conservative Group in Dumbarton District Council. In 2001 he became Honorary President of Helensburgh Heritage Trust and sadly died as this book was going to press.

Anne M Gray was brought up in Glasgow and studied medicine at Glasgow University. She then worked in general practice before becoming a consultant psychiatrist. Now retired, she has been secretary of the Helensburgh Heritage Trust since its beginning in 1996 and looks after the website. Anne comes from a Presbyterian family. Her father was an ordained minister but forsook the parish ministry for the academic life. Her late husband, Rev Ian A Gray, was minister of Drymen and Buchanan for twenty one years and retired to Helensburgh. She has two sons, two grandsons and one grand-daughter. Main hobbies are music, gardening, photography and grandchildren.

John Johnston was brought up in Helensburgh and trained as a Chartered Accountant. He then worked in finance in the City of London, but on retirement returned to live in Helensburgh. His wife, Penny, is a member of the Kidston family and he is currently treasurer of the Heritage Trust.

Sandy Kerr was born in Dundee in 1938 and then graduated BSc (Forestry) from Edinburgh University in 1960; he also gained the Diploma in Conservation and Ecology at University College, London in 1961. His career has been with the state nature conservation service in its various guises from 1961 to 1998, and included serving as Regional Director of the Nature Conservancy Council for South-

West Scotland (1975–92) and Head of Biodiversity and International Affairs for Scottish Natural Heritage (1992-97). He is a Life member of the Scottish Wildlife Trust and serves on its Council and Executive; he is also an Honorary Fellow of the Royal Zoological Society of Scotland. He currently works as a self-employed consultant on biodiversity issues.

Jimmy Logan OBE was born in Glasgow in 1928 and came to live in Helensburgh in 1989. He became the Heritage Trust's first Honorary President, and wrote a section in chapter 18 of this book on Jack Buchanan. Sadly he died in 2001 before the book's publication. He was one of the major figures in the world of Scottish entertainment for sixty years and was a major influence on many other entertainers. He initially made his name as a comedian and latterly as a straight actor, never however giving up his first love of pantomime. There is a section on Jimmy in chapter 18.

Patrick J McCann was born in Dumbarton in 1964, educated there and lives there with his wife and family. After graduating from Paisley College of Technology, Pat obtained the Diploma in Information and Library Studies from the University of Strathclyde, and is hence an Associate of the Library Association. He is currently Area Librarian and IT Systems Development Manager for Argyll and Bute Libraries and actually commenced his duties on the day the new Helensburgh Library opened on 5 October 1998. He is a keen football supporter, is interested in genealogy, and collects whisky miniatures.

Alistair McIntyre was brought up in Glendouglas where his father worked on the West Highland Railway, and he attended the old Hermitage School in Helensburgh. Since 1975 he has been employed as librarian at the James Watt College in Greenock, having worked previously at Clydebank College. He lives in Garelochhead and his interests include the local group of the Royal Society for the Protection of Birds, and Garelochhead Residents Association. His hobbies include local history, hill walking, cycling, natural history and industrial archaeology.

Neil Macleod has contributed in his capacity as the artist responsible for almost all the sketches. Born the son of an army chaplain, he spent much of his childhood abroad. However he finished his schooling in Edinburgh and graduated with a DA from Glasgow School of Art. He then worked as a graphic artist with advertising agencies, in industry, in educational publishing, and latterly in government service. He paints a wide range of subjects in a wide range of styles and a wide range of mediums, and is a past President of Helensburgh Art Club.

Catriona Malan was born in Devon, although her parents had married in the old Cardross Parish Church shortly before it was destroyed by a German bomb during World War II. The family came back to live in Cardross, and then moved to Helensburgh when Catriona was eleven years old. She was educated at the Hermitage School and then trained as a primary teacher at Jordanhill College. Her career took her to Clydebank and the Edinburgh area before she returned to Helensburgh, teaching first at Park Lodge and then from 1972 at Larchfield School (now part of Lomond School). She is a Helensburgh Community Councillor as well as President of Helensburgh Writers Workshop.

Pat Mitchell was born in Redruth, Cornwall in 1927 and then moved to Lancashire at the age of five. In 1944 he commenced his apprenticeship in John G Kincaid's of Greenock and his studies at James Watt College, moving from the workshops to the drawing office and by this time attending the Royal College of Science and Technology in Glasgow. In 1958 he joined the Admiralty Hydro-Ballistic Research Establishment in Glen Fruin, becoming head of the design team. He married his wife Jean in 1952 and they came to Helensburgh in 1971. Pat's hobbies are mountaineering, photography, and running (slowly nowadays!).

Brian D Osborne was born in 1941, and brought up in Helensburgh, where he attended

Hermitage School. After two years in a Glasgow bookshop he started work in Dumbarton Library. He then spent his entire career in the library service, finally retiring in 1995 from the post of Chief Officer, Libraries and Museums for Strathkelvin District in order to concentrate on writing and freelance work. Among his publications is *The Ingenious Mr Bell* and, in collaboration with Ronald Armstrong, he has written and edited a number of other books. They have also had two plays professionally produced, one being *A Voyage Round Para Handy*. He is a graduate of the Open University and served as President of the Scottish Library Association in 1992. He now lives in Kirkintilloch.

Alison Roberts was born in the same year as Mickey Mouse and Jimmy Logan, daughter of a Glasgow shipowner. Her childhood summers were always spent on the Clyde Coast and sailing became a lifetime interest which she shared with her husband. The family came to Helensburgh in 1960 and their four children were brought up and educated here. She has served on the Council of the Geological Society of Glasgow and on the board of Helensburgh Heritage Trust. She was co-author of *Around Helensburgh* in the Images of Scotland series.

Jenny Sanders was born in Helensburgh, being the fourth generation of her family to live in the town. She met her husband, Colin, a naval officer, in the West Kirk and married him there. Having qualified as a teacher of English, she taught in various locations. After a period living in England and Canada she came back to Helensburgh and finished her career as a principal teacher of guidance at Hermitage Academy.

Betty Stanton is the third generation of her family to live in Helensburgh, although she herself was actually born in Belfast. She was educated at St Bride's School and then St Andrews University, before starting work in her father's legal practice of Ormond & Stanton (now Macarthur Stanton). She acquired her legal degree from Glasgow University and spent her entire career practising as a solicitor in the town. She retired in 1980, and is a former board member of the Heritage Trust. In addition she was one of the founding members of the Abbeyfield Society in Helensburgh, having also served as its secretary and chairman. She has also been treasurer of Headline Helensburgh, and is a keen golfer, although no longer playing.

An aerial
photo of
Helensburgh
in 1966

Aerofilms Ltd

Ed. J Burrow & Co Ltd 1990

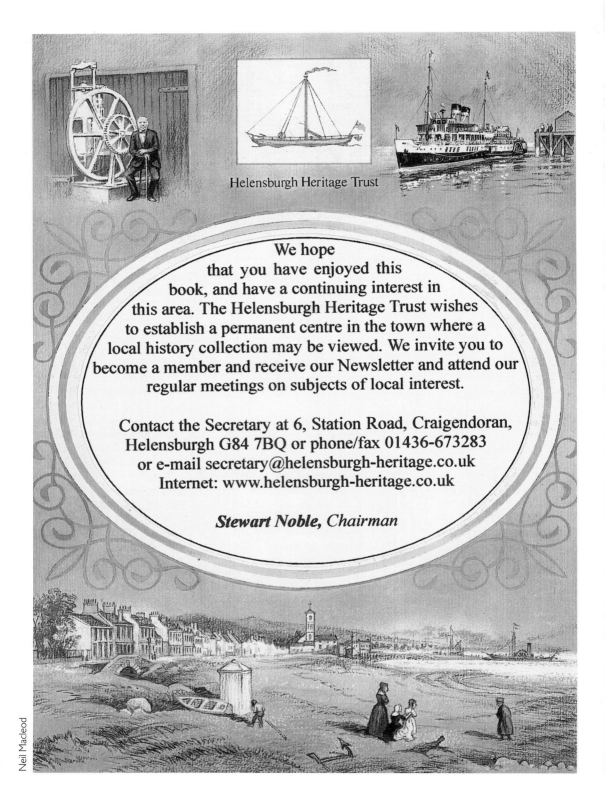

Helensburgh Heritage Trust

We hope
that you have enjoyed this
book, and have a continuing interest in
this area. The Helensburgh Heritage Trust wishes
to establish a permanent centre in the town where a
local history collection may be viewed. We invite you to
become a member and receive our Newsletter and attend our
regular meetings on subjects of local interest.

Contact the Secretary at 6, Station Road, Craigendoran,
Helensburgh G84 7BQ or phone/fax 01436-673283
or e-mail secretary@helensburgh-heritage.co.uk
Internet: www.helensburgh-heritage.co.uk

Stewart Noble, Chairman

Neil Macleod

Part of Ardnack

Cowel.

Innecher
Beoch

Stron-yalerach
Stroin
Kilching

Glen Molochan.
Achagain

Kreig na Skarrow
Kordaig
Inche
Launak

Carigow
Kowan
Inche chaille
Inche-crowie
Inche Zalda
Kuirnig

Goil
Loch
Castel Carrik

Ale na howa
Creigans
Corybuy
Tombuy
Hal of Fih: nes

Luz
Inche

Freuch Yl.
Yl. na Bock
Darrach

Loch
Loch Loung
Alt Achly

Inche-Connagan

Lacus hic supra angustias huius tabulæ porrigit se in Septentriones propemodum ad 14 milliaria: augusto tamen alveo: cæterum diversis insulis Sparsa.

Barry
Port
Ros duy
Nowach

Inche Daymain
Yl. na moin
Yl. na Castel
Lackow
Creinche

The Yle of Malmoir

Duchlass
Na Beg
Kean
Loch-gerr
Corling
Karrsk
Glen-Mac-heurain
Ross
Schy moir
Schey Beg
Yl. Rosh

Inche Merin

LOMVND LACVS.

Acham
Edinabin
Musk.

Commich hill
Balmacha
Gartruyn
Garsfairn
Mains
Ladey fses
Gart na gabhyr
Mill
Achaguil

Roseneth.
Roksewnish

Balarnaig Beg
Glen-Finglas.
Balarnaig moir
Din yn
Letyr O' wan Beg
Schanten
Pool dun boreach
Duchlaesh

Balenoachy
Boir land
Buchanan
Cast.
Drumyn
Druiss innadah
Ibbirt

Barranranan
C. Chachan
K. of Rosneith
Drumfald
Blair fodaig
Ardowil
Arnconnel
Achatullich
Glen-Mid Ross

Gherr Loch

Yl. Abbre
Gorty und
Kym
caronk
Mill
Mewy
Finarys

Cammer
Rosneith

Arn hagyil
Arncappill
Mullyis b.
Mulkys M.
Fruyn
Auon Freoyinn
Nether Ross

Abre
Airdoch
Ross
Perpmellen b.
Tullochan
Mill
Gart n
of Abre
Barower
Garteshop
Maines
Dunkrym.
Dunkryin hill

Yl. Portmellen
Yl. vealich

Ale wreiss nan b.

Kemmesamore
Kaildaruan

Stouck
Kirchmichell b.
Cosgrein
Kammezoshan
Slewna gowack hill
Nether Achindunen

Knochewyr
Pit wirrichs
Bellach
Ladyfsh
Shan
neghush
B. of Aleinerchach
Bleins
Balthom

Blairleish
Blairwyl
L. Breech
B. of Alcheyrachan
B. of
Dunchiyrachan
Standinghoppe
Dun

Ard dardan
Lyllstoun
Balenseanac
Blairhenne chann
Dyrtyth
Camron
Stochrethart
3 Tullichewym

Barw
Mill boish
Milleoun
Napersloun
Mill
B. of Binnuill
Seansal b.
Ladyton
Blackhrid
Edingchoyrachy
Noblestoun
Dyke
Glendissan b.
Colhaine b.

Ardgawa
Gorock
Grinock
Kars-bunet

Glotta fluvius

Ard-mou
Kilmahew
Achinshaw
Drumsadlach
Achinsaill
Kreitegash
Binnuill
Seooch
Middletoun
N. Dalwho
O. Dalwho beg
Kirkmichel
Kolnand
Arild
Naaddykein
Cusfoeoun
Gusfhoeoun
Cleroon
Ashrick
Morchamh
Maryland
Breechfeld
Gorsbeek
Quertoun

Wellacetoun
Mill
Krageud
Weletoun
Hall
Muschochs
Airdoch beg
Dashronoach
Ains
Dalwhorn
Cardos
Dumbarte
Stanyplan
Mains
Lonheed
Colhead
Milcoun
Barnbill
Chappeltoune
Cenelois
Middletou
Carmelbe

Kof Kilmahew
Achinheu
Castelhill
Maichorn hill
Clerkhil
Keuack
La-Kirktoun
Dunbarten Cast.
Barundeidain
Braa
Kilpattr

Air-doch

Neuwark

R E N F R O A N Æ   P A R S.

Cleuch stone uh: Clothain apertum mare exit

BARONIÆ

The   River   of   Clyd

Dunglass
Enc

Finlestoune
Bishop stoun

Part   of   the

Baronie   of

Renfrow.

Aeskyn cast.
Bedinbo

LEVINIA,
VICE COMITATVS.
The Province of LENNOX,
called the Shyre of Dun-Britton.